WALKING

WITH THE

ANALYSTS

A Wall Street Novel

David A. Mallach

Penhurst Books

For information contact: David A. Mallach.
dmallach@comcast.net

ISBN 978-0-9705684-0-3

Designed by Bob Wagner Design

Penhurst Books: Fax 305-675-0940
email: penhurstbooks@usa.com

Pen**hurst**Books

Printed in the United States of America by
Signature Book Printing, www.sbpbooks.com

About The Author

David Austin Mallach currently resides in the Philadelphia, Pennsylvania, area, where he has devoted his entire professional career since 1973 to helping investors develop strategies for income growth and capital appreciation. David has lectured to investors and professional investment advisors in Europe, Scandinavia, the Middle East, South and Central America and the United States.

From The Author

    This book is a work of fiction. Therefore, it should not be assumed by any reader that any specific investment or investment strategy made reference to in this book will be either profitable or equal historical or anticipated performance levels. It should also likewise not be assumed that the performance of any specific investment style or sector will be either profitable or equal its corresponding historical index benchmark. Finally, different types of investments involve varying degrees of risk, and there can be no assurance that any specific investment or investment strategy made reference to in this book will be suitable or otherwise appropriate for an individual's investment portfolio. To the extent that a reader has any questions regarding the suitability of any specific investment or investment strategy made reference to in this book for their individual investment(s) or financial situation, they are encouraged to consult with the investment professional of their choosing.

Forward

When I undertook writing my first novel, *Dancing with the Analysts,* I had no idea how popular the book would become. I knew the investing public was hungry for a new methodology that was time-tested and successful, but also something they could understand. But how to best spread the word about my earnings-growth strategy, that was the trick. I wanted to write something engaging and entertaining rather than some sort of dry primer on modern portfolio theory. Simply put, I wanted to write something that everyone could understand and also trust as an accurate depiction of what can be done with their investments to secure a better life for themselves and their families.

That's why I decided to write about my earnings-growth strategy in a novel. The dramatic form of the novel gave life to my ideas in such a way as to bring to life far more than just the mechanizations of my earnings-growth strategy. Everything you need to know about my earnings-growth strategy is there for the taking but in such a way as to provide themes for *better living* as well. Obviously, I struck a chord with the investing public. Indeed to this day, I still get mail from readers attesting to the veracity of my tale. Receiving feedback like this serves as a constant reminder of the good we can do when we approach wealth in terms of *opportunity.*

On the face of it, there was so much in my preceding novel, *Dancing with the Analysts,* that appeared too good to be true. And yet, I remained true to fact, at least to the extent allowed by the requirements of anonymity, regulatory compliance, etc. The story is indeed amazing, as is the earnings-growth strategy itself. It has created so much opportunity for people, I felt compelled to write about it. For me, making money is always about creating *opportunities* to experience more of the vast palette that humanity has to offer. Accordingly, both *Dancing* and this latest offering, *Walking,* weave a true story of investing success into the rich tapestry of human struggle.

In this latest offering, I present my second strategy – one focused on *growth of income* – but do so against a backdrop of human emotions much more intense than those in *Dancing....* Again, I suspect readers will think at first that I am writing pure fiction when, to the contrary, I am writing the facts as I have lived them. Or perhaps better put, *Walking with the Analysts* is my version of a fictionalized reality few of us ever glimpse. Without question, I am better for having done so. The names and places have been changed to protect the innocent (and the guilty), but the implications are as real as the success of the growth-of-income portfolio described herein. The challenge for you, the reader, lies in your ability to read this book with a mind wide open to the vast possibilities of life even when the truth of things is rather ugly and distasteful.

I came to understand this challenge more fully while working with my friend and former colleague Todd Napolitano. As with my first book, *Walking with the Analysts* has been brewing in my mind for many years. In both instances, Todd showed me how to transform ideas into literary being. His deft handling of structure and theme, form and idea, allowed me to more fully express my vision for dramatizing a series of events that changed my life and touched tens of thousands of people whom I will never even meet. Todd's ability to capture the essence of things breathes life into these pages in the way a good joke lifts the weight of the world from our shoulders. Todd was with me in Africa as the seminal themes for this book were taking root. To the best of my knowledge, he is still out there somewhere, having disappeared mysteriously a few months after the completion of this book. I guess some people were just meant to live in the wind, to be searchers. I don't know if I will ever hear from Todd again. All I know is that his spirit lives on in these pages.

Dedication

Walking with the Analysts is imbued with a second spirit, that of Dr. Stephen Gluckman, Director of Infectious Disease Clinical Services at the Penn Presbyterian Medical Center. Stephen's work with the Botswana-UPenn partnership symbolizes the impact one person can have in alleviating human suffering. Stephen is perhaps the most brilliant man I have ever met. When one refers to "the best of the best in internal medicine," Stephen is at the top of the list. Graduating at the top of his class at the top of all medical programs, Stephen could have taken the road *most* traveled by setting up shop in Midtown Manhattan and reaped significant wealth for himself and his family. Instead, Gluckman chose to dedicate himself to a wider range of medical practice including research, teaching, and, most notably for me, administrating the Botswana-UPenn program at Princess Marina Hospital in Gaberone, Botswana.

What is so inspiring about Stephen Gluckman is his level of self-sacrifice. Truly, his is a life replete with meaning, significance, and spiritual importance to a degree that many of us aspire. While we are dreaming of acting on a scale such as his, Stephen Gluckman is actually doing it. You are an example for all of us.

DM
Philadelphia, 2008

Acknowledgments

This book would not have been possible without the help of many people. When I started this book several years ago, Jeanette Freudiger was a champion of the story at every turn. She has also been extraordinarily supportive and is an outstanding example of someone who understands that the best way to help people is to make them feel comfortable in difficult times and successful in good times.

This book would not have been finished without the continual help, support, and encouragement of my family.

I am also more grateful than I can express to:

Scott Blanche, my Resident Director at Merrill Lynch for his management guidance over the last five years;

Shingai Chodeva, a gifted graduate student from Zimbabwe who helped me better understand the culture of Southern Africa;

Joe Bass, for his continued literary support and help;

Sharon Cromwell, my editor whose vision turned the manuscript into a readable document I believe it has now become;

Mike Spear, my aviation copilot in the skies over Botswana;

Ted Durkin, my Managing Director at Merrill Lynch;

Jack Haraburda, my former Managing Director at Merrill Lynch for believing in me and my process;

John Sasso, a friend and neighbor. I am inspired and awed by his struggle to succeed;

Harvey Friedman, Chief of Infectious Diseases at the Hospital of the University of Pennsylvania;

Gill Jones, Business Administrator for the Botswana/Penn Partnership. Gill has lived in Botswana since 1954. She is the daughter of the last remaining LMS Missionary in Botswana, having been brought up in Maun on the Okavango Delta. Gill is also the guardian of the *Mallach House* in Botswana.

Lastly, I thank all the wonderful investors, who in their quest for wealth and happiness chose to honor me with their trust.

Chapter 1

For the first time in a long time, Austin Montgomery woke up alone. Here was the dawn of a new day, a new beginning. He took in a deep breath. Then another, and so on. Each time he exhaled, Austin was left feeling something exhilarating. Something was gone. Her name was Cathy. But, think of all the opportunities to do something brand new.

Austin met Cathy not too long after his mother died. He could still remember that long flight home from Stanford. At 35,000 feet, things were easy to control, right? Just like when he played his sax. Music was easy to control. Seeing his mother in her coffin, though, was too grounded, too visceral for him to feel comfortably in control. His father, John, had died when Austin was young, so that was different. His mother filled Austin with warm stories of his early childhood when both parents were alive and everyone was together. Soft, nice, no problems, right? His father had died so long ago that he was really only a memory, comfortably ethereal so high up among the clouds, somewhere around 35,000 feet.

Weird as it was to say, arriving in Philadelphia for his mother's funeral had actually kicked off a whirlwind of life changes. Over the years that passed, so much had happened to him he simply had to wonder what on earth he did to deserve it all. For starters, there was the document spelling out which person would receive the possessions commonly provided by a will. *A will*. It came out of nowhere, boy. He grew up with modest means, not millions. His mother worked, but they did not have any money to speak of. He got a music scholarship to Stanford, thank God. Of course, along with the will came an estate to be settled, lawyers to meet, issues to be addressed, binding decisions to be made. These things were not part of his common parlance back then as they were now.

Looking back, what a shock it was to learn of his father's financial legacy, a secret gift from the grave that reached down to him like a hand from heaven and rested upon his shoulder. And how could anyone forget Johnny Long? *Johnny Long...* what a name for a guy who worked in the stock market. What challenges he faced those eight years ago. How he rose to the occasion in ways he never thought imaginable. What a father to be able to provide this from beyond the grave after so many years gone. And what a mother he had. He smiled briefly. What a mother he had to keep it a secret all those years. He was angry at her when he first found out about the money.

Some things you only come to see after time. Unfortunately though, people to whom you want to apologize may be long gone by then. He took in a deep breath. Well, at least he was fulfilled for a couple of years. What heady times those were. And now... now he was free to delve into whatever he wanted. Completely unencumbered, he could work as late as he wanted, go out with whomever he wanted, focus completely on new business development without having to worry about short-selling his girlfriend on "intimate time."

It was surprisingly evident – when Cathy told him she was leaving, he was filled with dread. Important people leaving his life did this to him. But something must have happened while he slept because this morning he was feeling insane for ever having given up any freedom to begin with. Back to work 100 percent at last. The relationship thing didn't really suit him. He had so much more to achieve professionally and spiritually, that it felt great to be moving forward again. Moving in circles takes its toll.

Lying there in bed, Austin had one of those moments of complete self honesty. It would be really easy to be pissed off at Cathy, work from anger or resentment or something else not really genuine. The truth was that there was no need to be angry at Cathy. She did nothing wrong. Neither of them did anything wrong. If the truth be told, Austin had long ago given up on the relationship in favor of juicing up his career some more and working with Johnny again. OK, so what? Wasn't she doing the exact same thing by moving to Atlanta for the Coke job? Not wanting a long-distance relationship was just an excuse they both used to let each other off the hook. They were both ready to move on, one before the other perhaps, but the order was of no real importance. Austin was content to allow both of them to have their own opinions on the timing and the who dumped whom stuff.

Cathy was an analyst with degrees in both database management and finance. That made her *highly* desirable. Who *wouldn't* hire her away? Of course, it also made her desirable to other men of ample charms and means. But lying there in his moment of self honesty, Austin acknowledged (if only to himself) that plenty of mysterious phone calls came his way from women he barely knew. The simple fact was that Cathy was perfectly free to pursue her career *and* find a husband and have kids if that's what she wanted. Austin wasn't in that frame of mind and might never be. And so that was that. A little bit scary, but cool all around.

Into the bathroom he went. The hot shower loosened him up quite a bit. Spending the extra money on the six-head shower system was the right choice, that's for sure. It was Cathy's choice actually. She had a knack for knowing what Austin would like, dislike and love. He had to give her that. But again, he reminded himself of how desirable he was. He was back on the market... no more Saturday nights watching *Howard's End* or *The English Patient*. Austin filled his mouth up with hot water and spit it back out for emphasis. Who was he kidding? He laughed at himself. From here, getting older meant hitting physical potholes and a long series of blowouts.

Austin spit out another mouth full of water. Lifting the in-shower shaving mirror off its bracket, he strained to see his handle bars. It occurred to him that maybe he stopped watching his figure because he *wanted* Cathy to find him unattractive. It would make things easier, right? Happily, though, Austin wasn't angry or sad or particularly happy. He just felt vague. He put the mirror back on its hinge and stroked his face. "Time for a shave," he thought. Yes, he would definitely have a shave. He tapped the pearl-handled safety razor against the mosaic shower wall. Cathy bought him that razor at Harrods two years ago. It was her first time abroad other than Mexico. She was so excited. As he lathered up, Austin remembered the first time he went abroad. It was actually to the Bahamas to start work on the Johnny Long Foundation Hospice Home. *That* was something, man. Cathy was always thrilled whenever he bought her something, especially if she could show it off. But the Foundation and the home were totally different. He felt like he was actually making a *difference.*

Austin looked at himself in the shaving mirror. He was starting to break out. He decided on a haircut. Better give Lisa a call and get a chop. Something stylish. Something entertaining. Austin kept people entertained. Austin Montgomery – Stanford grad, musician, millionaire investment guru, wooer of young women, and now, workaholic once more! "What a joke," thought Austin as he gently tapped the razor against the wall again. "This has *got* to be someone's idea of a joke." Austin Montgomery – potbelly, getting hairier, and just free again." He turned off the water and stepped out onto the cold marble floor he and Cathy handpicked in Italy.

Austin Montgomery was certainly free at last. Free to do what, though? That was the question.

Chapter 2

When his father died, Austin was only five years old. When his mother died, however, he was a junior at Stanford University, quite old enough to feel the loss poignantly. Of course, most people who knew Austin leveled the same general criticism – he could be "emotionally unavailable." Exactly what degree of availability they sought was not usually quantified, but that was sort of the point. For his part, Austin never really challenged the assertion. Why bother? And maybe a billion Chinese can't be wrong, so to speak. After all, it was entirely *his* choice to attend college way out in California. He got into Cornell and Columbia. He didn't *have* to venture off to the West Coast. He did so by choice. Was that telling? He wasn't sure. One thing was for sure, even when he was home, he never made much effort to really connect with his family. His advisor in the music department, Professor Tony "Chops" Pickett once wrote of his young sax playing student: "Austin has the gift of music... He has made excellent progress in several different musical genres.... With time, perhaps Austin will develop more depth of emotion in his playing... that certain something that makes Charlie Parker Charlie Parker or Mingus Mingus."

Chops pretty much summed up not just Austin's music but his personal life as well. He still remembered his mentor's parting words on graduation day like they were uttered yesterday – "You gotta earn your chops, boy. You gotta earn the cred," and then he would go into his world of sharps and flats. Coming into so much money so fast could have derailed Austin. It was certainly understandable for a young man to take the money and run, so to speak, and not worry so much about working hard. Who could chastise him for this? Who would not consider doing the very same themselves?

But Austin felt compelled to do something more, to be something more. He couldn't isolate any particular driving force or principle for feeling this way. He just did. If anything, he was driven to earn his "cred." In retrospect, that could have been why things didn't work out with Cathy – he stopped trying to earn her respect. Maybe he just expected it to end and stopped working hard at the relationship. He figured there had to be something to this theory. Otherwise, why was he so motivated to become a workhorse again? He simply couldn't deny the possibility that maybe, just maybe, he was getting a bit too soft. It was definitely time for another project... a mega project like the hospice home. He wanted to do something he could sink his teeth into.

Nor did it escape Austin that he was incredibly privileged to be able to look ahead with so much enthusiasm and optimism. Yes, it was definitely a privilege to view one's life from a perspective of foresight and control rather than from reaction and despair. When things got started, it was quite a different matter altogether. The notes of life picked up tempo so fast after that flight home. Money, maybe even more so than death, has a way of speeding up life's tempo. After that meeting with Clark Parkinson, his deceased father's long time lawyer, Austin realized he had entered a different world, a world in which he had no cred, no chops. He was a little scared. Just how different things would become he would not realize for some time, and even then, only after tremendous stress and anxiety. There was no question that he earned his chops over the years that followed.

Scrambling to keep up in a strange environment can reach a frenzy, at which point something must give. It's not easy to make one's way in the world of high finance. The music can float away, a sort of unbearable lightness. In short, some structure is always needed. Yes, an order of things is needed to harness the absolutes... God, Tone, Idea, and so on. Understanding the theoretical side to music was never a problem for Austin. For him, it might have sounded complicated, but it was very controlled, safe. When his mother died, though, he was stepping into the unknown. Clark Parkinson, and more so Johnny Long, would provide for Austin the structure he needed to find his own way and eventually become a leader himself. It was precisely *this* he sought again now that he and Cathy had split up. Austin wanted once again to reach new heights of living. He wanted to fly higher and in an odd way, he felt relieved that he still had a burning sense of ambition.

The analogy to flying worked in a number of ways, mostly in that Austin was about to soar to new heights. The analogy was not lost on Austin. He was always attracted to flying. There was something about it that held a lot of meaning for him. In fact, Austin had wanted to get a pilot's license since he was a teen. For him, flying his own plane was somewhat ironic. He always felt safely above life's turmoil up at 35,000 feet. But that was as a passenger, not as a pilot. If you're actually flying the plane, that's far from carefree and aloof. Maybe that's why Austin was attracted to it. He didn't actually know *why* he wanted to learn to fly. He just did. It wasn't like he had ever been up in a private plane as a kid. And he wasn't looking to learn how to fly as some sort of status symbol either. No, for Austin flying his own plane became a *symbolic* activity.

After he inherited the money and satisfied some challenges – after he became really rich basically – Austin started taking flying lessons at Wings Air Field near Blue Bell, Pennsylvania. It's one of the oldest airports in the country, and it seemed to Austin as good a place as any to dig in and learn to fly. He took to it right away, actually. Contrary to his fears, flying his own plane was not all that difficult. By the time he and Cathy broke up, he had about 100 hours under his belt. Not too many, but enough to feel comfortable taking passengers up for a glimpse of their world from above. In fact, Austin was a bit surprised at how *relaxed* and *peaceful* it was up there by himself. Of course, there's the old adage about flying being 99% serenity and 1% panic. Other than the inevitable moment of panic when a problem arose, though, flying was quite soothing for him.

As any pilot knows, there's much more to flying than altitude even if Austin preferred the world from high above. What's at issue, fundamentally, is one's *perspective*. When you're flying, you're oriented toward *what's ahead*. If you stop and think about it, this distinguishes the pilot from most of the people on the ground who are largely preoccupied with the past – what has passed – and that which they cannot leave behind. How do you fly looking backward? You could ask the same of people trudging their way through life – how do you live always looking back? But they do, or at least they try to. Austin flew a Diamondstar DA40. A new comer among planes. The DA40 was all composite, in other words, plastic. Composite material was all the the new rage of advanced airplanes. Double the strength of aluminum and prettier to look at. The advanced avionics was above the average flying machine. The GPS was now the norm, not VOR to VOR. Just plug in your destination and follow the line on the screen. It was hard to get lost, the cause of so many deaths in previous years. Modern weather maps saved the day too. Now Austin could fly anywhere and avoid nasty turbulence. Austin's radar screen was in the front of the plane. Exactly where he wanted it. Austin wanted to know what the weather looked like 20 to 30 miles ahead of him. Flying and investing have so many similarities. All the risk of flying is ahead of the pilot. Pilots do not want to know about yesterday's weather but rather the weather they will be flying into. The same as investors. The risk of flying is ahead of the pilot, just like the risks of investing are ahead of an investor. If a pilot is flying on a Tuesday, it does him little good to know what the weather was like last Tuesday or a month ago. The risk of failure is ahead of the pilot, not behind him. Austin always wondered why investors looked at the past as a guide to the future. The only guide to successful investing was in the future because that was where all the risks were. Since there is no risk in looking at the past, the returns of tomorrow should be zero. Imagine asking an airline pilot what the weather is like along your course, and the pilot says that last month the weather was fine. Travelers would exit that plane and ask another pilot for the weather over the next three or four hours. Austin's radar was in the front of the plane, not in the back.

There was a sound analogy to be drawn between flying and investing as well, although Austin had been completely unaware of anything regarding money, investing, "the Market," and so on. When Austin first met Clark Parkinson, it was to discuss his mother's will and estate. Back then, Austin didn't even know about the *S & P 500* or 401(k)s, stocks, none of it. And now, in contrast, he had actually *lectured* to professional money managers about growth-stock investing.

Things seemed to happen so much faster seven years ago. For that two or three year period, the tech boom drove the market higher and higher. People were making literally millions in no particular stock at all so long as it was either an IPO or the sexy eight-point flip of the day. Sure, people made a lot of money. However, as Austin was fond of citing, most people won and lost in their discount online gambling accounts after the tax man was paid his pound of flesh.

As a money manager, Austin was forged from fire in a time of tumultuous market activity. The tech bubble of 2000. There was Fed Chairman Greenspan... waiting, it seemed, for the market to make new highs on the rubber legs of Mr. MARGIN, before pronouncing that the investing public suffered from an acute case of "irrational exuberance." Like a chain of contagion, the markets began their long, excruciating journey downward, having contracted a strange disease with "recession-like" symptoms. As for Dr. Greenspan, he gave us repeated doses of castor oil by leaving rates untouched for some time when what we all really needed was a lifetime prescription for Valium.

Finally, the Bears were right! Well, vindicated is a better word. Wielding the vengeful and bitter sword of the Short Sale, the Bears punished the world for having the gall to make money in complete deference to logarithms, PE Ratios, and that sacred cow "CASH." Indeed, the Bears had been so wrong for so long, a perfect storm of resentment was about to explode. Add a bunch of terrorists flying planes into the World Trade Center and the Pentagon, and that was that.

Sooner or later, the Bears were going to be right. It was inevitable. Like with Chicken Little – when you see only impending doom, all you see is... well... impending doom. Money managers like Johnny Long – men with a discernable, time-tested plan for exactly what to buy and exactly when to sell – remained mildly amused by the never- ending battle of words and dollars between the Bulls and the Bears. For his part, Johnny never cared for either side. In fact, he found both equally misguided and focused on irrelevant issues regarding a stock's valuation. The one thing that Johnny *did* find distasteful was the sometimes intense negativity and bitterness exhibited by those who wanted the market to drop lower and lower; namely, the Shorts and Bears. One of the first lessons Johnny imparted to Austin was the importance of remaining future oriented and positive about the market.

This second point is very, very important to understand, and Johnny took great pains to ensure that his young mentee understood the importance of remaining positive with his clients about what he was doing. For Johnny, being positive with his clients was not merely a façade for marketing purposes. It was not about commissions, or looking good, or any of the other crap salesmen worry about. Johnny Long was positive about investing in stocks because he was positive that his strategies worked. He was positive that his buy, sell, and hold criteria were squarely focused on the right numbers – earnings-estimate revisions and dividend increases. He was positive that leadership in investing revolved around standing firm on one's proven successes amid the chaos.

Of course, this made the brokers in Johnny's office either insanely jealous and bitter or else blindly sycophantic. Those who squeezed out a living by trading stocks for short-term gains swore there was no such thing as a "strategy" for investing. To them, Johnny Long, and soon enough Austin Montgomery, were over-glorified. The fact that Johnny was successful and made both himself and his clients millions upon millions in his strategies only added fuel to their flames of jealousy. Johnny put up with his share of sycophants as well. Many of the brokers sniffed around Johnny's office for some sort of handout, some pearl of wisdom that they could trade. Oh, how they missed the point entirely. Johnny would lecture them till he was blue in the face on how to incorporate his strategies into their business. But of course, they never could fathom what he was talking about, despite its great simplicity.

Before 2000, nobody cared much about what anyone else was doing, though. It seemed everyone was making money somehow. But even Austin was quick to point out that the Bulls were let loose to run rampant through the proverbial china shop. It was one thing to focus on earnings-estimate revisions; it was quite another for companies to actually *falsify* earnings. The great problem for Austin back then was deciding when to *sell* a particular stock and what to do with the proceeds. Johnny Long showed him the way. And now, after the dust had settled on the great correction of 2000 to 2002, who was still in the market now that things were back? More to the point, who was *still holding* that one stock which is significantly higher now than it was when others were selling it off? As the bubble burst and brokers scrambled for their excuses, Johnny and Austin entrenched deeper into their strategies despite mounting short-term losses. In the years that followed, and as a result, their clients steadily *made money* again.

It would be easy and so tempting for Austin to rest on his laurels and simply revel in the glory days, use it as a crutch for not achieving new successes. In the last few months before his breakup with Cathy, he had the sneaking suspicion he was moving toward just this. But as Johnny always taught him, what good did it do to linger on things passed? To successfully navigate the market, one had to remain forward looking always. Believe it or not, this required more discipline than most people realized... that is, until they tried to do it themselves. "The More Things Change, The More They Stay the Same." That was the title of the presentation Austin gave at different brokerage offices. The manager would spring for cold, crappy pizza, and the brokers would all fall asleep... except the ones who understood. They inevitably ended up calling Johnny Long and, in many cases, transferring to his office for continued tutelage and even partnerships on their books of business. It was the least Austin could do to repay Johnny for his invaluable guidance.

The point was simple... when hasn't the Market undergone a continuing series of technological booms and corrective pains? In retrospect, would you rather have remained in the market consistently and with a specific plan for the last 25 years, or would you rather have been jumping in and out of this and that stock or bond while playing the futile game of market timing? If you choose the former, you probably have known wealth-through-investing. If you choose the latter, you are probably divorced... and still telling your bartender "would-a, could-a, should-a" every night.

Johnny Long's clients – and later Austin's clients as well – all had a distinctive calm about them. While others were freaking out over this or that short-term correction, clients who had money with Johnny had an entirely different perspective on the market. Like Johnny, they were totally focused on *the future* rather than the past. If you were going to invest money with Johnny Long, the first thing you would have to come to terms with was Johnny's unique approach to stock prices in general. Things were very simple for Johnny. Perhaps "intuitive" would be a better word. For Johnny, the markets were efficient. There were no grand arbitrage opportunities he was going to discover through advanced analytics and logarithmic analysis. He was just a money manager and not looking to reinvent the wheel. Instead, as he so often did, Johnny saw the lowest common denominator in stock-price movements: namely, earnings estimate changes. Johnny's clients knew full well that the reason any one of their stocks would move higher consistently over the course of, say, two or three years was that there were numerous and consistent earnings estimate increases providing the wind in the sails. For his part, Johnny tracked this information very, very carefully and leveraged it to make himself and his clients wealthy beyond their wildest dreams.

Knowing what to buy, when to sell, and what to do with the proceeds – that was the simple discipline behind Austin's wealth and Johnny's success as a professional money manager. And yet, few money managers could emulate it. That was the thing that differentiated Johnny Long from the thousands of others – he simply kept looking forward. Johnny kept his clients looking forward as well, and this, more than anything else, kept his clients loyal and disciplined enough to allow Johnny the space he needed to make them rich.

Before meeting Johnny Long, Austin knew next to nothing about investing, maybe even *less* than nothing in that what he "knew" was actually all wrong. Stocks were things his rich Stanford friends somehow owned from birth; investments were things like real estate or coins. Having millions of dollars at one's disposal... well, that was something Austin never really bothered to think about. Why bother? It would only get you in trouble. Before meeting Johnny, Austin had a pretty skewed perspective of money in general. It might have had something to do with losing his father at such an early age. He was fundamentally risk averse. He didn't want to lose anything most likely because he had lost so much so early. When you lose a parent like that, *control* becomes a major issue, a driving force.

Once, when he was about nine, Austin stole a stupid little *G.I. Joe* flashlight accessory from a toy store display because it was the coolest thing, and none of his other friends had it, and it only came in an expensive *Bolivia Coup Adventure* action pack featuring the brand-new *Kung Foo Grip* Joe (Austin also had his eye on the tiny beret that came with the *Hero of the People* limited edition, and much smaller in size, the *Che Guevara* doll). Back then, the $16.99 retail price was no small issue for a single mom living modestly. At any rate, Austin's uncle saw him pocket the thing and quietly confronted him away from his mother. Uncle Doug made Austin put the miniature flashlight back, although without telling the shopkeeper.

The humiliation was enough for Austin. At the age of nine, betrayed by the good people at Mattel, Austin learned that money and doing bad things were cause and effect, so don't even worry about it. It only made him bitter and resentful, and he couldn't very well play good music that way. As Chops Pickett used to say, "Negative thoughts, negative notes. The hope the great blues men had for the future made the so-called "blues" totally *un*-sad."

So again, when you lose a parent at a very young age, control becomes the issue. Stocks, well... you absolutely cannot control the stock market. This was the first thing Johnny taught his clients. You've got to look forward and act on new information as it comes out. You can't control the news, at least not legally. You have to accept the fact that new information about earnings will come out and you are relegated to acting accordingly. What made Johnny Long such a successful money manager was his ability to take this simple fact of investing life and turn it into a dance. It was like dancing with the analysts and Johnny Long was a great dancer.

Chapter 3

Austin went down to the kitchen wearing a pair of plaid pajama bottoms and an oversized designer shirt. He snatched the Sunday paper off the kitchen island right where the maid left it and headed to the fridge. He could do it all by now with his eyes closed. He took out the cold latte Maria made him earlier that morning and added a few cubes. Iced latte in one hand, paper under his arm, Austin headed right and took his breakfast out of the oven -- eggs over medium, onion bagel double-toasted, one slice of fresh tomato, and two slices of American cheese (white on the top and yellow on the bottom), salt and pepper, cut it in half.

Sitting down at the island, Austin looked almost dwarfed. The island was huge. As with the granite for the countertops, Cathy and he picked the handmade tile when they were in Italy. The bold Romanesque sun inlaid in the middle would make Versace jealous. The highlight of the island's design was a built-in fondue station which Austin hadn't used in months. It was Cathy's brainchild, although she would later complain (incessantly) that both chocolate and cheese alike were making her fat and zitty. All things considered, Austin was in particularly good spirits for someone who just broke up with his girlfriend of several years. When he went to sleep last night, he was worried about how he would feel this morning. But it was a beautiful morning and Austin was amped up and free to focus on work again.

While sipping his iced latte, Austin reviewed the closing stock market numbers and news. Every time he heard people talking about the closing price of this or that stock or the pre-market activity for this or that company, Austin felt great sympathy. If it were up to him, everyone would follow Johnny's strategy instead of worrying about things they could neither control nor be inside on. There was an article wondering whether Zectec Technology would be the next Krispy Kreme. Austin shook his head. Sometimes, he thought all the so-called pundits and talking heads actually *wanted* bad things to happen to people. For both Austin and Johnny Long, the question was not *what* you owned but *when* did you sell it.

Over the last year or so, Austin and Johnny hadn't been as close as usual. Cathy demanded a lot of Austin's time. Back in the day, Austin and Johnny would spend hours discussing things... not just stocks, but life issues as well. Austin had built a great business along side Johnny at First American Investors. Austin was looking forward to spending more time with Johnny again, especially now that he was up and on his feet as a money manager in his own right. Johnny would surely welcome spending more time with Austin. His mentee's success was no small delight. To see a young man like Austin "get it" so quickly and so fully was very fulfilling to Johnny. And truth be told, having a young sparkplug like Austin around kept Johnny motivated and working hard, too. It was good all around.

The highlight of Austin's mentoring relationship with Johnny Long had to be the hospice home in the Bahamas. Together, Johnny and Austin helped fund a beautiful home for terminally ill cancer patients. Not only did they raise the money for the home, they also managed the perpetual endowment. The entire project was funded by profits made in Johnny's strategy. Think for a minute about how truly amazing that is... to be able to do something like that for people. The donors came from Johnny's and Austin's client bases. These folks made money over the years following Johnny's investment strategies. The initial money for the foundation came largely from Johnny's earnings-growth strategy. The remainder of the trust was managed using Johnny's Growth of Income Strategy and generated the yearly income and capital appreciation necessary to cover operating costs.

Needless to say, taking work to new thresholds of philanthropy was something very, very special for both Johnny Long and Austin

Montgomery. Austin would never ever forget the first wave of terminally ill people who visited the home. Their families, their children, and *their* children always had tears in their eyes as they strolled around the grounds during visitor orientation. But not the patients themselves. No tears there. That was what Austin found so amazing, so motivating, so awe inspiring. Even though they were terminally ill, these folks were actually happy and excited. There was an odd sense of calm about them as if they were completely unbound from the sad facts of their past and present. Today was today... tomorrow, another day. The patients were always looking ahead, focused forward, and this made all the difference.

The lesson for Austin – one which he remembered poignantly to this day – was to make every day a step closer to achieving something great. We spend half our day at work. And if you spend that time just waiting around for a paycheck, you are wasting precious time. Those terminally ill patients knew all too well how precious that time really is. In meeting Johnny Long, Austin not only received a means to his own personal wealth and satisfaction, he also received a very precious gift indeed: the opportunity to turn his career into a means of spiritual fulfillment. Although Austin didn't know exactly what lay ahead in this regard, he was filled with general excitement to get cracking again. Now that he was single, he was free to do far more than just work. He was free to once again work on projects that, as in the case of the hospice home in the Bahamas, brought joy and satisfaction to those who needed it most. And in return, Austin would witness the awesome power of *optimism* as practiced by the very people who had the most cause to be anything but optimistic.

As he thumbed through the business section of the morning paper, this all rushed to Austin's head at the same time. He was ready to go, ready to start something, something big, something meaningful. That inevitably meant hooking up with Johnny Long. They may have worked in the same brokerage office for the last several years, but they hadn't really worked *together* for the last year or so. That was about to change.

Chapter 4

Parkinson took Austin by surprise at their first meeting. Never in a million years would Austin have guessed that his father, young as he was when he died, "lived a charmed life" as Parkinson put it. Austin pretty much figured the whole inheritance thing was a joke. He was suddenly rich through a secret inheritance left to him by his father? Come on, this Parkinson guy had to be up to something. The morning he first met Clark Parkinson, Austin was having none of it. At first, he was pretty pissed, actually. Funny, even to this day, Austin was somewhat embarrassed by his initial response.

"I had nothing for college," he quipped, still in disbelief. "I've been through some pretty hard times. Not all financial, but struggles sure enough." Actually, what made him most upset was thinking that this Clark Parkinson guy knew his parents better than he did. He had always maintained a very specific image of his father in his head. Now, that stability was threatened, and he didn't like it one bit. Even his mom turned out to be someone entirely different from the person he thought he knew. That hurt, it really hurt. It left Austin feeling quite unsure of himself and quite devoid of stability. He didn't like teetering.

"Why didn't my mother ever tell me about my father or about her own money?" Austin asked Parkinson.

After a brief pause, Parkinson answered. "Austin... what you've had to do is *no different* from what your father had to do to make his mark in the world, I assure you." Parkinson remained quiet for a few minutes. Austin was too embarrassed to start the conversation back up. Here he was complaining about the fact that he had just inherited – or so he was told – one million dollars. In the awkward silence, Austin reminded himself that this is the sort of thing that happens when you get too close to people or to an issue. He would always let others down somehow, even if only in his thoughts. It was only logical. If he suddenly had money, couldn't he then suddenly lose it all? Back then, Austin didn't know about opportunity or about managing risk. He didn't know about staying focused on the future. He was still driving by looking in the rear view mirror, so to speak. Accordingly, he would initially underestimate Clark Parkinson and what he was saying.

In time, however, that changed. Successful men like Parkinson are not to be dismissed as corrupt or greedy or sinister as if everyone wearing a suit thinks like Ivan Boesky or Ken Lay. Men like Parkinson are to be understood first and then emulated. This takes time and interaction. For his part, Parkinson did not care about money *in and of itself*; rather, he cared about people doing the right thing with money once they were fortunate enough to have more of it than they felt they needed. In this sense, Parkinson and Johnny Long would make a natural pair. It remained to be seen how well Austin fit in. For his part, Austin never forgot Parkinson's parting words that day: "Do the right thing and money will always follow one way or another." Put another way, *Bad thoughts make bad notes; good thoughts make good notes* – Tony "Chops" Pickett.

For Parkinson, doing the right thing – playing good notes – involved being far more than the executor for his father's and mother's will. It meant starting a long-term relationship with this young man upon whom he was about to bestow enough money to either make him *or* break him. It meant providing support for Austin, who had a lot of challenges and a lot of mad money ahead of him. Sensing Austin's discomfort, Parkinson continued with the details. "When your father was alive, he set up a special trust for you. It was intended to be a secret until after your mother died, which is why you never knew anything about it until today. It was your father's wish that the trust remain a secret to you, and your mother remained faithful to his wishes."

Austin was struck by the word "trust." He shifted in his chair. Now he was engaged. The idea of newfound money – and a lot of it? – started to take him over. It was an uncomfortable feeling, but intriguing nonetheless. Looking back all those years later, Austin was still embarrassed that he was so enticed by the thought of new found wealth resulting from his parents' demise. Still, who could blame him?

"So what's left over from my mother's estate goes to me, right?"

"Actually no," answered Parkinson. "Your father's trust was set up... with some tests." Austin sat and listened dumfounded by what followed.

Chapter 5

Austin brushed aside some bagel crumbs and scribbled a few quick calculations on the stock pages. He was still doing *great*. He was comfortable with his returns despite the volatility. In fact, as Johnny taught him, risk and return must be in an acceptable ratio. Otherwise, book ahead for the triple bypass. This morning there were two pieces on how the Market "was back." New highs, what's hot, what's not, you should have held this, you should have sold that. Austin always laughed a bit at the *Barron's* arm-chair quarterback types. Hindsight was so easy, being fixated on the past so tempting. Is it really helpful to tell your audience that they should have sold *after* it's too late? Now, Austin found it mind-numbing really. Thanks to Johnny Long, however, Austin was spared all of that. He jotted down a note to make a lunch date with Johnny. It had been almost two months since they last had lunch together.

Austin tossed the Business section on the counter and grabbed the Arts. A little change of pace. Fact was, Johnny's clients never, ever became fixated on the news of the day. None of them had CNBC disease. It was funny, back in 2002, the office sometimes resembled more of a panic room than a place of business. Clients – *not Johnny's* – would call incessantly, demanding to know what was going on with their portfolios. The brokers were sometimes on the verge of losing it. What could they tell their clients? Most of them knew less than their clients did about the stocks they held. They made decisions based on price or P/E or Buy/Sell recommendation or some other such irrelevancies. As Austin would learn from Johnny, none of that had any real effect on portfolio value over the long term. What drove stocks higher and lower over the long term would be a lesson as completely eye opening for Austin as it was for each and every one of Johnny's clients.

Quickly scanning the paper, Austin caught a quarter-page review of a new Coltrane collection edited by none other than Tony "Chops" Pickett of Stanford University. In this particular review, Pickett outlined quite succinctly his theory about the "intertwining complements" shared between blues and jazz. "You see," he wrote, "Jazz is like pulling notes in from some other dimension, somewhere in the interstices between flats, sharps, and so on, and so on. The jazz master – for there can be no Master of Jazz -- pulls a note *into* this world precisely to point out its ultimately ephemeral being. It's ironic."

What made Pickett a popular instructor at Stanford was that he seemed to embody the dichotomies he was always talking about. There was always some other force at work, not just the obvious. As he explained in his review, "Blues, yeah, blues is like taking something miserable and this-worldly like everyday human suffering – wake up, suffer, sleep (repeat unto death) – and turning it into a rhythm, a chug, a beat, a three-chord progression so you can *expel* it out of your world. Again, it's ironic."

Austin finished the review and laughed to himself. He started the day thinking he had the blues. Now, after reading Chops's review, he wasn't so sure he could even say that. Talk about irony, how about that one? Then Austin just sort of stopped in his mental tracks. He tapped his fingers on the island for a moment. He was thinking. If systems of any sort were always inherently flawed, why did he have to grow up and get over it…just dream every now and then, the answer is a *compromise*. We may not be able to understand truth in itself, but that shouldn't stop us from believing in things.

Austin downed the rest of his latte triumphantly. He was thinking again. It felt awesome. That's when it dawned on him that his growth-stock strategy (well, Johnny's strategy really) was *just that*. A compromise. As Johnny always says, "We can't possibly know everything about a stock just like we can't possibly determine from a stock's price whether that stock will go to zero or go up one thousand percent over the next three years." Austin felt a rush of energy surge through his body. It was more than the caffeine. He was onto something here. The only thing we can know for sure is that a stock's current price is a reflection of future earnings. We can actually *monitor* these changes as they occur behind the scenes to create a strict discipline determining what to buy, when to sell, and what to do with the proceeds.

Austin and thousands of other investors were living proof that such a pragmatic approach to growth investing can make you wealthy. A simple three-question system based on certain rules for earnings estimate revisions. It was a golden goose precisely because Johnny figured out a way of bringing *something certain* – an estimate revision up or down – as a means of approaching the uncertainty of the Market. Austin was immediately quite proud of himself. He had just created a bridge between his very expensive college education in music, of all things, and his financial success. For the last several years, he felt this unending need to reconcile things like this because both of his parents were dead and gone. He had nobody to give him parental approval. More importantly, though... he had an idea, a big, bold, exhilarating idea. True, he wasn't quite sure what it was. Nevertheless, something was pulling him, something important, something bigger than his bank account or his love life. This in itself can be motivational.

Under Pickett's byline was his e-mail address. Austin hadn't spoken to Chops since graduation. Why? No particular reason. Just moving on, doing his own thing. But that was just it. He felt totally free again to do whatever he wanted. So he walked briskly into his office, logged onto the Internet, and pulled up Pickett's web site to see what the cat was up to. Then he called his travel agent. Only one seat needed this time. At last, he was on the move again.

Chapter 6

Getting into Stanford meant that doors would open for Austin, not just after graduation but for the rest of his life. Exactly how a young person deals with this kind of opportunity varies, of course, from person to person. Austin knew plenty of arrogant people at Stanford. They *expected* things to come their way... friends, dates, grades, money, success, privilege. Definitely privilege. On the other hand, Austin had plenty of friends who were pretty down to earth despite coming from rather wealthy families. Obviously, Austin didn't come from money – well, not that he knew of anyway (how funny *that* was in retrospect). So he was basically like a walking barometer for good people. He was basically a normal kid from Philly. People who hung out with him were really not interested in pretenses. Quite the contrary, in fact, Austin's friends were the kind of people who sought *escape* from pretense. Johnny Long was one such person. So was Cathy.

Many people would agree that Palo Alto is an ideal place to go to college. Whatever your interests, if Stanford doesn't have it, chances are something in the greater Palo Alto area does. That part of Northern California is idyllic – lovely scenery, energizing climate, an engaging mix of people and ideas, and a financially secure populace who actually *want* to be there. Lest this seem too urbane, the Stanford Cardinal football team recently boasted Bill Walsh as its head coach.

To this day, Walsh remains one of the greatest NFL coaches of all time. The shadow of Stanford University loomed large over Palo Alto. Similarly, many Stanford grads made it a point to get back to Palo Alto as often as possible.

Now that he had graduated and moved on, though, the prospect of his triumphant return was exhilarating. Yes, he was a little arrogant. But he had not returned since graduation. After graduation, he fell right under Johnny's wing. Then the money started to flow, and he got involved with the hospice house and traveling. All this was rewarding in its own way, the hospice house especially. But not a day went by that Austin did not feel a sense of continuity, a grand design behind it all. He once told Cathy that he "always felt fragmented" despite all his achievements. If he could only put it all together, most of life's petty annoyances would simply whither away. For Austin, this short trip out west was a step in that direction. Sometimes, "moving on" meant going back (not backward) in an odd sort of way.

He was back now, though, and he wanted to make the most of the opportunity. Being a musician, Austin was less dependent on linearity than most. He was comfortable going with the flow, which prepared him quite well for working in the stock market. When he read Pickett's review, dropping in on him seemed like the obvious thing to do at this point in his life. Sometimes moving on is going back. Why not? As Johnny Long told him time and time again, sometimes the answer is so much simpler than we may think. It's like Poe's *Purloined Letter*: The clue we are looking for may very well be dangling right in front of our faces. Naturally, we never notice it because we are so busy searching for something far more complex than things really are. Visiting Pickett was the obvious thing to do at this point in Austin's life.

This is not to say that the good old days were all wine and roses for Austin just because he was a music major. Despite his jovial demeanor, Tony "Chops" Pickett was a hardass about playing music "the way it is supposed to be played," so right away you knew you couldn't just throw some notes at him and expect a rave review. Pickett felt it was his personal responsibility to weed out wanna-be's. He was especially hard on Austin. Stanford was Stanford after all. He felt Austin had the raw talent to be a professional musician. But he also felt that Austin lacked the focus and drive, and *that* really bothered Pickett. "Play or get outta' the way," was Pickett's mantra.

Actually, Johnny Long was the same way. He allowed Austin to make his own investment decisions at the outset, but once Austin came on board as his client, Johnny was very cut and dry about it – they would use his growth-stock strategy or nothing at all. Moreover, if Austin had recommendations of his own, he'd better have sound reasoning behind them. When Austin began actually *working* with Johnny as a money manager, Johnny demanded complete focus and discipline to the tenets of his strategies. Come to think of it, even Austin's father was a hardass. Why else leave his son a million bucks with hurdles – actually return-on-investment hurdles – on another *five million*? Some people might actually find this a little warped, a little bit too Truman Capote.

Even though Johnny's strategies were simple in their premises, managing so much money and doing so successfully required consistency and attention to detail. The one crucial point about the growth-stock strategy was this – future events *will* change things. You could count on this. Likewise, those changes may be positive or negative. A stock's price would respond accordingly. The only thing was… you can't tell a *thing* about unknown *future* events from the price of that stock *today*. So what do you do? Well, that was the whole point of Johnny's growth-stock strategy… what to do given that reality. During his flight out to the West Coast to see Pickett, 35,000 feet above the earth, Austin realized that there was a grand symmetry here. He was worth what he was worth *today*. Likewise, he was who he was then and there in time. Of course, future events both good and bad would determine what he was worth and who he was in the future. So then… how could he apply the lessons learned from his successes in the market to his life in general. That is, how could he better understand the continuity of his life thus far and *look forward* into the future?

The three most important men in his life – his father, Tony Pickett, and Johnny Long – were all very, very disciplined men. They each had a well-defined plan for tackling inheritance, music, the stock market. Most importantly, they had a *strategy* for *life in general* that was a natural extension of this or that smaller project. There was the continuity in it. In fact, the more Austin thought about it during that six-hour flight, the more he began to realize that his father, Pickett, and Johnny all shared a common thread. Namely, they were *patient*, patient enough to let the future develop as it always will. And no matter what happened, they lived their lives focusing only on what they could control.

It's difficult to teach patience. Music was definitely a good vehicle for teaching patience. So much of playing well depends on timing. As it turned out, so too were Johnny's strategies. Austin was not the impetuous type, but as a kid neither was he remarkably patient. It was something he worked on. Losing his father definitely drew him toward the rasher side of decision making, perhaps because there was no physical authority to appease. Clearly, Austin's father had some insight into this sort of psychology because nothing could have been better planned that required his son and heir to master self-discipline before inheriting the bulk of the money. Hooking up with Johnny Long brought this plan to fruition in that his strategies required the exact sort of patience and discipline Austin's father envisioned for his son.

When Johnny first got his hands on Austin Montgomery, he sought to teach the young man an essential rule of thumb - As the future happens, make changes accordingly based on a disciplined way of making decisions. This was a total paradigm shift for Austin, just as it was for each of Johnny's clients. Austin was so accustomed to looking backward to make decisions about the present or future. To Johnny, this was the fatal flaw of investing. What a stock is worth today or who we are when we wake up is based on things we *already assume* about the future based on what we already know. This is true enough. And of course, if we make *no* assumptions about the future, we'll be nervous wrecks, like the stereotypical day trader or the neurotic – always second guessing, always self-doubting.

However, if we can develop a strategy for acting on future estimate changes *as they happen*, as new information comes to light, we can better understand the here-and-now of a stock's performance. It may be ironic. But does that mean it's not true? As in "The Purloined Letter," the answer may be right in front of our noses. We just have to see the obvious. To Johnny, it was obvious that a stock's long-term future performance boiled down to the stream of *new* information that would emerge over the years to come. Specifically, Johnny was concerned with earnings-estimate changes and dividend increases that were themselves the direct result of new information. Analysts would make revisions and, in the long term, these revisions would drive a stock's price higher or lower over a five year period.

Keep in mind, around this time, everyone had a theory for "cornering" the market. The bottom line was that in 1998 and the couple of years that followed, a blind man could have picked stocks and made money. The old adage that a rising tide lifts all boats was applicable here. But there was much more to Johnny's success than the relative strength of the markets. During huge growth spurts like this, Johnny's clients garnered a disproportionately high return. Over time, of course, this would level out. But in the long run – the only run that mattered for Johnny Long and his clients – the *downturns* were less severe.

Johnny had two strategies, a growth-stock strategy and a growth-of-income strategy. And while most people were panic selling into 2001, Johnny remained disciplined and focused on *when to sell and what to buy with the proceeds.* Sure, he had relatively high volatility – higher than the market average and higher than a certificate of deposit (CD). But remember this, he also had a consistent record of higher-than-market returns over a twenty-year period. The risk-to-reward scenario remained intact and prudent. Simply put, Johnny Long realized that *selling a big gainer too soon* is what drives underperformance. Volatility, then, was secondary to a stock's sound underpinning in earnings.

In 1999, everyone had a sure-fired method of success. Everyone with an idea marched through the array of financial networks touting this or that stock, this or that strategy for reaping huge rewards. Yes, Austin was walking into a market where the so-called pundits and talking heads would pontificate on the unique value of their particular investment discipline. And there was no shortage of cash flying around. Markets can make careers... or break them. Newcomers would experience *both* turns of fate in the years that followed 2000. The gut wrenching was excruciating. Adding fuel to the fire was the lack of experience and focus. Most money managers were newbies with no clearly delineated strategy for what to buy, when to sell, and what to do with the proceeds. It was copy-cat investing where new money followed older successful money.

At times it seemed nobody knew *why* a transaction was being made. Moreover, what were the guiding principles for reinvesting the money? Most of the pundits never bothered to say. The fact was, they had no idea themselves. They just followed the market and reaped their huge bonuses... until the market turned on them. Of course, it was never their fault. It was always the specter of something or someone else – Greenspan, a Soros-driven currency crisis, the analysts' faulty estimates. When times were good, money managers touted themselves across the airwaves; when times were bad, however, they quickly pointed the finger at someone else, never looking in the mirror to make a frank assessment of themselves or their methodologies.

It would quickly become apparent that jealousy, cronyism, and bitter competition were the norm throughout the financial world. This was especially true of the haughty proprietary traders, who, with math degrees under their arms, would use esoteric algorithms for making millions of electronic trades a day. But even fancy algorithms with millions of I.T. dollars behind them fell victim to underperformance in highly volatile markets. Had they looked, they would have seen that Johnny Long outperformed them. So naturally, they didn't look. All the time, Johnny Long kept chugging along doing his own thing and making money for himself and for his clients. A wonderful trait about Johnny was that he would never disparage the others. He stayed focused on the *positive* elements of what he alone was doing. Of course, Austin would inevitably stir a hornet's nest everytime he debated with other money managers throughout the world. All this, of course, was unknown to Austin when he first graduated college.

It was no wonder then that Austin welcomed a return to the relatively innocuous environment of Palo Alto and academia in general. He arranged to meet Pickett at the Coupa Café on Ramona Street. They hadn't spoken for a while and Austin was a bit nervous. More importantly, though, Pickett – like Austin's father and Johnny Long – had expectations... disciplines... strategies. What's more, they were all very demanding, Pickett perhaps most of all. Austin couldn't remember ever being yelled at by his father. His father had died when Austin was young. But he certainly could remember Pickett yelling at him. It came back to Austin in a flash as he drove past the Compton Lazben Hotel on Artesia on his way to the Coupa.

The Compton Lazben was home to the Indigo Jazz Club. It was also home to Austin's first professional gig. Pickett used to play to the local scene with a quintet called the *Redwave*. *Chops and the Redwave* had a nice local following. Pickett played piano and sang most of the tunes, Frank "The Fingers" Deason on guitar, a semi-retired Lee Taylor on drums, Pluckin' Don Bush on double bass, and a guy who just went by the name of Bubbles on alto and tenor sax. The name Bubbles for a sax player was obviously some sort of puny joke dating back to before Austin was born. Bubbles was like eighty-two years old and the fact was that nobody who was still alive knew his real name. In fact, it was often conjectured that even Bubbles himself had forgotten. Bubbles didn't believe in bank accounts, and he'd long since stopped driving, so you couldn't even rifle through his wallet to find out.

"Bubbles, what's you name?"

"Bubbles."

"No, I mean your real name."

"If that's what you call me, then that's my name." And that was that, time and time again for decades on end.

One night, Bubbles was M.I.A. leaving the *Redwave* short a sax player. So Pickett called Austin to sit in. Austin jumped at the chance. He was on his way to a blind date when the call came in. His date might well have been blind because she never saw him. After speaking with Pickett, Austin pulled a New York u-turn right in the middle of Hanover St. and sped off for the Indigo Club. This was the chance he'd been waiting for.

What followed was a perfectly typical first gig unless you're Mozart. That is to say, it was a near-total catastrophe brought on by an apoplectic fit of nerves. There was just too much pressure. Austin was completely afraid of messing up and disappointing the crowd. More importantly, he was terrified of letting Pickett down. Pickett was the closest thing to a father Austin could remember. Having grown up without a father, Austin never learned how to be proud of himself for himself. He was always worried about pleasing other people. As you might imagine, then, he overplayed something terribly and kept losing the beat.

It figured that Pickett was a stickler for exactitude and discipline in music. By the end of the gig, Pickett had turned more shades of black than a freshly-poured pint of Guinness. The guys in the band still remember that night. No one had *ever* heard Pickett curse like that before. In fact, they had never even heard of some of the more... shall we say "colorful" expressions Pickett used. Divine would have blushed. There was one bit involving a comparison between Austin's playing and some sort of mix between Pickett's third wife's mother and some beast common only to the backwater swamps of Pickett's imagination. To this very day, Frank Deason refuses to repeat it in mixed company ("mixed" meaning any person who believes in God). Poor Pluckin' Don Bush still stutters profusely whenever he tries to retell the story and requires at least four shots of Johnny Black to get all the way through the unexpurgated version.

Chapter 7

Austin cleared the memory from his mind when he saw Tony Pickett sitting at a corner table. It was the usual Pickett sitting there – cotton turtleneck in any color but white or red, tasteful gold bracelet instead of a watch, earth-tone slacks, and his trademark ostrich boots. Their eyes met, and Pickett rose to greet Austin.

Smiling that ear-to-ear, toothy smile of his, Pickett gave Austin the hug-and-shoulder-slap. "What's up, man? I am really happy to see you, man."

Austin blushed a little and took a seat across from Pickett. He ordered an iced latte and loosened up immediately. As much as he feared Pickett, he also became kind of laid back around him too. Sort of like a hipster affect. "I'm sorry it's been so long, bro. I don't know."

Pickett laughed and shook his head. "The first thing out of your mouth is an apology! Ain't that fitting."

Austin ignored him and returned fire. "I see you got a little fro thing going on up top there." He motioned to Pickett's hair.

"Yo, that ain't right. I'll have you know I flow with the fro, baby." They both started doing their best Commodores impression. Pickett trumped all with his impression of Lionel Richie being stabbed by his ex-wife. "Brother must have done some *bad* shit for that one. And anyway, you're still pale and ugly."

Austin blushed. "You're just mad about that night at the Indigo. Admit it."

"Admit it? When did I *not* say it, man. You gotta' be shittin' me with that. I never forgave Bubbles for that. Bubbles died by the way."

Austin cocked his head. "Really?"

"No, Austin. I'm making it up. What do you think. He was like ninety. Great player. Better than you, that's for damned sure, man!" Pickett slapped his hand on the table for emphasis.

Austin made a sarcastic grimace. "I know. I mean I'm sorry to hear that. It's just that you sort of expected him to live forever, you know?" He picked up his drink. "To Bubbles."

"To Jackson Alleluia Reed," said Pickett.

Austin was surprised. "You know his real name."

"I knew that cat for a long time, man. But I never knew his name until one of his kids gave the eulogy. Jackson Alleluia Reed. Great name for a tune, huh?"

Austin pursed his lips. "Hmph. So he had kids then?"

Pickett laughed. "Had kids? Get this. Turns out there were like a dozen 'Lil Bubbles running around through the years. Man made Larry King look like a rookie."

Austin almost spit out his latte laughing. "Alleluia! Can I get a waitress?"

Pickett gestured for the waitress. "Check out this chick. Her name's Cara. Anthropology student. She's dating one of my grad students, so I made a few calls for her."

"What can I get you, man?"

"We'll take two Johnny Black. Mine with Coke." She looked at Austin.

"Rocks," he said.

Pickett took Cara by the arm. "Baby, get this cat whatever he wants. He's rich you know. And *he's* paying." He looked at Austin.

Austin grimaced. "How did you know that?"

Pickett laughed. "Do I look like an anthropology student to you?"

"Hey now!" said Cara with her hands on her hips. "You watch it or I'll put Visine in your drink, buddy." Off she went.

Pickett turned back to Austin. "Seriously, well done, Austin. I'm very proud of you."

Austin smiled and looked down at the table for a second. "Wow, thanks Tony. But how did you know about that?"

"Well, after you e-mailed me that you were coming, I Googled you. You're all over the place. Not for music, though."

"Ha! Too true. I can't even begin to tell you."

Pickett leaned in closer. He had something on his mind. There was something about the hospice home that had special meaning for him. "Tell me a little bit about the place in the Bahamas, man. It sounds like something... really something, man."

Austin saw right away that Pickett had ideas on his mind. Starting out with his mother's death, Austin recounted his tale. The secret estate, the multi-million dollar challenge, Johnny Long, Cathy, the break-up, all the money. Of course, Austin spoke of the *ennui*. Pickett listened quietly for the duration, interrupting Austin from time to time only to reorder another round of drinks. Austin was actually weirded out a little. Pickett was *never* quiet for very long. Being a university instructor suited him well. He could talk a mile a minute for what seemed like hours. What was Pickett so interested in? Instead of chiming in with this or that comment, Pickett seemed to be adding something up in his mind. You could literally see him putting two and two together, so to speak.

The end of Austin's tale came somewhere around the seventh round of Johnny Black. Wisely, Austin followed Pickett's lead and started cutting the booze with Coke. He knew Pickett would explode with commentary sooner or later, and their get together would run its next leg at any time. The one thing about musicians – when they drank, they talked. And when they talked, they drank even more. Repeat as necessary.

Pickett cleared his throat and excused himself for a minute. When he returned from the bathroom, Pickett put his right elbow on the table and rested his chin in his hand. He cleared his throat again. Neither one would be driving home at this point.

"You've got a lot to be proud of, Austin. Do you know that?"

"Huh….," Austin thought for a moment. "Thank you."

"Good God, that was a good story. Is it true?"

"Hell yeah! Gimme a break, man. Would I make up a story about my mother dying?"

"Would I make up a story about Bubbles dying?" They both laughed. "What I mean is the part about the Bahamas? Is the home really doing well? I mean, doing well is kind of a freaky way of referring to a hospice home, but you know what I mean. How do you Wall Street cats put it – delivering on its anticipated intent?"

Austin smiled. "Yeah, it is doing really, really great. I mean, like you said… it's sad and stuff." Austin laughed. "But yes, it's 'delivering on its anticipated intent,' as you academic cats say."

"So you donated the cash to get it going?"

"Actually, I gave some of the money to build it and some more to operate it."

"Geez, they're still running off your *original* money? What are you, Rockefeller?"

Austin did his best Gangsta pose. "Yo, yo! I got *mad* dollars, yo!"

Pickett was quiet for a second. "Did I ever tell you that you are still pale and ugly? And trying to pull a bad *Fiddy Cent* don't help, yo." They both laughed, ordered another round from Cara, the anthropology student, who was doing lab work apparently by being a cocktail waitress, and continued right along into the third hour.

"Seriously," said Pickett. "You gotta tell me how much that sort of thing costs. I'm not prying. I have a reason for asking, so fess up." Austin gave him the number, but Pickett seemed incredulous. "But that's not *that* much. I mean, I'll take it, but still….shit, it's a hell of a lot more than I make in ten years, but you know what I'm saying." He did some quick calculations in is head. Given his blood-alcohol level, he just rounded to the nearest hundred-thousand. "I still don't see how they live off what was left over after they built the place. Construction's not cheap, right?

Austin buzzed his lips. "It's ridiculous what it costs, especially in a resort area like that. But I guess they made enough, right? It's still running great."

"Well, don't you manage their money, or the foundation or whatever – by the way, I'm sure you named the foundation after me. Thank you."

"No, I named it the Foundation for the Pale and Ugly."

Pickett laughed. "Yo, that ain't funny when you're talking about cancer patients, man!" Austin put his face in his hands. "How is it," continued Pickett, "that you manage the money and you don't know how they get income? Are you like *that* lucky? 'Cause if you are, man, spread that over here."

Austin shook his head. "No, no, no… *I* don't manage the money now. I only donated it. Well, some of it, actually. The guy, Johnny Long, I was telling you about manages it. Some of his clients also donated money. Now *those cats* are loaded. He's the guy who showed me how to invest. I guess I never really inquired how he was squeezing out so much income. I've been kinda focused on my own clients. Hmm… And why are you interrogating me and showing up my ridiculous ignorance?"

Pickett nodded his head. "Ahhh… I see. I'll explain in a minute." He took a sip of his drink. "So that guy Long runs the money. But I thought you said you made it with some growth-stock strategy of his or something?"

Austin cocked his head. "Yeah, that's right. But then… I'm not really sure how they get income after that. I thought I just said that. Are you trying to belabor the point about my being a knuckle-headed rich kid?" They looked at each other.

"So I'm not totally out of my mind. Either Johnny made some ridiculous amount of money for them in growth stocks or he is doing something else with the money to get some sort of income out of it."

"No, no, you're right I guess. But rates have been dropping for the last, like, I don't know how many years. To be quite honest with you, I have no idea what he's doing."

Pickett laughed. "I want to be reincarnated as *that* guy! Geez, I hope you know more about your own account. Ha! Come to think about it, maybe I ought to be reincarnated as *you*. Looks like money just follows your ass." He slapped his hand down on the table, much louder this time than when he did it three hours ago. "Maybe you should just write me a fat check. You know, for being your sounding board here."

Austin shrugged. "Actually man, you're right. With the Bahamas place, I just let Johnny do it all. I mean, I totally understand the growth strategy thing, so I know *why* he makes investment decisions. And – I might add – I have done quite well for *my own* clients using it, thank you very much. And you know, if I quickly glance at the Bahamas account statement, I'm sure we have income from dividends or something, but I honestly have *no idea* where that comes from. Honestly, I never really worried about it. This guy Johnny Long is like that. You never worry."

"Maybe you have bonds or something like that? You're lucky, dude."

Austin shook his head. "No, I am *sure* that I don't have any bonds. Johnny's always inveighing against them. But hey – that's enough about my money. I feel like you're arranging my marriage or something weird like that. What the hell are you scheming about? I'm not building a new wing in the music department, so just forget about it. You Stanford folks have enough bread of your own."

Pickett looked serious again. "First of all, you *are* one of us Stanford folks, as you say. And we will *definitely* be having a talk about a new wing. But that's not what I was thinking about. You know your timing is impeccable... ha, much better than your timing when you play! It's so amazing that you just thought of me and popped out here like this. It's amazing. A week ago, I wasn't even in the country. Did I tell you that? No, probably not."

"So what makes this some sort of magic moment then?"

Pickett leaned in. "I was in *Africa*, man. Dig *that*."

Austin sat back in surprise. "Really? Wow, what was that like?"

Pickett's face lit up. He had told his story of Africa daily for the last week, but he never grew tired of retelling it. He would play it slightly differently each time as if he was doing a standard number on tour. A different hook here, a different tie-in there. It all depended upon the audience... who they were, what they were about. For Austin, Pickett jumped right on the Bahamas home theme. That was the connection for him between past, present, and future. Here was continuity.

"I had an amazing time, man. The people are *awesome*! I would definitely go back."

"What sent you out there in the first place? Trying to get back to the Motherland? See what sort of turtlenecks the African cats wear over there?"

Pickett laughed. "Funny, but lame. And it's like boiling hot over there. Even the heat sweats. Anyway, I was in Jo'Burg playing back-up for a bunch of bands. Bono's always doing some sort of AIDS concert series, so I jumped in on this one."

Austin grimaced. "What the hell is Jo'Burg?"

Pickett laughed. "Don't worry about my turtlenecks, man. Study a map instead. Yeah, Johannesburg. As in South Africa, right? You heard of it. Nelson Mandela... even you pasty cats heard of him."

Austin rolled his eyes and groaned. "Oh, really? Thanks, I'd never heard of him. Anyway, is Bono cool? I would like to meet him. Can you hook it up?"

Pickett made his *you've got to be joking, right?* expression now famous among his grad students. "Uhhh... I'm sure it would make his day. Spare me, man. Bono can wait. He spends most of his free time shopping for the perfect pair of sunglasses anyway. No, no, be serious for a second. I'm talking about *whole populations dying off over the next fifty years!* Isn't that the most bizarre thing you've ever heard?"

Austin tried to think as literally as possible. The implications were staggering. "Like literally?"

Pickett became more animated. "Bitch running rampant. Just think about it. Also, to the North is Botswana. They have... I think like one-and-a-half million people, right? Over *half* of those poor folks are HIV positive. Think about that for a sec. Think about it like this. Let's say you were visiting and you went out one night. OK, all those chicks you're looking at... *flip a coin* and heads they got it, tails they don't. A stupid damned coin. That's screwed up. Creepy, isn't it? Heads they got it, tails they don't. Which means, heads *you* got it, tails you don't. Real Russian roulette stuff, man. And what... are people just gonna stop having sex? I don't think so. Not in the hard wiring."

Austin sat back and was quiet for a moment. Pickett was looking at him and nodding his head as if he was reading Austin's mind. "What's really disturbing," said Austin, "is how they have generations being born with it then? It's like a downward spiral sort of thing. It's hard to break the cycle."

"Let me tell you, man, you can really get lost in the sadness and political rumble. But think of it like your Bahamas project. There's something else going on there behind the scenes, right? Like you said, the optimism and positive thinking where you least expect it. For example, they're making amazing breakthroughs like preventing HIV from passing to fetuses. I guess that's the key."

Austin agreed. "Yeah, you've got to stop babies being born with it."

"Otherwise that's it. End of game for an entire country. Doesn't that just totally blow you away?"

Austin nodded. "Yeah. I don't think about it too much honestly. So then you're into this cause now?"

Pickett rubbed his face. "Ah, you know me, man. Not really into causes." He made quotation marks with his fingers. "Not my bag, you know?"

"Mmm... I hear you there. I can't tell you how many people hit me up for donations and stuff like that."

"Yeah, we should all have your problems, man."

Austin rolled his eyes again. "What I mean is that I need to feel some sort of personal connection, even if it's only money—"

"Precisely *because* it's *only* money! It's not *you*. Hey, I like that one, man. Very Schoenberg."

"How do you mean?"

Pickett laughed. "I have no idea, man. Anyway. The whole AIDS thing seemed kind of old to me. I'm not trying to be a jerk or anything, but it's like out of sight, out of mind, you know? I mean, who in their right mind can imagine an *entire country* disappearing from AIDS?"

Austin agreed. "Well yeah. That's what I mean. I need to... *feel* it to be in it. I see it on T.V., but it doesn't really make an impact on me."

Pickett started snapping. "Like Gil Scott Heron said, 'The revolution will not be televised.' Whatever your politics, that's definitely the word."

"So," said Austin. "You're getting into the Africa AIDS thing?"

"Well..." Pickett was searching for the words. "For me... this is going to sound a little whacked, but for me... it's the sheer *size* of the thing."

"Africa?"

"No," continued Pickett. "The math involved. You know me, I love the order of things. What staggers me about AIDS in Africa is the *math*. Whole countries dying off? Can that possibly be? The math says so."

"Yeah," said Austin. "Problem is, it's still about sex for most people, so they're not going to care very much so long as they don't have it."

Pickett's voice got serious. "I'm telling you sure as Muddy Waters is old... AIDS is really the second Great Plague. Did you know that the first plague killed over *half* of Europe? Isn't that amazing? Who even thinks about it any more, but it's unbelievable. I'm telling you. AIDS is the same thing, but this time in Africa and parts of Asia. *That's* what really interests me." The Berklean in Pickett started to come out now.

Austin smiled. "This isn't going to be one of those Numerology rants of yours, is it?"

Pickett made a face. "Whatever... it works. But anyway, we're in the midst of the next Great Plague, and nobody seems to really be approaching it this way. *That's* what clicked for me when I was over there. The *scale* of the thing. It's *bigger* than we are, Austin. There's a cycle at work here, like it or not. There is. The planet has a way of shaking us off from time to time, and *that* scares me, man." They were both quiet for a moment. Then Pickett continued. "Look, it's no coincidence that you suddenly just up and thought to yourself... 'Gee, I think I'll call Tony.' There's a greater order to things, man."

Austin shrugged. "And-?"

"I need your help. Africa changed my life. I don't even feel goofy saying it, so I know it must be right. But I need your help."

"Oh God," cried Austin. "This isn't about money, is it?" He really felt uncomfortable.

"Austin, man, everything's about money. Good God, what else have you talked about since we sat down." Pickett held up his hands. "And I don't mean that in a bad way, you know that. It's a major thing in your life... for us all. But I don't want your money, man. Give me a break. I want your *help*. I want to open a center here that focuses on the big *historic* picture."

"You think that will help?"

"First of all, like I said, Africa changed my life." Pickett grew more intense. "Second... there is an ancient cycle in motion here, like it or not. And third... putting this thing into a *historic* context rather than a sexual one *will most definitely catalyze millions and millions of people.* Trust me, it will. That's what I can do for the world as a 'thank you.' We're all in it together, you know. I *need* to fire it up again, Austin. Know what I mean?"

Austin was quiet for a minute. He couldn't believe what he was hearing. He had been looking for something to fire him back up for a while now. He needed to *feel* again, like when he and Johnny were working on the hospice home. Was Pickett actually right with all his Numerology crap? Actually, did it even matter? Of course, not. Facts were facts. His point about history and plagues and stuff was dead on, pun *intended.* Maybe this *was* no coincidence. Then again, did that even matter?

Here they were, sitting together, making things happen. It had been a while. And come to think of it, Austin recognized here the *exact* sort of thing he was now free to investigate since breaking up with Cathy. He wouldn't have to do any explaining or rationalizing. He could just *do.* That's what he loved about working with Johnny and about working in finance in general – you could just *do.* Show results and people leave you alone. No nagging or haranguing. There was definitely a project here, an opportunity to do something positive and good and make some money doing it. That's the win-win we all look for. Everything else is falling short of the mark. But like anything else, you had to recognize the opportunity and then actually *seize it* where most people let it pass right by unnoticed or, worse yet, uncaptured.

Austin leaned forward. "So what can I do for you, Tony? To repay *you* for everything you've taught me."

Pickett shook his head. "Thank you, but don't worry about little ole me, man. I don't expect people to do anything more than what people do... namely, *be arrogant and self-interested.* That's the key."

Austin wasn't sure if Tony was being sarcastic or not. "Really?"

"Oh yeah," continued Pickett. "Think about it. Who cares about something happening in Africa. But tell a rich cat that he can have his name plastered all over some African town and be the Great White Hope *for real*! Now *that's* how to get stuff done over there. That's what I want to do."

"Oh... well I guess you're right. Speaking for myself, when I opened the hospice home, I *did* get a total rush like that. I've got to be honest."

Pickett reached across the table and slapped Austin's shoulder. "And there's not a damned thing wrong with that, man. Good for you, that's what I say. More power to you."

"So again," said Austin. "What can I do to help?"

"I don't want your money. I want you to help me raise funds for this center. We really don't need a big building or anything like that. Just a modest facility. But we need cats with money on board. That's where you come in. I can get the famous cats, but you got to get the money guys. We'll do cool fundraisers and stuff. We'll work it out later. But it'll be the right thing to do. And you can maybe get some business out of it, too."

Austin was surprised. He could make money off this with no problem. But more importantly, Johnny jumped into his head immediately. So did the idea of leaving a legacy larger than oneself. Is that what his father had in mind when drawing up his will? Austin was overcome by a flood of emotion that only surges when one's past is redeemed – yes, *redeemed* – by being incorporated into one's present. For the first time in a long time, Austin began to feel that he actually *wasn't* banished from a life of symmetry and meaning. Austin suddenly realized that, just as with Johnny's stock strategy, what has happened has already happened. That's all "priced in," so to speak, in who he was right then and there. After this talk with Pickett, Austin saw his future as bright again. His stock in himself was going up again because his future was looking better than it had yesterday.

He wasn't expecting this at all. He only thought he should get together with Pickett. Who knew? Maybe things would fit together after all? Austin's eyes were glassy. He looked at Pickett. "I really need this. Thank you."

Pickett smiled. "Hey man, I *know*. From the moment you walked in the place, I knew your ass was stuck in neutral."

Austin laughed and wiped his eyes. "Let's just say that I recently replaced my clutch and got a tuneup and cleared out some blockage. Ready to put the pedal to the metal again."

"Ha! Sounds like women trouble to me. So romantic of you… but no. I've seen cats with blown clutches, man. And until you got a needle in your arm or a bunch of household chemicals up your nose, man, you are just fine." Pickett paused for a minute. He could tell his former student needed to speak his troubles. It was a lot like playing music actually. He goaded Austin. "You know, I'm just surprised you didn't take up a new project after the Bahamas place got going… if I'm being honest. I feel like I kinda lucked out finding you in between projects and available to help and all that."

Austin looked up. "Mmm... I don't know. I'm scared, I guess. You know, whenever I get a large windfall or a great client or a lot of success, I am a little afraid of losing it."

Pickett pursed his lips. "Scared of *what*? What on God's good Earth do you have to be afraid of? You're limo getting caught in traffic? I thought you Wall Street cats were all risk-to-reward and all that ice in veins, cucumber-cool stuff."

"Yeah, yeah... what I mean is when I first got the money from my father, I could just take the million and walk, or invest it for certain benchmarks and possibly get five million more."

Pickett followed along. "Yes," he said. "You told me that part. Interesting dad you had. I could of used one like him!"

"Well," continued Austin, "I was totally afraid of what to do. I've had that same feeling for a couple of years now. I don't want to lose everything now that I have it."

Pickett jumped in. "You mean like money? Which is important ..."

"-exactly. I never really had any growing up. Now that I do, it's like I'm almost paralyzed with fear of losing things."

Pickett shook his head. "So by doing *less*, you actually intend to get more? I'm not sure about all the math and finance, but it doesn't pass the smell test to me. Just sounds wrong. And anyway, that's not why we're on this Earth, Austin... to live in fear. No way. What a waste. And it might not seem like it now, but when you're old and looking back, you're inevitably gonna take inventory of what you did and saw."

"But," said Austin, "what if I try something and it doesn't work out. What if I, like, can't do it? I'm really not up for failing. Why bother now?"

"Man, you gotta be kiddin' me. So you're telling me that your life is pretty much done then?"

"No, I didn't say--."

"Sure you did. Think about it. You already have what you have. You're too afraid of losing that to try new challenges. So you tread water. I got news for you, man—"

"What?"

"Treadin' water ain't swimming, and it ain't drownin' neither. It's bullshit, it's *limbo*, and that ain't livin'.' That much I *do* know. So you might as well just die. But you know what?"

Austin was somewhat annoyed. "What?"

"Ha! Try going to Africa and telling them folks that you're afraid to take risks. Why don't you try that?" Pickett was a bit fired up now. "Go ahead. Try telling them. Do you have any idea how much they would love the chance to *live* in the way that you and I – winners of the birth lottery being born in America – are sitting here enjoying the luxury of philosophical debate. Philosophy is a privilege, man. You should know that."

Austin lowered his head. It was obvious to Pickett that he had touched a nerve.

Pickett thought for a second. "Well, it's interesting that you said you were afraid of *what to do*. That is a nightmare, let me tell you. Take me, for example. When I'm sitting behind that piano playing a solo or whatever… just riffing… *fear* never enters my mind! Anticipation… excitement… self-confidence… *that* is what fills me. How do I know what's going to pass through my fingers? As soon as I lay down one note, I know what to do with it, I know where I can play next, I choose, and that's that… and so on, and so on." He waited for a moment, but Austin didn't seem to get the parallel. "Doesn't that sound a lot like—"

"Like Johnny's stock strategy. Yeah!"

"You were telling me that he focuses on three questions – umm… what to buy, when to sell, and what to do with the proceeds. It occurs to me that that's the kind of general question you can apply to anything."

Austin was exuberant. Only a few people had figured out how to connect Johnny's investment principles to other areas of their life. Truth be told, it was how Austin decided he and Cathy should part ways. It was time to sell and move elsewhere to invest the proceeds of his life and time. Same for Cathy. Earnings estimates for their relationship had been cut, so to speak.

"Yes, that's right!" exclaimed Austin. "I've never really figured out how to explain that to people. So how do you think that applies to me right now?"

"Well," said Pickett, "here you are looking for something to... invest yourself in, right?" Austin nodded. "OK, then, let's follow along. What to buy?"

"Oh," said Austin, "picking a new project. OK. What to buy? Well, I'll have to think about it I guess."

"Of course you do! And when you finish that project, you'll have to take your reward or disappointment and move on to new investments of yourself... new projects. Right?"

"That's it exactly. Yeah."

Well, here it was. Austin flew clear across the country only to have a *musician* school him on applying his *own* investment strategy to life's challenges. Austin knew then and there that his old self would have been totally depressed by this fact. Sitting there with Pickett, however, Austin felt safe. He didn't feel like he missed something or disappointed someone at all. Instead, he felt exhilarated. After all, he *did* think to call Pickett. He *did* fly out there. Geez, he *did* go to Stanford.

He and Pickett had been talking for almost four hours. They had been drinking for most of that time, and Austin needed to grab a cab and go to bed. Nevertheless, he was so happy he met up with Pickett. They would talk next week about planning the first fundraiser. One of these days, he would get to meet Bono. In the meantime, though, Austin felt he really needed to pay Johnny a visit. It had been several weeks since they last spoke. After his conversation with Pickett, Austin realized he needed to be more involved in the workings of his own life. If there was some sort of grand system at work, then he would be involved in oiling the gears. If there was not, and life was simply a series of random events based on the decisions we make... well, so be it. He would still be involved and spend his cocktail time debating fate versus free will like he did as an undergrad.

There was no denying, though... this all sounded to Austin a lot like Johnny's strategy applied to life in general. Pickett was right. Austin had a sneaking suspicion that there was actually more to

Johnny – and more to his relationship with Johnny – than he imagined. Austin had the strange feeling that there were things which involved him in the past that he did not even know about. Perhaps Johnny held the key.

Chapter 8

The rest of the week in California went quickly. Austin visited all his old haunts around town. He even got to see Pickett play with his new trio. The flight back east was the best flight Austin could remember. He jotted down a quick list of affluent and connected people to start out with for Pickett's first fundraiser. He was also excited about seeing Johnny. Thinking back, Austin realized Pickett was on to something when he extended the growth-stock strategy to include life in general. It made perfect sense really. Austin ran it through in his head.

Johnny applied three basic questions to every investment decision. *What do you buy? When do you sell? What do you do with the proceeds? The most important one of the three is when to sell. That represents about 95% of an investor's long term success.* It was so seemingly obvious. For Johnny Long, things usually were. The man had an aura about him that said "consistent" and "reliable." This is true of many successful people. They aren't necessarily smarter or wiser than other people. Rather, they seem to have figured out a discipline that covers all aspects of their lives, whether work, personal, or spiritual. Thinking about what Pickett had said, Austin wondered if this air of consistency and reliability came from Johnny actually applying these three questions to his general decision making in life.

48

Johnny lived his strategy. He could talk about it for hours with strangers on a train. And his client base included some extremely wealthy people including a Saudi Prince among other dignitaries. Nevertheless, Johnny was unassuming. He was neither brash nor arrogant. Quite the contrary, he was generous and valued human *connection* as much as anything else. Johnny Long was one of those people whose success enables them to seek meaning in life's finer distinctions – the value of family, teaching others to teach themselves, one's soul.

Back when he first had to make important investment decisions per his father's will, Austin put immense trust in Johnny Long. For Austin, this was perhaps the highest compliment he could pay someone – putting complete trust in another. It required him to be more intimate than he liked. He felt vulnerable. Similarly, Johnny took very seriously the trust his clients placed in him. It didn't matter a lick how big their account was, so long as he could employ his investment discipline appropriately. In fact, he often reminded his prospects and clients alike that his way of *repaying* their trust was to employ a strict investment strategy. When Austin first heard this, it clicked. He had visited with a number of so-called financial advisors before choosing Johnny and recognized right away that Johnny was different. As hard as it was for Austin to believe, no one he met before Johnny had a clearly delineated strategy that could answer the Big Three questions.

There was nothing fancy about Johnny's strategy, at least not with the Big Three questions. Johnny never professed to be some sort of clairvoyant. As Johnny was fond of saying, "The point is not so much *what* strategy you employ but rather that it is logical and makes sense." Having a strategy that is bad and non-logical is believing in a false god. It made perfect sense to Johnny Long that, as an investment advisor, he'd be able to answer just three basic questions. But so few others did. Of course, his growth-stock strategy was more complex than this, but the point remained – have a strategy that you believe in.

Austin remembered the time he first walked into Johnny's office on Walnut Street in Philadelphia. At first, he was intimidated. There was no doubting it, the money establishment presented a formidable front as if to say "Interlopers Beware." The venerable halls of Wall Street – the very same halls once patrolled by the historical giants like

J.P. Morgan, Rockefeller, Gould, Getty, the entire pantheon of capitalist gods – were by no means easy to access. The world of high finance appeared formidable indeed from the outside. But for all its cronyism, for all its "insider trading," so to speak, in who knows who, no business allowed for such flat-out *opportunity*. Because in the end, when it gets down to cracking a nut – and it *always* gets down to cracking nuts – performance rules the day. The markets recognize performance. It's the basis of a company's success. Well, so too with people. What the system lacked in transparency it more than made up for allowing in personal achievement, and you can't ask for anything else.

Johnny seemed to understand this principle intuitively. As a result, he always seemed so comfortable not just with himself but with his profession as a whole. Austin was immediately at ease when he first met Johnny. Naturally, Austin was very anxious not having any sort of background in finance or investing. But Johnny's three questions seemed so easy to understand. Austin expected something far more complex and over his head. Looking back now, Austin felt confident that things in life *could* actually be kind of easy. Life did not *have* to be dangerous and frightening as it was for so many of the intellectual sort running around campuses. Pickett made a good point the other day – "Look at Kierkegaard or Heidegger, or Nietzsche," he pointed out. "Were they any happier for all their brain pain? Naw, that detective in one of those Poe stories who just walks in, takes in the facts, and puts it together is the really happy dude. It all makes sense for him. It doesn't matter if it's some sort of ultimate Truth with a capital T."

This strategy of Johnny Long's – these Big Three questions – could actually be some sort of philosophy for living. *This* he would have to explore when he met with Johnny. In the meantime, though, Austin just sat back and enjoyed the last leg of his flight, the best flight he could remember. Just a week or so ago, he was rolling out of bed alone and getting ready to take on the world again. Now, he felt connected to the world and re-energized. This AIDS project had him going again and he hadn't even started on it yet. Really though, it was getting together with Pickett again. For the first time in a long time, Austin believed that he *could* actually connect with people, despite what Cathy kept telling him. She was right about one thing though – he had to make the *effort*. For that insight, he would always be thankful.

As his flight made its final approach back into Philly, Austin caught himself humming *The Girl from Ipanema*. Pickett's new trio had played a cool, slinky version for about thirty minutes the other night. That used to be Austin's favorite tune to play. It took him away to someplace far off and happy... some place where no one ever suffered. If he had a couple of guys playing with him, Austin could play that tune for hours before coming back to reality. He had neither played nor hummed that song for quite some time. And yet there he sat, buckling his seat belt and returning his tray table and seat back to their full upright positions... humming *The Girl from Ipanema*. He was about to arrive.

Chapter 9

When Austin walked into Johnny's office, they all knew him by name, even the other brokers, who never tried to poach him. How could they? Even if they *had* access to Johnny's strategy, they saw themselves more as asset gatherers rather than money managers, not to mention the fact that it was much safer to stick money in mutual funds or something like that. Or so they supposed. Austin had his own flourishing business. But even so, everyone knew he belonged to Johnny Long. He was Johnny's boy, and that gave him huge credibility.

Austin's office was on the other side of the building from Johnny's. When he first started, Austin had a cubicle more or less outside Johnny's office. But as he became successful in his own right with his own client base, the office manager decided to keep a safe distance between Austin and Johnny. In brokerage, an office manager had to approach his pool of brokers like a portfolio itself. Each had to be managed like a stock, bought up and sold off accordingly. Austin's manager didn't want too much power being concentrated with any one advisor, especially Johnny Long. If Johnny Long left the company, for example, he might try to take Austin with him. This had to be prevented. Moreover, Johnny seemed to have a way of staying above the office politics and the general market fray that consumed everyone else. Managers will always find this threatening. Office politics are what keep people in check, after all.

So when it came time for Austin to be promoted and given his own office, his manager saw to it that it was situated away from Johnny's. Accordingly, Johnny and Austin didn't necessarily see each other every day. It used to be Austin would make several trips daily to Johnny's office for consultation. But since things had been going so well for Austin on his own, he found himself tied to his desk a bit more than he preferred. Hey, nothing to complain about... being too busy managing money. Not in this business. Still, Austin went to work that Monday after seeing Pickett determined to spend more time with Johnny. The long weekend out West did him good. It was back to basics, back to his roots for Austin. If he was doing this well on his own, thought Austin, just imagine how much more he was about to achieve hooking up with Johnny again.

People can have synergy. Most of the jealousy Austin encountered when he first started was more or less unfounded. The fact was that Johnny *always* made himself available to his colleagues. But he was intractable when it came to compromising on his strategies. He was always quick to offer advice when asked. The problem was that most brokers didn't want to take it. Instead, they wanted to hear what they wanted to hear – insights on short-term trading techniques, how to sell managed-money products, what mutual funds where favored at the time.

Austin and Johnny hit it off because Johnny's strategies made intuitive sense to Austin whereas other brokers found Johnny complex and, quite frankly, too dangerous. Why would they risk taking responsibility for investment decisions when they could gather assets and pass them to the "pros" who ran mutual funds, etc.? What they didn't understand – and what Austin did – was that having a unique and successful approach to investing set one apart and allowed one to prospect and accumulate massive amounts of money under management. Just as Johnny taught Austin the premise of risk-to-reward in managing money, he also taught the boy about incorporating a risk-to-reward strategy in developing his own business as well.

So the jealousy was unwarranted. Anyone at First American Investors could have followed Johnny's strategies. They chose not to. They chose *not* to manage their clients' money but rather to pass it off to other people, to "professionals" who allegedly knew more. And maybe they did. Maybe, too, Austin's flat out ignorance of the investing world made it easy for him to see the value in what Johnny was doing because he was untainted, un-pressured, free to make his own decisions. The trick now was to remain as free even though he had a large income, lots of money under management, and a sizable net worth of his own to protect. Optimism was the key. It always was. It always will be.

Indeed, remaining optimistic and positive made Austin likable even to those who were envious of his success. Moira, Johnny's personal assistant, adored Austin because he was like a breath of fresh air in the office. She saw him come around the corner toward Johnny's office right away and beamed him one of her gracious smiles. "Hey there, hot shot," she called out and gave him a wink. It had been a while since they flirted.

Austin winked back and slipped into an awful Sean Connery imitation. "Yes, Miss Moneypenny. You're looking marvelous this morning." He leaned in and kissed her on the cheek. He was hiding something behind his back. Moira caught it right away.

"And what do you have behind your back, your little black book perhaps?"

"Now Miss Moneypenny, there is only one book with you in it, my dear."

Moira smiled and cocked her head. "Oh, really. And what, pray tell would that be?"

If he was going to stoke things with Johnny, this was the place to start. Austin handed her the bouquet of calla lilies he was hiding behind his back. "The Good Book, dear Miss Moneypenny, for you *are* the angel."

Moira took the flowers and made enough noise for the other secretaries to notice her (of course, they had been watching the whole time). "Well, dinner some time would be nice, too," she said.

Austin made it a policy never to become intimate with co-workers for any number of reasons. Nevertheless, he blushed a bit. "*That*, Miss Moneypenny, would be *far* too enjoyable for the likes of me."

Moira shrugged. "Oh well, your loss I guess. And by the way, thank you for the flowers, hon. They're my favorite."

Austin bowed slightly. "But of course, Miss Moneypenny."

Just then Joe "The Tuna" Marentona popped into the office. Marentona became The Tuna because he was always caught in some sort of net. He was always stuck in this position or getting trapped by an option expiration. He was always, always impeccably dressed. Yet at times, the Emperor wore no clothes. He was always, always tan. Yet, inside he was white as a ghost whenever option expiration day came around. Today was option expiration day, and The Tuna was seeking Johnny's advice.

Moira intercepted him per usual. "Hey Jo-Jo. How's it going, love?" She shot a glance at Austin and they both smirked.

The Tuna was sweating. He was *always* sweating. And not just a little perspiration. Big, salty droplets of sweat rolled down his face in a steady stream throughout the day. "Dude, you're sweating like a madman," said Austin.

The Tuna patted Austin on the back and wiped his brow with the tissue Moira handed him as if on cue. "Sweatin'," he said. "Sweatin', I sold calls on Google for God's sake. I sold calls on Google for all my guys. Oh yeah, they loved the income, but now what? Like I never explained it to them. Give me a freakin' break. I'll tell ya' what... it's my ass, that's what. I picked the wrong day to quit drinking." He turned to Moira and gave her his sweaty tissue. She disposed of it with two fingers. "Is the Big Man in?"

"Now Jo-Jo, you know very well what he's going to tell you."

The Tuna started looking around frantically as if the secret were written somewhere on the wall. "I don't want to hear about three questions right now, man. I really don't. The stock can't go any higher. There's no way. I picked the wrong day to quit taking Valium. Where's the irrational exuberance stuff? Huh? Huh?" He turned to Austin. "Dude, Heavy Hitter, what are you doin'?" The Tuna was sweating on his top lip.

Austin looked at Moira. He couldn't resist the opportunity. "Short it. Turn around on all your positions."

The Tuna's face lit up. He started snapping his fingers and popping his hands. "Yeah, yeah. You're right. It's not going higher, no way. Thanks, player."

Moira clicked her tongue loudly. "Joey, don't pay attention to a word he says." She shot a look at Austin. But the Tuna was already down the hallway popping his head into any open door. "Google's topped out... Google's topped out... Google's topped out. I'm short. I picked the wrong day to quit smoking."

Moira frowned at Austin. Then they both started laughing hysterically. Austin's side hurt. Johnny Long emerged from his office, arms outstretched. "So this is how you distract my staff?" He and Austin embraced. "It's good to see you, Austin. Or is it Player? Where were you all last week? I heard this rumor you were in the market and available again."

Johnny stepped out of his office, saving Austin from having to reveal personal details to coworkers, especially when they wanted a piece of him. "Did I hear Joe out here?"

Moira chocked down a laugh. "You mean Sweaty Sweater? Yes," she said.

"Clammy Sammy," said Austin.

"Sticky Ricky," said Moira.

"Mr. Moist."

Johnny held up his hand. "OK, OK."

"He's getting crushed on Google," said Austin. "Go figure. He must have gone through like a box of tissues already today."

Johnny shook his head. "Let me guess... not interested in the strategy, right?"

"Not right for the Tuna," chimed in Austin.

"Huh... Christ," said Johnny. "Next he'll be shorting the thing." They all chuckled. Johnny turned to Moira. "Call him and tell him we raised estimates again. He might want to add to his long position." He took Austin by the arm. "And you..."

"Me?" said Austin with mock surprise.

"Come in and sit down before you cause any more trouble. Something tells me you've got quite enough on your hands now. Stop distracting my secretary. She has enough trouble. What have you been up to? How was California? Weird being back at the old college campus, right?"

As Austin and Johnny went inside, a buff, well-dressed young man was just leaving. A little over six feet, he had short brown hair tousled just enough so he looked a bit vain. He nodded at Austin on his way out. Austin took a seat at the table. Johnny joined him. Johnny preferred meeting with his clients in as comfortable an environment as possible, so he always sat down with them at the table. Thus, he never sat behind his desk and spoke *at* a client or prospect sitting in his office like so many other brokers did. In the end, results spoke louder than words. That's what really mattered, to his clients most of all, anyway. Johnny had seen his fill of brokers who simply didn't understand this. Johnny always found it strange that so many of his colleagues assumed their clients wanted their brokers to act snobbish, always too busy, and arrogant, as if one could actually corner the market or something.

Johnny's office was like a museum of client satisfaction. The place was filled with keepsakes interspersed among the numerous First American Investors awards. They were small but meaningful gifts from his clients. If they were over the maximum value allowed by the NASD, no one mentioned it. It was all innocuous enough. There was a little ivory statue of a flower arranger from one of his people in Japan... a bottle of crude oil from one of the Saudis... an autographed picture of a Swiss client arm-in-arm with Pavarotti... a hand-carved wooden Baobab tree from Africa? That was new. There must be a story behind that.

These items were not meant to be boastful. True, Johnny was very proud of them. For Johnny, though, there was no point in intimidating his clients. Why should he try and make them feel insignificant? He knew full well that the brokers who did this were really just trying to buffer themselves from the inevitable conflict that follows making investment decisions without a strategy of some sort, let alone one that actually produces.

And produce results Johnny Long did without parallel. You see, having those Big Three questions put him and his clients on the same side – commissions and fees notwithstanding – because it was clear throughout why he made the investment decisions he did. Everything followed a clearly delineated strategy so his clients tended not to feel taken advantage of, out of the know, or exploited. If, at some point, they decided that they no longer believed in Johnny's rationale for growth-stock investing, they could transfer their account. It was not *personal* for Johnny, and he did not take it as such.

Johnny always felt sorry for the multitude of brokers who took every up and down as some sort of comment on their personal ego. Take the Tuna for example. He was only forty-two years old, but he could easily pass for fifty. If you looked closely enough, you could see the stress and pain hidden behind the perma-tan. For people like the Tuna, a losing stock means that *they* too are losers. And inversely, a winner means they are winners! What invariably ends up happening is that investment decisions are based solely on short-term market price changes. What people like the Tuna never realized is that this is a no-win game. It's Russian Roulette and no tanning bed can ever hide the look of fear and anxiety plastered on someone's face when there's a gun pointed at his head from the minute he wakes up to the time he goes to bed.

For Johnny, buying, selling, and re-investing was simply a strategic process. And it worked very well. The art in Johnny's office was all gifts from his clients and other advisors, tokens of their genuine gratitude. Johnny had a little story about each, of course. Each piece was a wonderful little icebreaker depending upon who was sitting at his table. Johnny worked with a Middle-East contact in the First American Investors offices in Bahrain. Aref Kamal, one of the top producers in the office, had numerous wealthy clients in the growth-stock strategy. He and Johnny managed the money together, but Johnny usually flew out to give the really important presentations... royalty, audiences of a few hundred, twenty million in investable assets, and so on.

One client, A Saudi businessman named Mohammed Talal, sent Johnny a beautiful painting of a bustling marketplace set against the backdrop of gleaming office buildings. The juxtaposition nicely captured Talal's world of dichotomies. Whenever he studied the painting, Johnny could instantly transport himself back to the desert. Talal was worth "only" fifty million, his account opened with thirty million U.S. dollars. For people like Talal, though, "wealth" was not an adjective, and it was not life's goal. It was a means to an end. Arabs view wealth as a creative force, a way of life that generates thoughts and acts befitting the religious beliefs they hold so dear. That Johnny had a strategy – a tool – for achieving wealth was a perfect cultural fit in a world so culturally different.

But Johnny's favorite "thank you" hung in a frame next to the table. It was a letter of appreciation from Saudi Prince Abdullah. The Prince wished to convey his sincere appreciation for all Johnny had done with his account. It was a small percentage of his assets – one hundred million dollars – but the results were the thing. Always the results. And it didn't matter to Johnny if you had one hundred million or one hundred thousand – *you would get the most suitable strategy.* Look what he had done for Austin Montgomery.

Johnny smiled at Austin. "It's good to see you, Austin. For the last couple of days, I've been thinking about you."

Austin sat back. "Really?" He noticed how comfortable Johnny looked in a suit. He might just as well be wearing pajamas. That's the value of a fine, hand-tailored suit. "Well, are you going to tell me what you were thinking about?"

"Whenever I don't hear from you in a while, I get a little worried. Call me paternalistic. I suppose you're just over there on the other side of the building cranking away, huh?" Johnny stated.

Austin grinned. "I'm fine. Things are going great as usual... thanks to you, of course. I had a great time in California actually. I have a couple of ideas for new projects. I wanna try and get something new going."

"Fine... see, whenever you say you're 'fine' there's something going on."

Austin looked at Johnny. "No, I'm in a great mood lately. Like I said, I want to get going on something new. I'm in the mood for a big project, you know."

Johnny nodded. "Of course. You forget who you're talking to! So what have you been working on lately? Oh, remember that trip you took to Bahrain?" Johnny gestured to the painting. "Mohammed Talal sent me that."

Austin looked it over. "Wow, very nice. It sums the place up pretty well, huh?"

"Yeah. Speaking of which, I was talking to Kamal the other day. You remember Aref Kamal, right?"

"Sure. Nice guy. We spoke like a month ago. What a great book of business he has, huh?"

Johnny laughed. "Well sure. In fact, he has been trying to get me to go out there for a big seminar he wants to set up. He says he has another three hundred people."

"Geez, word travels fast, huh? Good God, I'm lucky to get like twenty five people coming to see me speak."

"Well, you're not as handsome as I am, naturally." Johnny cleared his throat. "Look, I can't get away right now. I'm just too busy here. I thought maybe you'd like to go again. Kamal says the last time you were in Bahrain you did a bang-up job. I got the Prince's account, by the way."

"Really? That's great. I'm glad I could help. It just happened to work out really well in my schedule. I would love to go back. Whatever you want."

"I put the accounts I got from your presentation under our joint production number. I was waiting for the end of the month's production check to surprise you, but I might as well tell you now. "

"Awesome. I'll take it."

"There's like fifty million dollars coming in. Should mean about seventy, eighty grand in income for you. I know how you spend money. You can run the smaller accounts. Under ten million. I'll manage the others."

Austin grinned. "Does that mean you put the Prince's account in the joint number too?"

Johnny laughed. "Ah... no, but nice try. I admire that."

"Yeah well... I *am* persistent if nothing else. Which reminds me, remember when we did the Bahamas project?"

Johnny nodded. "Of course. It's going great. You should get out there some time soon. Maybe I'll pop out with you. I'll fly us to Miami, then we can meet my friend Carlos and we'll take his boat out to Grand Bahama."

"Sounds like a plan. Let me look over my schedule. I have to catch up from being out a few days. And I really do want to get cracking on something new."

Johnny was impressed. "Good. I like to see people working hard even when they have money in the bank. I always admire how you keep on trying to pull your own weight even when we share accounts. That's how things work, Austin. People work together, they help each other out. It's about *connecting* with other people. And if everyone helps with the heavy lifting, it works out great."

Austin folded his hands on the table. Moira popped in with a wicker coffee tray. She winked at Austin and poured out two cups. She always tried to keep Austin in the vicinity as long as possible. She left, leaving a whiff of perfume lingering in the air.

Austin stirred cream into his coffee and watched it swirl in. "As a matter of fact, Johnny, I recall when you told me just that at the ground breaking ceremony in the Bahamas. That was very nice of you. I appreciate your noticing. I try to work hard. I'm actually getting fired up to throw myself into work again."

Johnny sipped his coffee. "Well, we'll see what comes of it, eh? Look—" Johnny gestured for Moira to close his door. When it was shut, he continued. "Look Austin, I totally understand your wanting to achieve things on your own. I've always said that. Like you just pointed out. When I started out, I was determined to do it for myself. So I know what you mean, believe me, Austin. At the same time, though, a little help – when deserved – never hurt."

"You know, you were absolutely right when you said positive people gravitate naturally toward positive projects. One of my old professors I met out West was really interested in the Bahamas thing." Austin said.

"Hmmm... Well, I haven't seen you take much interest in that project for a while now. You should get more involved with the regular operations. Life is much easier if you have continuity."

"You know, it's funny you say that, Johnny. This guy I met up with, his name's Tony Pickett... he was saying how your strategy could be applied to anything, not just to stocks. I thought that was interesting. He just plucked it out of the air. He's not even a client."

Johnny took a loud slurp of coffee as if surprised to hear Austin say that. "Really? I don't see why not. I'm not really looking to be a philosopher or anything like that, but I suppose you could apply the questions to general decision making. You know, it's funny... I had a client call the other day. We were talking about his portfolio and stuff... changes we had to make because of his divorce. At the end of our chat, he thanked me for helping him move forward with his life. I figured he meant splitting up the account and such. But he told me that the strategy was the reason he got divorced!"

Austin laughed. "What, he made enough to give her half and *still* had enough left over to find a chippie?"

"That's what I thought," said Johnny. "But it turns out, he said, that he applied the three questions to his life and realized it was time to cut loose—"

"To 'sell'." Austin made quote marks with his fingers.

"I guess so. He said that if it weren't for me, he would still be languishing in pain waiting for things to get better. So there you go."

"Maybe you should become a marriage counselor in your next life, Johnny?"

"Who knows. But my point is this – there has got to be some sort of strategy to investing—"

"Got that part."

"Sure. But I have always thought... well, let me say that I made as many mistakes as the next guy when I started out in this business. Likewise, I made a bunch of *stupid* decisions during the first few years I was married to Mandy. I had no plan for the future or anything like that. I just went at it the same way I went about investing my clients' money. This sounds good, this looks interesting. You know how it goes. And so there I was... clueless in marriage, clueless in life."

Austin took a deep breath. "Yeah, well, sounds familiar. I broke up with Cathy."

Johnny winked. "Oh, I know... Moira told me. Somehow the Tuna found out. He must have overheard you on the phone or something. I don't think the phone was back on the hook before Moira knew. Sheesh... so anyway, this guy Pickett is quite right. And, by the way, so am I!" They both laughed. Austin poured himself another cup of coffee. "Look, you can't be afraid—"

"I'm afraid to mess up," Austin interjected. "I don't want to be broke. I want to settle down a bit and do some stuff that is good for the world. *And* I have a project in mind. It involves Pickett, as a matter of fact. Go figure. So I get what you mean, Johnny. The analogy to the strategy is great, it really is. I totally believe in it, and I definitely get how I need to 'take stock,' so to speak, in my life. Make changes when necessary. I'm trying to do that."

"I feel the energy, man. Good for you. You know some people would be very jealous of your energy." said Johnny.

"You think? I really, really want my life to be-"

"Less chaotic?" suggested Johnny.

"Yes! I need *balance.* I want to make more money. You know I love that, man. But I also want some stability like spiritually, too... this way, I can do like any project I want. Think about *that...*" He poked his finger on the table for emphasis. "Think about being able to do whatever you want."

Johnny smiled. "I do, Austin."

"You think about it?"

Johnny laughed. "No, I do what I want. I know exactly what you are talking about. You know, the Arabs are like that. All that money... you know, millions and millions... but like you told me when you got back from that trip, it's like money for them enables them to express some sort of higher religious sentiment. Right? I'll always remember that insight of yours. You hit the nail on the head. Totally right."

"Well," said Austin, "if I could only follow my own insights instead of being blind to them. Wouldn't that be something? So then, I guess I should ask you how the accounts are doing... mine and the Bahaman."

Johnny got up and walked over to his desk. He took a manila folder off the top and sat back down. "Funny you should mention balance, Austin." He handed Austin some papers to look over. It was like something out of Mission Impossible... *your assignment, should you chose to accept it...*

Austin never really looked too closely at his monthly papers. His father's lawyer, Clark Parkinson, took care of things. He settled the estate for Austin, and Austin trusted him. Parkinson's office took care of the bills, the accounting work, and so on. "You know," said Austin. "I really should be looking at this stuff more closely... at least monthly."

"What, so if you aren't making commissions on an account, you don't follow it? Even if it's your own money, huh? Amazing. Simply amazing. Do you still have your um... *people* keeping track of things?" asked Johnny mockingly.

"Yeah, you're right. You know I used to like reviewing all this stuff. It can get obsessive, though." Austin continued looking over his papers.

"Don't think. Just turn to page twelve," instructed Johnny. Austin flipped pages and followed along. "Your growth-stock portfolio is doing well."

Austin looked up. "Which is amazing considering everyone is screaming about how bad things are. Fifteen different stocks, right?"

Johnny nodded. "In seven different sectors, right. People complained all last year, too. Your growth-stock portfolio was up about 15% a year ago, 18% last year, and you're up about 20% so far this year. We have to make some changes, though, which we'll discuss later."

Now Austin was *really* glad he came in to see Johnny. His money kept compounding and actually growing at an immense rate even though he was living a rather high-end lifestyle. He wanted for nothing and was *still* making money. Simply amazing. Everything Johnny had promised back when they first started out had come true for the most part. "Johnny, I owe you so much it's unbelievable. Thank you so much for everything. I'm going to buy you a painting!"

Johnny laughed. "We'll see. So it looks like this. I haven't done your returns going all the way back to when you started. Parkinson's guys should have all that for you. In fact, I know they do. I was just talking to him the other day. Maybe while you were in California. Anyway..." Johnny shuffled some papers. "Let's see...

OK, here we go. Two years ago, you had about seven million in the growth-stock strategy. You made about one-and-a-half million in gross profits. Not too shabby, eh?"

Austin was excited now. In all honesty, this *was* more fun than working. "Realized or on paper?"

"Well, some of each. But your *growth-stock* portfolio was worth a little over five million. And... let me see... last year, you did almost 18% I think." He looked back at page thirteen. "Yeah... so that was another—"

"Damn, boy. You go, man." exclaimed Austin. "I just use my debit card. Money's always there. Kind of ironic that I pine away over my clients' accounts but not my own. Too funny. But hey... I can afford to be funny, can't I? Yes I can!"

"Yeah, don't you love this? Gets that fire going again. Doesn't it?"

They agreed the income portfolio was worth a little over two and a half million dollars. "More like a raging blaze! This is gonna go right to my head. I hope not, though." Austin said.

"We'll find something to keep you focused. OK, so you are worth about another... whew, almost two-and-a-half million. And now up another twenty percent... Excellent." Johnny looked up and smiled at Austin who was busy doing a little shimmy in his chair. Whenever he got news like this, he began to dance a little bit. Well actually, his shoulders and hands danced. And he always bit his lower lip. They called it the "White Man's Overbite." It made Austin look like he was about to be overcome with intense gastritis. But he danced nevertheless.

Johnny shook his head. "Did you dance like that for your musician friend Pickett?" Austin didn't speak. He just shook his head and kept shimmying. "Well then," continued Johnny, "I think it's safe to say that your *growth-stock portfolio* is doing just fine!" Johnny waited for Austin to pick up on the fact that he kept stressing the words "growth-stock portfolio." Nothing. Johnny cleared his throat. "Ahem... If we could turn off Soul Train for a minute, Austin, I would like to mention something about your *growth-stock portfolio...* consisting only of *growth-stocks...* which pay little or *no dividends* because they are *growth stocks....*"

Johnny finally got Austin's attention. "Yeah that's right, Johnny. How much principal have I spent on total crap? Go ahead, give it to me straight. I'm rich, single, and ready to mingle." Austin stated.

"*That*," said Johnny, "I'd rather not imagine. I'm sure Parkinson is distressed when you buy things like – what was it-"

"My three-hundred horsepower dune buggy? My robotic kitty-litter scooper? The seven-room ice fishing cabin I had built by the Joaib Construction Company? It sank."

"No," answered Johnny. "I was thinking of that stuffed panther you bought on E-Bay for, what was it, ten thousand dollars?"

"It has emeralds for eyes, man!" said Austin.

Johnny laughed. "Lovely. My point is that you live quite well, yes?"

"Thanks to you."

"Well, the most amazing thing about your account is *not* the growth-stock portfolio. Did you know that?"

Austin was taken aback. "It's not? What is it then."

Johnny shuffled through some more papers. "Turn to the second packet, page three." Austin followed along. On page three were listed ten stocks with which he was totally unfamiliar. He never owned any of them for his clients, nor did they ever appear on the growth-stock buy list in Johnny's strategy. Some, like Dominion Resources were obviously utilities. Austin found this totally strange because he had never thought of utilities as growth stocks. He read through the list and scratched his head. He looked up at Johnny.

"OK, so what are *these* stocks. I haven't really heard of these before. Since when are utility stocks in my growth-stock portfolio? Did I miss something?"

Johnny laughed. "Austin, since I met you, you've been missing something." He winked at Austin. "Anyway playboy, the whole point of stocks is growth. Why own a stock if it will *never* appreciate?"

"Umm... I got that part, thanks."

"Well then, it follows that capital appreciation—that's capital appreciation – should be at least *one* of the goals when buying *any* stock, *even...*" He put his papers down and looked Austin in the eye. "*Even* in an *income portfolio.*" He was silent for a second.

"Income, huh?" said Austin. "When did you come up with that?"

"Many years ago, Austin. What am I, a one-trick pony? Is that what you think? Or that I limit myself to just aggressive growth money? That's not where the *real* money is, anyway. The big money is sitting in fixed income, and I go after it with a second strategy. A growth-of-income strategy. And where do you think you've been getting your income from? Actually, where do you think the Bahamas Foundation has been getting its income from every year? You haven't given them any more money, and you haven't put any more into your accounts here. Didn't you ever wonder where your income came from?"

Austin smiled. "Yeah... it comes from the mailman who brings me my checks. I'm just kidding. I figured you sold stuff off and always left some cash."

Johnny rolled his eyes. "Man, oh man, I love you *noveau riche* guys." Johnny moved in closer to the table. "Think about this, though. You have been sitting here telling me about how you pine away worrying about balance in your life. You said that you wished you could figure out how to make your life satisfying and easy like the growth-stock strategy."

Austin nodded. "Yeah, I would love some continuity. My friend Pickett was saying that too."

"Yes. Wise man that Pickett. Look Austin... I have been in this business a long, long time. When I first started out, I made all the dumb mistakes. I was no different than anybody else. But when I started doing the growth-stock strategy, there was a lot – I mean a *lot* – of money out there earmarked for fixed income."

"There still is. Millions." said Austin.

"Hundreds of millions, Austin. *Even hundreds of billions.* And remember, these people were about to see their income steadily decrease over the years due to a declining interest-rate environment."

"That blows."

Johnny closed his eyes and shook his head mockingly. "Yes... it blows. I'm telling you Austin. One of the saddest things to watch is a retiree's income go down by over *half* as they get older. I'm being facetious, of course. But think about it. What are they going to do? Can you imagine. Then you start eating up principal, so you get even less income, and so on."

"Vicious cycle," said Austin.

"Yes," continued Johnny. "Vicious cycle. It's very sad. Do you know that they used to have us cold calling on CDs... paying fifteen percent! Can you imagine that?"

"My God," said Austin. "I wish!"

"Yeah, yeah, who wouldn't cold call. It was actually fun back in the day. A few drinks, then we all got on the phones for the night. You could actually build an asset base by cold calling on CDs. Amazing. But remember the old adage... you don't get something for nothing. CDs eventually had to mature. They didn't go out too far. And even if you held bonds paying, say ten percent, they were almost always callable. So what good did it do you? No sooner did you get a nice, fat coupon, then they called in the bond a couple of years later. It was like slowly dying of dehydration. You can only squeeze so much out of the cactus before you are out of luck. You can eat the cactus toward the end... like using up your principal... but when that's gone, too... *game* over!" Johnny pounded his finger on the table for emphasis.

"So," asked Austin. "So you started working on a fixed-income strategy?"

"No!" exclaimed Johnny. "That's my point. *Not* fixed income. *Increasing* income... growth of income. Big difference."

The hair was standing on Austin's arms. This happened whenever he was on to something. He was starting to see a cycle. He shook himself out of it. "So anyway, you were saying?"

Johnny thought for a moment. "It wasn't long after you were born, Austin. I was thinking a lot about providing for my family back then. Pretty weird looking back now, huh? It was clear that *fixed* income would be a losing endeavor in the years to come. But *growth of income*... that was a career. If I combined the growth-stock strategy with a growth of income strategy! It simply occurred to me – that *growth of income* would be a crucial issue for the investing public over the years to follow. So I applied the Big Three questions to the problem of income."

Austin was impressed. "Balance…"

Johnny smiled. "Yes, Austin. Balance. I have the growth-stock strategy for the aggressive-growth portion of a portfolio, and I have a *growth of income* strategy for the income component."

Something occurred to Austin suddenly. It was a flash of insight during which a piece of his past was revealed. "Wait… so you're saying that I've been in *both* strategies since I met you? That's where my income comes from? That's where the hospice home gets its income? And I didn't even know it? Man, I'm out of the loop. You know what I like about you Johnny? It seems like every time we get together something totally cool happens. So I gotta hear about this." Austin stood up and poked his head out the door. "Moira, my sweet." Moira was on the phone but gestured for Austin to go ahead talking. "Order us all some lunch. Whatever you want. It's on me. And get some pizzas for the office, too. The Tuna looks like he's gonna pass out." Moira smiled and nodded.

Austin went back inside. "Thanks for spending time with me."

"Don't mention it," said Johnny with mock joviality. "You don't look at the bill anyway!" They both laughed. "So where was I? OK. I applied the three questions to the problem of income. What to buy, when to sell, and what to do with the proceeds."

"That's my mantra, man," chimed in Austin.

"But remember, I wanted to *increase* income, not just get a decent income."

"Bonds," said Austin, "won't do this, right?"

Johnny nodded. "That's exactly right. And like I said, no sooner do you get a good interest rate, then it gets called and you're stuck having to buy a bond with a *lower* interest rate… assuming you want to stay with the same A-type rating and not risk it in junk."

"Sure, sure. I follow you."

"So you have a sort of law of diminishing returns, so to speak. For that same, say, million dollars, Mr. and Mrs. Client are getting lower and lower interest rates over the years. Thus, they will either have to diminish their lifestyle, spend *principal*, or work at McDonalds."

"Don't laugh," said Austin. "Have you ever noticed how many older people work in fast food?"

"I'm not surprised," quipped Johnny. But remember, if we're talking stocks – and we are -- we should invest for *capital appreciation, too*."

Austin leaned in. "So this is like a total return approach."

Johnny held up his hand. "Yes, exactly! Just as with earnings-estimate revisions in the growth-stock strategy, I found a direct correlation between *future dividend increases*—"

"Income *growth*," said Austin.

"Yes, income growth... a direct correlation between dividends and the stock price of a utility. In fact, the utility strategy – the Growth of Income Strategy – is the best example of capitalism I can think of. A utility issues stock for a number of legal and organizational reasons. But in terms of investments, the future dividend that a utility pays out will be intrinsically reflected in the current stock price. Investors are being *rewarded* for their investment risk by being paid dividends. Now, the stock will develop a sort of floor market price based on how much this dividend is and will be. Bonds, on the contrary, will often *penalize* you for lending them money at a higher rate by *calling in* your bond. Do you understand that?"

"Yes, I think I do. Basically, the amount of the dividend will give the utility stock an intrinsic value—"

"Yes," said Johnny. "For your investment of X dollars into, say, 1000 shares, you will receive Y in income as a return on your investment."

"No matter what the price of the stock?" asked Austin.

"So long as the utility stays in business and continues to pay a dividend. But here is the really important thing to remember... There is a *phantom line* you can draw between a utility stock's dividend and its market price."

"Ahhh, that's the key."

"Bingo!" said Johnny enthusiastically. "As a company increases it's dividend, as it *rewards* its investors more and more, the market price of its stock will increase also over time. Get it?"

Austin was excited. He loved the sound of this. "There it is," he said. "Growth of income *and* capital appreciation. Total return!"

"Now combine this with the growth-stock portfolio, and you have a formidable allocation plan... a strategy for growth, income, growth of income, and capital appreciation. It's all in there!"

Moira came in with a large tray-full of sushi, seaweed salad, and some steaming *miso* soup. She set the tray down in the center of the table and gave Austin the bill.

"One hundred and twelve bucks!' cried Austin.

Moira grimaced. "Well, it's for three of us. And The Tuna. Tuna for The Tuna. That's kinda cannibalistic. They just got the Toro in this morning. It's supposed to be awesome. And they have *fresh uni*."

"This morning?" replied Austin. "Then sometimes they serve yesterday's *Toro*? I don't even want to know what old *uni* tastes like."

"Probably a lot like fresh *uni*," quipped Johnny.

"Quit it, both of you. You know I mean not-frozen *uni*," said Moira.

"I'm just busting your chops, girl." Austin handed her a hundred and a twenty. "Johnny will make it back for me in about a minute."

Moira turned to leave. Over her shoulder she said, "And anyway, this is the closest I can get to you taking me out, Austin. So I'm gonna enjoy myself, thank you very much." And she left, closing the door behind her. "And I'm going shoe shopping later. I'll send your, ahem, *people* the bill. God, I love that."

Austin looked at Johnny and exhaled loudly. "Well," he said. "I guess you'd better keep that growth-of-income strategy working if we're talking shoes like Prada and Jimmy Choo. Johnny laughed and bit into his *hamachi* hand roll. "Wow, fresh *wasabi*. Hard to find. So this thing is really, really interesting, Austin. I love doing the income strategy."

"I thought you would rather do the growth stock strategy."

"Well… this kind of investing has both components, right?"

Austin sipped his *miso* soup. "Go over that again."

"OK," said Johnny. "First of all, the Growth of Income Strategy is intended to be a bond substitute. I'm going after bond money with this strategy. If you're in bonds, this is an amazing alternative."

"Got it," said Austin.

Johnny continued. "As with the growth-stock strategy, I rely completely on First American Investors research for the Growth of Income Strategy. It's still the best on the Street."

Austin scratched his chest. "But aren't people still pissed off about analysts?"

Johnny rolled his eyes. "Look, there are always going to be problems like that. One thing, though, will *never* change… At the end of the day, the analysts will *always* have earnings estimates, and this is what really matters. This will *never* change. Growth stocks will move accordingly. *This* will never change either. Just look at your portfolio. Did all that controversy change anything in the long run? Not a thing."

"Imagine all the people who stayed away because they didn't trust the analysts."

Johnny shook his head. "I know. I've talked to several. And I tell them – look, investors are buying something."

"Stocks and bonds-"

"No! That's either a stock trader or a bond saver. Just buying based on price. An *investor*, on the contrary, is buying research, buying information. I think it's crucial that people have access to good information. Without good information, my twenty-five years says you can't make any money. I think it just turns out to be luck, it turns out to be random. I often tell people, Austin, if you have great research, great performance is not far behind. If you have no research, I don't know how you do what you do."

Austin was right with Johnny. "That's why you work for First American Investors?"

"Right. They have the best research. And to be honest, I sell research. That's it. I'm not Einstein here. I'm no analyst, I'm not trained to be an analyst, don't want to be an analyst. I probably couldn't be if I wanted to."

Austin jumped in. "Successful investors have strategies. That's what I learned right off the bat with you. Even so, aren't bond investors—"

"Bond *savers*," corrected Johnny.

Austin cleared his throat. "Sorry. Bond *savers*... aren't they usually too conservative for stocks, especially utility stocks?"

Johnny seemed nonplussed. "I tell them, call your broker. Ask him why he recommended that bond. Ask him when it's time to sell it. Like you said, Austin, successful money managers have a strategy. Mine *works*. More to the point, though, if you're not buying the best research or maybe you don't even have a strategy at all, Mr. and Mrs. Client... aren't you taking a big risk?"

"But their triple-A bonds are pretty much guaranteed," objected Austin.

"Yes. But their *income* will continue to decrease, so they're losing income and risk having to eat into principal at some time in the future when rates go even lower. And again, I don't care *how* sophisticated the client is, if they don't have access to an analyst's data, there's no way in the world they can make any money."

"Well, not a lot of money," said Austin.

"Right, certainly not like what you made. Lucky gains are not what we're looking for here."

"Hmmm... so you are saying that you tell your clients they are *buying* First American Investors research?"

"Yes. I own only stocks in both strategies, yet if someone asks me 'What stocks do you like, Johnny?' I tell them that I don't have any stocks. I explain to them that I have a *strategy*. If you ask any successful money manager, they can answer the Big Three questions, they know why they are doing what they are doing. And as with growth stocks, *all stocks* – even utility stocks – are *pulled up* by some event in the future. They are *not* pushed up by things that have already happened. The markets are far too efficient for that."

"Ahhh, so by 'saver' you mean—"

"Anyone who bought a fixed-income investment. They're a saver."

"And an investor?"

"Mmm... Investors have a strategy, a discipline."

"And they have information."

"Exactly!" said Johnny. "It goes without saying that anybody who has inside information on Wall Street is going to make *a lot* of money because they have access to information before anybody else. Crass but true." Johnny bit into *Toro* sushi. "Excellent *Toro*." He pointed his finger at Austin. "In-for-ma-tion, Austin."

"That's what you've always said. But I figured that was only for your growth-stock strategy. I never realized that you could apply the same system to income."

"Let's clarify something," corrected Johnny. "This is a *second* strategy. It's different than my growth-stock strategy. Remember, this is meant to replace bond portfolios, and there are plenty of them out there."

"Oh, sure," replied Austin. "But this would complement the growth strategy pretty well."

"Yes, you're right."

"So then *that's* what you developed by applying your three questions to other areas of life?"

"Think about it, Austin. You, of all people, should realize that having money provides opportunities for you to shape your life however you wish. But it's so easy to get consumed in worry about *losing* it."

Austin thought this over for a moment. "Huh... I can only imagine all those poor people whose nest egg started off yielding like a hundred thousand and ended up kicking off only like thirty thousand. What a nightmare."

"And I dare say," added Johnny, "it becomes too much of a preoccupation to enjoy or do much else. *That's* the sad part."

"That's kind of what I am trying to tell you about my own life."

Johnny nodded. "Yes, I sensed that right away." Johnny laughed.

"Well, it works, man. How people buy stocks out of a newspaper is beyond me. How they buy 'em out of an article in *Fortune* magazine is beyond me. How they use a discount brokerage firm is beyond me."

"Just to buy and sell based on price, I guess," said Austin.

"It reminds me of a client I had when I was starting out. Ask anyone. Every broker has a story like this. I went to see an attorney. I profiled him on the phone. He said he had half-a-million dollars. I went to see him. Made my recommendation for three stocks I liked. He wrote a check out for fifty-thousand dollars."

Austin laughed and tossed a piece of tuna roll into his mouth. "Feedin' on the little guy," he said.

"Yeah well... I was the little guy," responded Johnny. "So I said I thought you had half-a-million dollars? He said, 'John, as much as I like you, there's no way'...." He took a sip of *miso*. "There's *no way* I'm giving you five hundred thousand dollars to buy three stocks.' I asked... Well who has the other four hundred and fifty thousand? He said, 'That's my serious advisor. You get the play money, you get the stock-jockey money.'"

Austin choked on his soup. "He called you a 'stock-jockey?' For real? That's so funny."

Johnny shrugged. "Something crystallized for me right then and there. I can even tell you to this day what his office looked like. I realized right then and there I had to do something else. Whatever I was doing back then was not working for me. Somebody else was getting the real money, I was getting just the play money."

"Hey," said Austin, "and now *you* get the four hundred and fifty thousand."

"Exactly, my boy. And I'm telling you *one thing* – once bond savers realize that *there is another way*, a better way, they jump on board and reap the rewards. Excuse me Mr. Prospect, would you like your retirement income to increase ten percent a year? Of course they would. Who wouldn't? Basically, It's crucial that I know the person, build a *profile*, learn if they have an investment strategy or whether they just buy and sell based on what their broker says and so on."

"Even with fixed income?" asked Austin.

"Absolutely. But you have to have *information* above all else," replied Johnny.

Austin nodded. "So you need an *analyst's* information?"

"Yes, Austin. It's important to remember that this is a *strategy*, this is a discipline. I rely entirely upon First American Investors analysts. I dance with the analysts… they lead, and I follow. Remember that – *they* lead."

"And you follow."

"Yes. And my research has shown that *growth* of income is really the key for fixed-income investors. Which means utility *stocks*. Again…" He sipped some more soup. "Again, I use this strategy to replace bond portfolios because they have been getting *less and less income* over the years."

"And using up more and more of their principal."

Johnny nodded. "This all comes out in their profile. Ironically, most people think that utility stocks are more risky than bonds. But that's because they don't understand what makes utility stocks move up and down. It's so simple, some people don't believe me at first."

"Well," said Austin, "in your growth-stock portfolio, you focus on earnings-estimate revisions."

"Right," replied Johnny.

"And with this growth of income strategy?"

"I focus on dividend estimate increases."

"*That's* what moves utility stocks." Johnny smiled and nodded. "Wow," continued Austin, "that's awesome."

"And let me clarify something here," said Johnny. "I'm not

the only advisor who uses analyst's opinions... buy, hold, and so on. But that's not what I'm talking about."

"One of my friends is always telling me his broker said their analyst said this or that about some stock," said Austin.

"Well, yes. But I'm interested in the nuts and bolts. I'm not interested in the analysts recommendation. I'm interested in the data that usually never makes it into an investor's strategy."

"If they even have one."

"Yes, if they even have one. Buy, sell, hold doesn't help me or my clients. Earnings-estimate revisions and dividend-estimate increases are what I focus on."

"OK, Johnny. Give me an example, though, because I'm not sure what you mean by dividend estimates."

The phone rang, and Moira picked it up. A few seconds later, she buzzed Johnny. "Johnny, it's Cristina Miller. Should I take a message?"

Johnny held up a finger. "Ohhh... perfect, Austin. Let me put Cristina on the speaker phone. Her husband worked in environmental services or something like that. He was actually pushed onto a subway track by his sister-in-law. It was terrible. I remember her name like it was yesterday—Denise Paul. She pushed him right onto the tracks. I still think they were having an affair, but what do I know? Her account was the only one I've ever had seized by the government. Poor Cristina was about twenty-five or twenty-six. Their daughter, Jina, was about two I think. He had insurance, though, so check out what we did."

"That makes Jina about... twenty-eight? Is she cute?"

Johnny nodded. "*And* wealthy... thanks to me. But forget it. She's involved with that crazy guy on TV who throws himself down stairs and stuff like that. I guess she likes scars. Anyway—" Johnny hit the speaker phone. "Johnny Long."

"Hi Johnny, it's Cristina Miller. I'm returning your call."

"Yes, Cristina, how are you? I have you on my speaker phone with my partner Austin Montgomery. Austin found himself in a similar circumstance to you when your Randy died."

"Oh," said Cristina. "I'm sorry to hear that, Austin."

"Thank you, Cristina," Austin replied.

"At least," she continued, "you're in good hands. I've known Johnny for a long time. He's great."

Johnny jumped in. "Cristina, We need to make a couple of changes in your income portfolio, but I'll call you later about that. In the meantime, though, when did we start? The early eighties?"

"Hmm... It must have been," she said. "Randy died in seventy-nine. I got the insurance money the next year. So yeah, that sounds about right."

"Do you remember what we bought?" asked Johnny.

Cristina laughed. "Not really. I can barely remember last week, for God's sake."

"Well, *I do*" said Johnny. "We put the million you got from Randy's policy into CDs, of all things."

"I remember I got a nice income."

Johnny laughed. "Eleven percent!" he said. "Three-year CDs"

"My goodness," said Austin. "Talk about easy money!"

"OK, Cristina," said Johnny. "I'll talk to you later today."

"OK. Bye guys. Bye Austin. Johnny, I volunteer at the Women's Exchange tonight, so call me before five."

"No problem." Johnny hung up the phone. *"Eleven percent. Can you imagine?* But let's trace what happened to her. Cristina got about one hundred and ten thousand dollars per year for three years. Nice income for her and her daughter."

Austin chimed in. "Why do I suspect that will change?"

Johnny laughed. "Because that always seems to be what happens. With fixed income, it seems like your income goes down much faster than it increases, doesn't it?" Austin shrugged. "Yes, well... we rolled the money over three years later, right? I think we got around nine-and-a-half percent, ninety-five thousand a year for the next three years. Rates kept dropping. Now, if she stayed in this strategy, by the time we got to 2002, she would have been at *four percent!*"

"Wow," exclaimed Austin. "That's like forty thousand a year! That sucks!"

"It's pathetic," responded Johnny. "And have rates gotten much better now, many years later? Please... not a lick. So all those people who were saying 'rates are going to go back up'... how wrong were they?"

"And how much income did they lose out on?" asked Austin.

"Exactly. It's funny, all those people who sat and waited for rates to go back to where they were in the early eighties... I ask them, do you *really* want an economy like *that*? But they don't care. They're miserable."

"Because they have no income any more!"

"And," continued Johnny, "they don't enjoy their life, they don't try new things... they're dead in the water, just like their portfolios. This is *not* what you want for yourself, Austin."

Austin nodded. "Well, that's kinda how I feel these days, Johnny."

"I know, Austin. That's why the three questions are relevant to more than just your money. Your money has a great impact on your life, even your spiritual life."

"Hmmm... So I'm guessing you put Cristina into the Growth-of-Income Strategy?"

"Once I saw the losing game we were stuck in, yes. And I started out switching over bond portfolios from there on." Austin looked confused. He felt like this when Johnny first explained his growth stock strategy, too. "I can see you have questions," said Johnny.

Austin put down his chopsticks. "Well, if triple-A bonds are pretty much guaranteed, don't people *expect* lower returns? Isn't this what they *want*?"

Johnny shook his head. "No, Austin. Not at all. Actually, I found it to be just the *opposite*."

Austin looked puzzled. "Really?"

"Yes. This is really important. Most bond buyers need *income* most of all. Look at Cristina… if we didn't switch her into the strategy, she would have been forced to either live like a pauper or use principal. Going from one hundred and ten thousand a year to *forty*? Good Lord, I would have ruined the woman. Or rather, the fixed-income market would have. So…"

Austin's face lit up. "Ahhh.. so how safe is *that*? I get it."

"Exactly," responded Johnny with a smile. "How safe is that? If you lose principal by selling an investment at a loss or if you are forced to use principal *just to maintain* your investment objective– in this case, your lifestyle income needs – is there *that much* of a difference? Again, I found that once people *learned about* an alternative to bonds, they jumped in readily."

"So then," added Austin, "most bond buyers are actually *too conservative*? Really?"

"I think so," replied Johnny. "I think so. Their investment objective – X dollars in income – is *not* being met. Plain and simple." Johnny pointed at Austin with both hands. "Plain and simple. Plus, it gave me something new to develop and work with. It was very intellectually rewarding as well. Which is part of your point, right?"

"Right… But still, it's not *conventional*."

Johnny smiled. "Over the past twenty-five years, Austin, I have learned something. Making a *lot* of money investing is not difficult. But it *is* unconventional… otherwise everyone would be rich. Conventional investing often just keeps people churning in place while others get wealthy. That's what I've learned."

"Ahhh… it's the information thing again."

"Well, yes, I access and organize very valuable information for my clients' benefit. In this case, I take the utility's yield and I add it to the percentage dividend growth. I come up with a number, and I rank *every single utility stock* First American Investors covers in this way. This is certainly not conventional. But it generates wealth. With the First American Investors research behind you, it's *well worth* taking the little extra risk."

Austin was a little lost. "Wait... run that part about dividend growth by me again please."

"Sure," answered Johnny. "Every month, First American Investors research department puts out an immense book containing their hard numbers – earnings, dividends, and so on – for *every single stock they cover.* For the utility strategy, I remove any stock from consideration that does not pay a dividend at all."

Austin chuckled. "Wait... there are actually utility stocks that *don't* pay a dividend? Why buy them then?"

"Austin, that's question number one, right—why did you buy the stock? Would you believe that about ten percent of the utility stocks we cover *do not* pay a dividend? Amazing. But I remove them right off the bat if they don't. Out of the remaining companies, I eliminate those with *no anticipated dividend growth* for the next fiscal year."

"So," asked Austin, "if they keep their dividend the same, you don't select them?"

Johnny nodded. "Sure, because I'm looking for *growth* of income, right? If there is no dividend growth anticipated, then—"

"Then you won't be growing your income in your portfolio," finished Austin. "Right?"

"Right," said Johnny. "So I remove utilities with no dividend and those with no dividend *growth*. Keep in mind, Austin, that I've now eliminated about half of the utility stocks we cover."

"Ahhh... half that people may otherwise be buying. Stupid mistakes."

Johnny agreed. "Stupid mistakes. From the remaining list, I calculate the year-to-year dividend growth as a percentage. I take that growth number and add it to the current yield. I rank them all accordingly."

Austin was still confused. "Johnny," he said. "I've been through the mill with you and even *I* am still confused. This sounds more than just a little bit risky?"

Johnny walked over to his desk and fished out a file from a stack sitting on top. "Well let's see," he said as he sat back down. "Despite your success with me, Austin, I made a lot of stupid mistakes for the first eight years of my career. I got used to losing money for people"

"Huh… better them than me."

Johnny shook his head. "Ah, Austin. The point is that now I don't make them. I let the analyst do all the work. Mistakes *are* inevitable, but they're not *stupid* mistakes. In the end, the *saver.*"

"The bond buyer."

"Right. The saver who just buys bonds never… *never* wins versus the investor in my strategy. The saver has a million dollars in tax-free bonds. They never write checks out of that account when the coupons come in. So I ask them, 'Why do you own tax-free bonds?'" Johnny raised his hands and shrugged. "Normal question, right?"

"Yeah, why do they?"

"Basically, they didn't know they had another choice, they didn't know there was something comparable to tax-free bonds."

"And they all just jump into the strategy?"

"Remember Austin, I may rely upon First American Investors research, but I still have to understand the person's tolerance for their portfolios moving up and down."

"Their risk tolerance."

"Yeah… but again, after I explain it to them, they usually see their own portfolios as either too safe because their principal never grows, or too risky because they can't maintain their lifestyle without eating up principal. But what I tell them is, 'Look, I'm not suggesting that a utility stock is as safe as a CD that is government guaranteed. It's not! It's not anywhere near as safe. It would be malpractice to claim otherwise. The *real* question is, is the extra reward worth the extra risk using First American Investors research? When I explain this to them, they usually let me take a small portion of their money and invest it in the strategy. It's like if I said to a real-estate investor that they could raise rents ten percent every year, they would love that. Moreover, by letting the analysts at First American Investors do all the work, I can say that. Remember, that whatever your personal opinion about First American Investors analysts, I tell people they are among the best on the Street. And I remind them that *all investors* merely *buy research*. That's that. With utility stocks, what matters most is our analyst's forecast for future dividends. Are dividends expected to increase, decrease, stay the same, or discontinue? If you don't know the answer, you don't know—"

"You don't know what to buy, when to sell, or what to do with the proceeds!"

"Yeah," said Johnny. "You are a saver, not an investor. Worse yet, you are at the whim of the interest-rate markets and this huge thing called The Economy which you probably don't know too much about. Yet these things totally control your life. How can that be?"

"But how do you demonstrate this to people?" asked Austin.

"That's the easy part," replied Johnny. "I take two hypothetical people – a Saver and an Investor – and I create two timelines. Take Cristina for example. Let's say she was the Saver starting out with a million. Assuming we get her in CDs. When we started out in 1980, CDs were paying... I think I told her eleven percent."

"Yeah, you said eleven percent."

"OK. It's like looking just at the price of a stock. It may be expensive, it may be inexpensive when compared to the company's earnings... but what do they know. They see a price and they make a decision without knowing what analysts are saying about *future* earnings. They sell it as the stock fluctuates, again not knowing what the analysts are forecasting future earnings to be. It's the same with savers buying CDs or bonds—"

"They look only at the coupon," said Austin.

"Right, they look only at the interest rate, and not at how First American Investors analysts are forecasting *future interest rates.*"

Austin chuckled. "That's actually pretty funny, Johnny."

Johnny cocked his head. "How so?"

Austin sat up straight in his chair. "Well, the current yield is the current yield. You get what you get for income and you pray to God that the stock price doesn't tank. But the funny thing is, the company's dividend changes *in the future* will determine what that stock does over, say, three to five years, right? The current income has *nothing* to do with your future income from that stock, right?"

Johnny put his hand in front of him like a Buddhist monk. "Ahhh my young paduan, you seem to be catching on."

"There's so much continuity between the two strategies... I absolutely *love* this," exclaimed Austin.

"It's gets better. So instead, we have another client put a million bucks into utility stocks because in 1980 the yield on good utility stocks was only around eight percent." Johnny shuffled through some papers. "Yes, here it is... eight-and-a-half percent. That's all they see. The current yield. So naturally, the bond saver opts for the $110,000 in interest income over the $85,000 or so in the utility dividend strategy. That's why they didn't do it."

Austin shrugged. "Can't blame them."

"No," responded Johnny. "That would be like blaming a person who wears glasses for being myopic. But they still can't see a long way off, can they? They say 'Ah, I don't want to take eighty-five, I want the one ten.'"

"Again," said Austin, "can you blame them?"

"Hey," said Johnny as he threw up his hands. "They're *conventional*! In fact, even in the mid nineties, savers would still take the seven percent in bonds instead of the four percent in utilities, and so on, and so on. Today, savers, *by definition*, will always take the higher rate. Nothing has changed, you see. That's what makes them savers. And it's what makes them plain miserable to have to watch their income keep going down."

All right, what about the investor?"

"It's unbelievable," said Johnny. "First, let me remind you that all dividends in both of these sample portfolios are totally spent. Money goes out."

"Hmm, so there's no compounding going on."

It's apples to apples this way. Both clients spent their income. So the investor's original $85,000 income – because of dividend *growth* – has increased to... are you ready for this?"

Austin was genuinely excited now. He loved talk of money, especially his, when the news was good. In the greater scope of things, it usually was with Johnny Long. But more than that, he was excited to be tuning into something *new*, something he could sink his teeth into. Maybe there was a project out there where he could apply this new strategy? Austin clapped his hands together. "Ok, lay it on me, Johnny."

Johnny cleared his throat and flipped through some pages. "The dividend investor's income has grown to about $250,000 per year! Is that amazing or what?"

Austin laughed. "Ha, in the meantime, the other guy is eating dog food on... what... $40,000? Good luck. And there goes their principal, too."

"Well, I'm not so glib about it, Austin, but yes... I don't know about dog food, but the saver is the person who is struggling to save up for two weeks in the Poconos instead of a month-long cruise. Seriously though, Austin, I make it sound much easier than it is. Knowing what to buy, when to sell, and what to do with the proceeds means actually *buying and selling* stocks based on First American Investors dividend estimates and changes to those estimates."

"That's what makes you unique, Johnny. Sooner or later, an advisor has to actually make decisions."

"And anyone who remembers the eighties will say to me, 'It all depends on what you bought. You could've gotten killed in utilities like so many other people did.' And they don't believe me. But I remind them that it is *always* a matter of what you buy and what you sell... and what you hold, actually, and I thank them for making my point! Ha!"

Austin scratched his head. "Explain to me how you take the analyst's numbers and make actual decisions in the trenches."

"Imagine a game of Pin Your Future on the Portfolio. In fact, I'm gonna make it real easy for you. Let's say that I don't even blindfold you. Instead of a donkey, we're going to have seven different million-dollar portfolios listing yields from, say, three percent right up to seven. And I told you to go ahead and pin your future on the income, right?"

Austin agreed. "That's what makes the most sense to them. Why shouldn't they take the one with the higher income?"

"Well, if you used that strategy in 1980," continued Johnny, "which is really no strategy at all, you would have gotten your head handed to you over the next ten years. So you can't say to me, 'Johnny, you made money in utilities during the 80's because interest rates *plummeted*."

Austin squinted. He was obviously confused. "I don't get your point."

"Well," replied Johnny, "interest rates went down in the 80's, and utility stocks got hit very, very hard. Due to new construction cost overruns. This is no secret."

"But you said your strategy did amazing?"

"It did," answered Johnny.

"How on Earth did you pull that off?"

"Have you been listening to a word I've been saying... think about the growth-stock strategy..."

Austin threw his hands up. "Oh.... *information*."

"Research, right! The difference between making all that money I detail with the sample Investor's portfolio is a *direct result* of following First American Investors analysts. I dance with them, I follow *their* lead, but I organize their research in my own unique way. That's *my* value to my clients."

"Good thing for them. I know firsthand. No wonder Cristina was so happy with you."

"Austin, a lot of people got their shirts handed to them owning utility stocks in the 80's. But it was because they *did not have a strategy*, let alone a strategy that *worked* as well as mine." Johnny pounded his index finger against the table to emphasize his point. "Plain and simple. I made a lot of money. But... in the 80's more utilities went out of business, changed their name, cut their dividends, canceled their dividends then ever before... even in the *Depression*."

Austin was shocked. He was amazed all over again. He remembered when he first met Johnny, how Johnny's growth stock strategy seemed so unreal to him, something he could never partake of for himself. Looking back, meeting Johnny was a gift from beyond the grave, the *real* value in his father's legacy. And as Johnny continued outlining his utility strategy, Austin couldn't help but wonder if great successes still lay ahead. Just thinking about the fact that maybe, just maybe, he had experienced only a *part* of what Johnny Long had to offer made Austin giddy. He was rocking his foot up and down as Johnny continued on with his explanation.

"Austin, someone will always pooh-pooh something that worked when their plan didn't... assuming, of course, that they even had a plan. In this case, you had to know which utility stocks to buy. And you *surely* had to know which stocks to *avoid*. First question... knowing what to buy. There were plenty of utility stocks yielding ten, eleven, even thirteen percent."

"Ha," said Austin, "pin your future-."

"Of course, those were usually the stocks that had the most trouble. Those people got caught looking because they didn't know what type of information to use. They made decisions simply on the current yield."

"Geez," said Austin, "so they not only saw their income go down substantially when these companies cut their dividends and stuff, they probably lost a lot of principal *also* when the dividends were cut. Wasn't that what you were explaining before?"

"Precisely. You can trace a line between dividend growth and stock price. They move together over time, and that's for sure. I've got thousands of pages of research on this. So if you didn't have the right information or didn't know how to use it, you could have been ruined. Conversely, however, if you focused on what *really* makes utility stocks operate on the open market – namely, dividend changes – you could have made a tremendous profit, even during the 80's."

"I'm jealous," said Austin.

"Huh, don't be. You're in it."

Austin smiled. "Oh yeah, I forgot. So that's exciting. Do tell, do tell. What else?"

"The numbers are self-explanatory. The saver who started with a million is now worth a million. The investor who started with a million is now worth *five million*."

"What?" Austin blurted out incredulously.

"Sure," said Johnny. "Remember, because we are buying stocks with growing dividends, and because those stock prices will trend upward accordingly over time, we are capturing *growth* in general. Total return!"

"You're not withdrawing anything in this model, though, right?" asked Austin.

"The client is withdrawing and spending the income. Remember too, that the saver is reduced to about $40,000 in interest income, while the investor is getting about $250,000. In the game of Pin Your Future on the Portfolio, the saver *always... always loses* versus the investor."

"So most people don't know there's another way."

"Yeah," said Johnny. "$250,000 versus $40,000... One million versus *five* million. Is it worth the increased risk? Sure it is."

Austin rubbed his chin. "There's a lot you can do with this, Johnny."

"The sky's the limit."

Moira buzzed in on Johnny's phone. "You have the University of Pennsylvania Hospital coming in soon. Just a heads up."

Johnny leaned toward the phone. "Thanks, hon. Just wrapping up here..." He hung up. "For now." He turned to Austin. "UPenn Hospital, Austin."

Austin first became familiar with the Penn people when he was working to open the hospice home in the Bahamas. UPenn was one of the best cancer hospitals around. What impressed Austin most was the way in which the doctors managed to find time to care about the *people* with cancer, especially children. It is sad to see children with cancer. The way they try to smile and laugh through the pain and humiliation, through knowing they are probably going to die... ironically, it's *other* people who are sad for them. Austin would get choked up every time he thought about it. Yes, what impressed Austin was the way in which the doctors tried to fulfill themselves *spiritually* through their work which was financially rewarding as well.

"They're great over there," said Austin."

Johnny sat back in his chair and smiled. "You know I manage quite a lot of endowment money for them... in the Growth of Income Strategy."

"I never thought about it," replied Austin. In fact, he never had. This was the big problem with him. His thinking – his strategizing – stopped with the growth-stock portfolio. And he wasn't even following that closely any more. Sure he wanted to make more money. He *loved* making money. But he had to get over this feeling of emptiness, despite all his new-found wealth. What had he really done *for himself*?

Both Pickett and Johnny said basically the same thing-- the answer was obvious, hanging right in front of your face. Austin felt like he was going to explode one of these days if he didn't get his arms around this thing. The frustration was totally consuming him, and that's when he usually lashed at people. Was it any wonder he and Cathy broke up?

Austin looked up at Johnny. "How'd you get hooked up with them?" he asked.

Johnny stood up and started cleaning up the table for his next meeting. He looked Austin right in the eye. "Austin, I don't just do what I do because I make a lot of money doing it. There's got to be more to it than that."

Austin smacked his leg. "*That's* what I'm struggling with, Johnny."

"I know, Austin. I know. The reason I like to do the Growth of Income Strategy, aside from the fact that it works so well, is that I can successfully replace fixed-income portfolios. And who usually depends on large fixed-income portfolios?"

Austin shrugged. "Older folks?"

"Who else?"

"Don't know... rich people?"

"Not-for-profits, hospitals, charities...*good people*, Austin. *Those* are the accounts I am trying to help. Do you know that in the last five years alone, the Penn Endowment Fund has grown enough to finance a new children's facility? Do you have any idea what that means to me? My name will never be on any buildings, but I'm in *every single brick* of that new facility, Austin. Do you know what that means to me as a father, as a man? Wealthy Arabs may send me valuable paintings, but the dying kids at Penn sent me a "thank you" drawing in crayon. There's no comparison."

Austin sat quietly. He felt like he was being scolded by his father... but he didn't even know what *that* felt like. He felt humiliated. Johnny continued firing away as he cleaned up. "The few times a month I go out in the city, I see a lot of these rich little guys zooming around high as a kite in their $100,000 cars. But I'll take the crayon drawing any day. They remind me of you, actually, Austin."

Johnny's last comment stung Austin very badly. Obviously, he was referring to the hotshots and not the cute drawings. "Ouch, man. What did I do to you?"

"Nothing Austin. I'm sorry. I didn't mean it that way. But *you're* the one who started on the topic when you first came in this morning. What are you doing to *yourself*? That's the question, eh? The answer's right in front of you, Austin. Why don't you *do* something instead of wallowing away? I have the two strategies. I could just sit back and rake it in. Instead, I use what is right in front of me to *help* other people who are less fortunate. How you chose to do that, and for whom, is up to you. But here it is right in front of you, man. And don't start thinking I'm some sort of bleeding heart or anything. I do it because it makes me feel good. And so what? I like it, and it helps people, bottom line."

Austin was tearing up. He just couldn't see it. He could sort of understand this new utility stock strategy, but he just couldn't figure out what both Pickett and now Johnny meant when they said the answer was "right in front of him." Austin was staring at his feet. He looked up. "I need help, Johnny. Please help me to see it."

Moira buzzed in again. It was time for Austin to leave. They shook hands. "Just think about it, Austin. Something *always* pops up. It's just a matter of seeing it right in front of your face."

There was that damned term again. "Great," said Austin. "Just lovely. Thanks, Johnny." Austin walked out into the sunshine. The sun felt good, but his brain was going to explode. For Austin, it felt like when he tried to solve the Rubik's Cube as a kid. He had no idea how to do it, yet there was that handful of kids who could blow through it like they were writing their names. "Just follow the system," they would say. Unbelievable. Needless to say, Austin's Rubik's Cube quickly collected dust on the shelf in his bedroom. Instead, Austin enjoyed conning the "smart" kids into trading him their gourmet lunches for his bologna on white bread. Then there was Pickett and his amazing ability on the piano. Austin had to work hard to improve his saxophone playing. For Tony Pickett, the piano was his Rubik's Cube— *he* controlled the medium, not vice-versa. When Austin first met Johnny Long, Austin couldn't tell the difference between a mutual fund and an ETF. But not Johnny Long... he was a master at investing. And now this new strategy! Austin was overwhelmed again. For Johnny, earnings growth and dividend growth were so obvious. How? How did he do this? It was infuriating.

Austin hated feeling this way. It set him at odds with the world. Instead, he yearned to flow *along with it*, to somehow be in unison with other people. Money wasn't the issue. He couldn't use that common excuse. For people like Tony Pickett and Johnny Long, the world seemed to offer a smooth path to great personal growth. And yet for Austin – or so he felt – the world was like a dense jungle and he had only a penknife to cut through it. But Austin knew in his heart of hearts that this simply *couldn't* be. It was the same damned world they all lived in. Therefore, he figured, it must be a matter of *perspective*, his and other people's. He must remain alert, focused, and ready for everything and yet nothing in particular. It was so Zen. That really pissed him off. Too contradictory!

Austin looked at his watch. He decided to work until the close and then spend some time organizing his thoughts. When he left Johnny's office a few minutes earlier, he was quite conflicted. On the one hand, he was enthralled with the Utility Stock Growth-of-Income Strategy. It was new and exciting... full of potential. On the other hand, he had been in it for some time without even knowing it. How embarrassing was that? Johnny must have thought him a fool, one of those rich hotshots he was disparaging, and rightfully so. Worse yet, the Hospice home had money in the Growth of Income Strategy. That's where they got their yearly income from, and still Austin knew nothing of it. What kind of commitment was that? On the one hand, Austin felt it was no coincidence that he stumbled upon the Growth of Income Strategy right after meeting up with Pickett. After all, Pickett *did* elaborate on the possibility of applying the Big Three questions to life in general. So did Johnny. This could *not* simply be a coincidence. On the other hand, it seemed to Austin sometimes that just about everyone else could figure continuity in life. It was the Rubik's Cube thing all over again.

Austin had to admit, though, that Johnny did give him a good kick in the ass at the end there. Austin might have been frustrated and a bit confused when he left their meeting, but if anything, he was even more determined to develop a sort of philosophy for himself. After the close, Austin headed over to Holt's Cigars and bought himself a fine leather-bound notebook. He would keep a journal. The leather smelled of ideas… aged, a bit weathered, idyllic. The pages were thick and rough-hewn. Speckles of fine colored threads were woven into the pale yellow paper. Austin hoofed it a few blocks to Rittenhouse Square and sat down against a huge oak tree. He would start his journal then and there. He pulled out the Cuban *Romeo and Juliet* Churchill *en tubos* he "borrowed" from Johnny's humidor, nipped off the end, and fired it up.

Nothing mellows you out like a top-shelf Cuban cigar. People say the high lithium content in the Cuban soil gives their cigars an almost narcotic effect. Lithium balances you out, calms your mind. Lithium is what they prescribe for bipolar patients. So the tobacco grows in lithium-rich soil. But there's more to it. There's a balance between nature and the human artisan as well. The construction is perfect… you get that nice, fat ash which you can grow on the end of your cigar like a pet glowworm. The taste is rich and vibrant… it progresses through several distinct flavor profiles as you smoke it down. If properly humidified, the cigar is neither chewy nor crackly… you may bite and suck as you wish without having to spit out little pieces of tobacco. Sometimes, a cigar is just a cigar. But a fine Cuban can hardly be called a "stogy" any more than a fine *Bordeaux* can be called swill.

By the time Austin realized he was hungry, he had written some fifteen pages. His thoughts flew out through the felt-tipped pen. Austin didn't censor himself or try to arrange his thoughts in any particular way. He just free-wrote. Austin relit the stub of his cigar and puffed a few times with a sense of satisfaction. He couldn't remember the last time he sat down and just wrote like that. The last time was probably after his mother died. A lot had happened since then and reading over what he had written, Austin was surprised by how much he spewed out.

When you think about the lithium-like effects of smoking a Cuban cigar, it comes as no surprise that Freud smoked them constantly. Call it a sort of self-medication regimen for dealing with the complexities of the human mind – Ego, Id, and Super Ego all fighting for Daddy's attention. It's enough to drive a man... well, crazy. Marx smoked his to declare his solidarity with a working class that was, by definition, inexorably at odds with the dominant socio-economic system in the world. Castro smoked his as a symbol of his unimpeachable sovereignty in the face of his American neighbors who would rather see him buried and gone. And then we have Austin Montgomery, sitting in Rittenhouse Square, smoking his cigar and trying to sort out his life on paper. He felt pulled in so many directions. The lithium leveled him out.

There are rare moments when we are self-confident enough to make honest self-criticisms. This was such a time for Austin. For as he read over what he had written, he realized he didn't have much to say after all. He thought for a moment... if he were to thumb through the world-news pages of the *Philadelphia Inquirer*, would his life really seem so bad? What did he actually *want* for? Nothing, really. Not a thing that he couldn't find within himself like Pickett and Johnny said. What he scribbled out really amounted to rich, white boy whining if he were being honest. And Austin was being honest with himself at the moment. That damned Cuban was getting the better of him.

If you were reading over Austin's shoulder, this is what you'd surmise. *We're all obese and lazy, but eating is a lost art... college costs too much, but thank God I went to Stanford... greed is at the root of the problems, but just think of how much good I did building the hospice home... women are selfish, but I feel totally lost without a girlfriend... work can be totally boring, a new project gives life direction.*

His thoughts were at odds with each other, conflicting, bouncing off the inside of his skull. He was sure this didn't happen to Johnny, or Pickett, or anyone else, for that matter, who had a sense of continuity in their life. All these thoughts, all these either-or's which filled his head... obviously, then the answer had to be somewhere in the middle. It was dangling right in front of his face.

Austin got up and flicked away his cigar butt. He snapped shut the journal with a thud. By the time he reached the *Black Bass*, he felt embarrassed by what he had written. He tossed the journal in the trash can and kept walking east toward the water. He started thinking about Johnny's Growth of Income Strategy. It was so... *easy*. Johnny was right. There was nothing particularly complex about it. It was not *genius*, it was...*ingenious*. Yes, that was it. Johnny Long was an ingenious man. His two strategies worked because they focused on what *really* mattered. It was so obvious. Growth stocks? Look at earnings-estimate changes, of course. Growth of income? Look at dividend-estimate increases. And that was that. All the information Johnny would ever need was printed for him every month by First American Investors analysts. All he had to do was follow along, dance with the analysts. The same was true for Johnny's clients. And like Ginger Rogers, they were rewarded handsomely for following so well.

It suddenly occurred to Austin that he might actually have done good with his father's will. After all, *he* accepted the challenge when he could have just walked away with a cool million. *He* interviewed other advisors before settling on Johnny Long. *He* had to see Johnny's ingenuity enough to trust him with all his money. And *he* was richly rewarded for *his* decision to do so. Then there was the hospice home, the utility stock strategy... maybe he hadn't done so badly after all?

His cell rang. It was Johnny's office. "Hey Austin, it's Moira."

Austin figured she was trying for a date again. "Hi there. Long time."

Moira sighed. "Ah... too long, my sweet. Actually, Johnny wants you in again tomorrow. Something interesting came up with the Penn people."

Austin was a bit surprised. "Really? That's unlike him not to have mentioned anything about it. I was in there for over an hour today." Austin was suspicious. "What's going on?" He figured Johnny wanted to show him his utility stocks or something like that.

"I really can't say, Austin. Knowing him, it's probably some big new client he wants some help with. He wants to see you tomorrow at eleven. He said he was sure you'd be available for this."

"Is that so?"

"Uh-huh. Oh yeah, he also said you're going to need to clear about a week or so on your schedule. You're going on a trip. He'll look after your accounts. Maybe they'll actually go up."

Austin was taken aback. "Very funny. This doesn't sound like the kind of offer I can refuse, does it?"

Moira cut him off abruptly. "OK, then. See you tomorrow stud boy. And you'd better buy some mosquito repellent." Then she hung up.

Austin crossed Walnut Street at Third. Time to pack again.

Chapter 10

The first leg of the flight was no problem. It was only six hours or so into Heathrow. It was the second leg into Johannesburg, a twelve-hour excursion, which would make you go stir crazy. If it were not for British Air's first-class sleeper seats, he didn't know how he would have survived. Flying from Philly to London was one thing. Flying twelve hours mushed into an economy seat was quite another. It only takes one look at a fully-booked economy cabin to realize that prisoners in Guantanamo Bay enjoy better conditions, and all they did was try to blow up the United States and kill every American they could.

For a rich guy, Austin hated to be flown by other pilots. He flew as infrequently as possible. True, once he reached cruising altitude some 35,000 feet up in the air, he felt completely above the world's problems. It was like he was on his own little cloud. What bothered him was the *idea* of being flown, of course. So typically Austin. He loved flying high, high above everything but hated the principle of being flown in general. To Austin, nowhere was this more obvious than during the pre-flight safety check. Did it *really* matter that his seat could be used as a flotation device after plunging ten... twenty... *thirty* thousand feet into the sea? What would be left to float? He liked soaring high above the clouds, and yet the very concept of being flown by other pilots appalled him.

Austin actually read in the paper that the European company *Airbus* had already introduced standing-room "seats" on planes sold to their Asian carriers. It seemed cramming a giant cigar tube with hundreds of people and hurtling it through the air just fast enough so it doesn't fall out of the sky was not insane enough. No, Asian commuters apparently had no problem actually *strapping* themselves to the sides of the plane (*in-side*, of course). Trying to imagine exactly what that would look like, Austin kept seeing images of Hannibal Lecter strapped in his straightjacket being wheeled around on a hand truck. The facemask wouldn't matter because they probably wouldn't be serving food on the flight anyway.

If eighteen airtime hours wasn't bad enough, Austin knew next to nothing about Botswana. He ordered a few books from Amazon, but how reliable were they? They turned out to be mostly picture books, anyway. He felt totally unprepared for the country. He studied Johnny's proposal nightly. He knew *both* strategies inside and out. But what of Botswana, the people of the country. If you are referring to the country, you pronounce the word as *Boats-wana*. If you are referring to the people, you say *Bats-wana*. Even that was confusing. Austin did not like the unknown, and nothing is much more "unknown" than flying off to the middle of Africa to talk with a client.

Austin was looking forward to his seven-hour layover in London. He decided to enjoy his time in London, by stepping out a bit to hit a pub. He didn't have time to go through customs and make it all the way into the city, so he settled for getting off the Piccadilly Line somewhere in the outskirts of the city. Checking his watch, Austin decided to get off at Holloway Road. In typical British fashion, each stop on the Piccadilly line had its own historical significance. A stop or two earlier was the Arsenal stop, so named for the world-famous soccer team which called the area home. It was St. Patty's Day, and Austin feared the pubs would be mobbed, packed to the gills with riotous wankers and larger louts proudly wearing the green or the orange, and brawling over which side was right. Austin was not sure if there was a match that day, but he didn't want to risk walking into a pub in the middle of a brawl. You see, there are three topics over which the English will start throwing punches—soccer, Ireland, and the Queen. It being St. Patty's Day, two of the three fuses would be lit. Wise to keep a safe distance.

The next stop, Holloway Road, seemed harmless enough. Nobody sinister getting off, no Sid and Nancy or anything like that. At the very least, he would be able to chat with the typical English Everyman. The historical significance of Holloway Road was this: Originally called *Hollow Way*, it started off as little more than a ditch (a hollow way) dug by some pauper. There you go... behold. And as Austin emerged from the red-tiled station into the brisk wind, he noticed that little had changed since then. It actually took him almost fifteen minutes to find a pub. This was quite unheard of, even to a ditchdigger.

Austin neglected to take out a jacket before checking his baggage for the next flight. Consequently, he was chilly. It was 7° Celsius which, roughly transcribed, equates to "nippy" in America. The English perma-cast gray skies choked out the sun just like cigarette smoke choked out any breathable air in the neighborhood pub. He didn't feel like hoofing around looking for just the right sort of pub to stir his memories of freshman literature class, so he picked the first one he came across – the *Queen's Head and Artichoke*. The connection wasn't quite clear to Austin. It would do.

Austin hadn't visited London in several years, and even then he never went to the outskirts like Holloway Road. As soon as he stepped into the *Queen's Head*, though, Austin could see things had changed. It seemed to him that *everything* was changing. It wasn't nearly as idyllic as he hoped. For starters, the pub was virtually empty... and it was only two in the afternoon. There were no crusty old Brits for Austin to eavesdrop on, no leggy birds for Austin to flirt with. The second thing he noticed – and this would be true of anyone who *ever* stepped foot in a pub five years ago – there was *no smoking*. It was shocking. It was appalling. Austin stood in the doorway wondering if he had stepped off a plane from the *Twilight Zone*. How on Earth, he wondered, can you have an English pub *sans* the thick cloud of cigarette smoke hanging about seven feet off the ground? Surely, this was seen as an injustice? It wasn't that Austin was a smoker. He wasn't. It's just that there are some traditions you don't mess with. Austin scratched his head, still standing in the doorway. The next thing he noticed – without even sitting down – was that all the beer taps were *chilled*. This was truly a crime against humanity. Had Labour gone so far this time as to upheave traditional *beer* as well? He could see requiring hard liquor bottles to have a pre-measuring

98

device hooked on to ensure no man was cheated his fair portion (a g*il*). But *Coors Light* on tap? He could have stayed at the airport for that.

This all reminded Austin of the time he tried to replace an old *Radiators* L.P. He walked into a huge music store and asked for the record section, but all they stocked were CDs. The chick standing near him wearing the retro-green *Adidas* shirt sent him down to South Street for his vinyl. Standing there in the doorway, lungs unencumbered, Austin wondered if things had once again passed him right by without his slightest knowledge. Pickett would get a real kick out of this, he thought.

"Whattaya have, love?" asked the barmaid. She was short and dumpy, not like the tall, leggy English girls Austin loved.

Austin bellied up to the bar. There were only four or five other people in the place. "Umm… I'll have a pint of snakebite."

The girl nodded and poured off half a pint of Fosters, half a pint of hard cider, and toped it off with currant. "Anything else then?"

Austin looked over his culinary choices… cold sausages, cold pork pie, cheese sandwich, pickled eggs, pork cracklings, assorted crisps. "Some crisps." He pointed to the wall behind her.

"Bacon, Beef or Cheddar Curry?"

Austin chose the least threatening. "Beef, please."

She handed him the bag of crisps and rang him up. "That'll be two quid then."

Austin handed her two coins. "Cheers," he said. The English may have no middle class, he thought, but they'll always be able to afford their beer. He looked for a seat at the bar. Then he looked at the barmaid.

"Sit anywhere you like, love," she said.

Austin looked around again. Aside from the stools lining the counter along the windows next to the bar, there were no actual seats *at the bar*. Austin suddenly realized that you couldn't sit at the damned bar. The stools along the window were the closest he would get. Austin pulled up next to a man of indistinct age. Smog, smoking, work, beer, and God knows what else had taken their toll on him. He could have been twenty-seven or fifty-seven.

Austin sat down next to him and raised his glass. "Cheers."

The man nodded. "Cheers, mate."

"Where is everyone?" asked Austin.

The man turned to face him. "Oh, I don't know. They'll be around shortly, I suppose."

"Wow, back in the States the bars are packed by six a.m.on St. Patrick's Day!"

The man thought deeply about this. "It's true then."

"What's that?" replied Austin.

"You Yanks are crazy. Gonna kill us all." He laughed. So did the barmaid.

Austin smiled. "Naw, it's just a St. Patty's Day thing. They like to start early and pass out late, that's all."

"Ahhh…" said the man. He turned to the barmaid. "That's right, it's St. Patty's Day, Liz."

Liz nodded. "That's right, it is." She continued washing pint glasses used by unseen patrons.

The man turned back to Austin. "I suppose it is here, too? What the bloody hell do I care. I'm South African, man. The Irish are pigs." Liz, the barmaid, laughed out loud.

Austin was totally unprepared for this sort of comment. He recognized right away, though, the man's different accent. It was not English. Not knowing what else to do, Austin laughed too. "Everyone's Irish on St. Patty's Day."

The man picked at his cracked nails. "Like shit, man."

Austin had traveled enough to know there were two different types of South African Whites. Those who acquiesced to the unstoppable tide of integration led by the African National Congress, and those who would *never* accept it. Almost always, both types flee to some degree. The racial geography of South Africa changes daily as sure as the wildlife migrates with the rains. Indeed, there is a constant ebb and flow of racial tensions that no American would readily comprehend if they had never been there. Generally speaking, there are the places the white people go. And then there are the places the white people *used* to go.

This man was clearly of the first sort. He was an Afrikaner, and he was pissed. Not "pissed" like the British say when they're drunk. No, "pissed" as in *you took away everything I had and now I'm gonna string you up and lynch you.* Johannes was his name. Many Afrikaner first names came from the Bible, but sometimes their ideas do not. By the time his trip to Botswana was complete, Austin would learn that whenever a person said "Naw, I'm South African, man" with that certain haughtiness, they were of the angry sort. Austin would meet many, but he was uncomfortable talking with them. They were obsessed with what "those damned savages" were doing to their beloved "homeland", or so they called it. Sometimes Austin felt sorry for them. They were out of place, the butt of jokes because they still felt entitled to speak however they wanted regardless of where they were. This was a privilege angry Afrikaners no longer had anywhere in the world. This made them even angrier. Ironically, Afrikaner nationalism was easily the most successful form of African nationalism. This made them angrier still.

Just as Austin was about to put his foot in his mouth again by asking a question about Nelson Mandela's role in the modern *ANC*, a second man jumped in to save him. "'Allo there, mate," he said holding out his hand. "Name's Simon, Simon Van Der Stel."

Austin shook his hand. "Austin Montgomery."

"Bloody Montgomery," added Johannes.

Simon jumped in again. "He means Montgomery as in Patton's World War II ally."

Austin nodded. Thank God he saw that movie recently. "Hmm, yes... quite a rivalry with Patton."

Johannes couldn't let this one pass. "Another crazy American with a gun!"

"A tank," corrected Simon.

"Big soddin' gun," fired back Johannes.

The triple-strength brew was starting to hit Austin. Drinking one pint in England was like drinking *three* beers in America. You could almost serve it in a shot glass. He motioned to the barmaid for another. While he was at it, Austin thought it a good measure of *detente* to buy the blokes a round, too.

"That's a good lad," said Johannes. "Cheers, mate."

"See," said Simon, "you found the way to Johannes' heart. That wasn't hard now was it?" They all clinked glasses.

Johannes smiled sardonically, took a swig which knocked off about half a pint, and said, "I'm just a misunderstood bloke."

"See, we were in the army together."

Johannes finished his pint in one more guzzle. "Bloody 'ell no, man. South Africa!"

Austin tried to change the subject. "I'm heading to Africa now."

"That so?" asked Simon. "Where 'bouts?"

"Not Jo'Burg, I hope," said Johannes bitterly.

"I'm flying in there, but I'm moving on to Botswana."

"Good... good," said Simon. "I really miss Jo'Burg, man, but it's really dangerous now." There was lament in Simon's voice. If Johannes represented the angry Afrikaner, Simon came from the group of white South Africans who just capitulated and went with the flow of history, the flow of something much bigger than the Boers themselves.

It occurred to Austin that these two men were the exact opposite of himself. Johnny Long sent him on a business trip to Africa. But it was also Johnny's intent to send his young protégé on a search for himself. What better place than the proverbial "heart of darkness?" The business opportunity was a fortuitous happenstance... sometimes things just happened that way. Who knew why? Did it even matter? So here he was, thought Austin, headed off to Botswana. To be honest, he didn't even know where the country was! He didn't even know who he was meeting. He just got his shots and off he went a week or two later. He could not pass up the opportunity, the pure adventure of it all. Just pick up and trek to Africa! *That's living.* Austin was out looking for his roots.

For these guys, though, it was just the opposite. They *pulled up their roots* and were trying to live hydroponically, so to speak. They were trying to survive *without* rootedness. Unlike Austin who was trying to shape for himself an identity that brought him together and gave him a sense of well-being and continuity, Simon and Johannes were struggling to *undo* who they were because it was too painful to live in exile within their own country. Little did they care, though, that the indigenous blacks they subjugated for hundreds of years might have felt the same way.

When you travel abroad these days, you are acutely aware of being American. The clothes you wear, the shoes you have on, the volume at which you speak... they are all incriminating, or so you feel. You may be the farthest thing from the Ugly American. Nevertheless, you worry. Austin could turn on the charm if he had to, though. When he came into money, he came into himself. He was more self-confident. Not arrogant really. Just confident that he could manage to impress a girl in any way she wanted. Whether she deserved it was a matter for later consideration. When Austin took the leap of faith and jumped right into the situation, he usually found people – even complete strangers – to be fascinating.

Listening to Simon and Johannes reminiscing about their army days, Austin realized that only an American would take it for granted that he would be just fine being dropped off in the middle of Africa. Some of their stories were startling, describing things that would not, that could not happen in the States. And thank God for that. Johnny trusted Austin implicitly with the job of talking with a new client. Obviously, Johnny had a very strong contact in Botswana, or he would have gone himself. Nevertheless, Austin took the trip as more than a challenge. He understood what Johnny was up to sending him to the middle of the "Dark Continent." Austin was determined not to disappoint Johnny Long. As a result, he was more focused than he had been in years. And it felt great. So great, in fact, that Austin barely noticed he was cut adrift to fend for himself. As much as he hoped to meet wonderful people with ancient customs and old souls, he knew some things would be all too modern -- a journey into a world of poverty, disease, and warfare as much as anything else. His meeting with Dr. Tony Stone, the Princess Diana Hospital Assistant Director, was sure to bring him face-to-face with this dichotomy.

Austin recalled the article he had read by Pickett. About halfway through, Pickett referred to a Mingus piece that exemplified what Pickett called "polyphonic dichotomy." For Pickett, this was achieved when two musicians play *against* one another. If done correctly, they resonate in such a way as to create what Pickett called a "third line," a sound that was actually in tune and therefore *resolved* the musical conflict between the two musicians. Austin wasn't sure if he believed all this, just like he wasn't sure if he believed in Pickett's "Great Wheel in the Sky" theory or whatever he called it. With Johannes on one side cursing the "savages" and Simon on the other talking about the inevitable flow of history, Austin felt that Pickett's theory of polyphonic dichotomy could actually be applied to life in general.

Austin shook the alcohol from his head. He noticed Johannes' hands shook whenever he extended them. Seeing him standing there, Austin felt sorry for Johannes. As Simon pointed out time and time again, things in South Africa – and Africa as a whole – were not so black and white, so to speak. People like Johannes were caught in the middle.

Both Simon and Johannes did time in the South African army. They were both special forces. They started off innocently enough, comparing Rommel's prowess with Patton's. Then they started boasting about South African tank technology, among the best in the world. Then Johannes decided he was going to tell Austin about "necklacing." Simon advised Austin to have another drink first. In Simon's words, it was the "bloody story about what happened to our Johannes here, man." Austin checked his watch. He had a few hours before he had to be back at Heathrow. He ordered another round for the three of them.

Austin had never heard of necklacing. As far as he was concerned, Johannes was about to tell him about some African custom of exchanging jewelry or something like that. Simon clarified things.

"It's not about sodding necklaces, man."

Johannes got a kick out of that one. He started laughing until he turned red from a thick, phlegmatic smoker's cough. "We was both all over Africa, Simon and me," he said.

"Somalia, Rawanda, uh… South Africa," clarified Simon.

"Damned South Africa," spit out Johannes.

Austin was confused. Why would they be deployed in their own country? "I thought you were from South Africa?"

Simon took a long sip of beer. "The sad fact, mate, is that we saw a lot of action in our own damned country. Believe me when I tell you, mate, things aren't as easy as people think."

Johannes sprung to life. "It's my damned country. My people been there just as long as theirs. Savages. We were doing a routine patrol in Soweto."

"Soweto?" asked Austin.

"A nasty, nasty shanty town," replied Simon. "You don't want to ever have gone there."

"Let me finish," said Johannes. "We were on patrol. The usual stuff. Watch out for crime—"

"Rape mostly," added Simon. Austin nodded.

"Yeah," continued Johannes. "Rape mostly. They rape their woman like they was taking a piss, man. But, you know, things were very tight there for a while. They would attack us every now and then when they were drunk enough to act like men."

"You'd always know beforehand," said Simon, "because you could hear 'em dancing around and chanting and stuff."

"Real crap, man," said Johannes. "You know, and every now and then they would find out one of their own was informing on 'em and stuff. So they would necklace the poor bastard."

Simon finished off his pint. "Nastiest thing you'll ever see, man. I can still smell it."

"Smell it?" said Johannes. "Sometimes I swear I can *taste* it on my tongue." He finished off his pint too. "So we were out on patrol, and we hear all this screaming coming from around the corner. That's different because if it's a rape or something like that, the women usually don't scream. Rape is kinda like a custom."

Simon jumped in. "But you could hear this woman screamin' bloody murder, man. I've never heard anything like it, and I've been lying next to guys that just had half their leg blown off, you know?"

Johannes started biting his worn-down, dirty nails. "Screamin' like you never heard before, mate. So we make our way around the corner. There's like a big group of people gathering. That's what they do. They all watch."

Austin swigged his beer. "Huh… like those public beheadings the French used to have."

Simon shook his head. "Naw mate, not like this."

Johannes cleared his lungs with another deep smoker's cough. "So we get there, right, and they're pulling this woman out of her house—"

"*Pregnant,*" said Simon.

"Yeah, pregnant bitch like this," Johannes outlined a belly about eight or nine months large. "Full baby in there, man. You just knew it. They threw her down on the dirt. She's screamin' at the top of her lungs. Then they all move away from her."

Austin was appalled. "So they threw this pregnant woman down on the ground?"

Simon and Johannes laughed sardonically. "When they all pull away like that…" Simon gestured with his hands. "Then you know a strike's coming."

"A strike?" asked Austin. He didn't like the sound of that.

"Yeah, a *strike,*" said Johannes. He was getting agitated now, agitated at Austin, at the story, at his fingernails. You name it. He motioned to the barmaid for another round. "So they move away from her. You can almost feel it coming. Then out of the crowd comes this guy with a machete. He doesn't even run up to her. Just-"

"Just walks up to her, man," said Simon.

"Right. Just walks up like he's taking a piss. He grabs her… she is still on the ground… he grabs her by the hair so she sits upright. Then the bastard cuts her head right off. He holds it up like a trophy or something."

"What?" asked Austin incredulously. "Something like that would never happen in the States. That is so disgusting." The closest thing Austin could imagine was a lynching or something like that, but that didn't even come close to what they were describing.

Johannes belched. "I ain't finished yet, boy. He takes the machete and cuts her right down the middle." He outlined a line from his throat to his belt. Austin put his hand over his face and pinched his eyes. He knew what was coming, and he was getting nauseated. Johannes was rocking his knee up and down nervously. "He slit her belly wide open, man."

"*Wide open,*" said Simon for emphasis.

"From *here* to *here,*" demonstrated Johannes as he once again traced an imaginary line from his neck to his belt. "Pulled the baby right out and just threw it in the bushes."

"End of the lineage," said Simon.

But Johannes wasn't done yet. To Austin's horror, he continued with his story. "Then they pull the guy out of the shack. He's screamin' like he was a woman, man."

"Must have been an informant," clarified Simon.

"Who knows with those people," said Johannes. "They give him a couple of good shots in the belly, yeah, so he can't breathe too well. A couple guys hold him up while some other guys pile tires over him."

Austin didn't understand. "Pile tires over him?"

"Yeah," said Simon. "They put like car tires over you."

"Oh," said Austin, "like the Michelin Tire Man."

"I don't know what the hell that is," said Johannes. "They put the tires so you're in the middle and can't move, yeah. You can't even fall down, really. If there's enough tires, you're just sort of trapped there. You can't move." He cleared his throat and spit on the floor. "Then they light the tires on fire and watch you burn to death."

Austin's jaw dropped. He closed his eyes. Immediately, the scene came alive in his mind. He opened his eyes again to make it go away. Now he understood what Simon meant by the "smell." Now he understood what Johannes meant by the "taste" on his tongue.

Johannes continued. "They start dancing around and chanting," he said. "Can you believe that, man. Bloody savages. I wake up at least once a night hearing that poor bastard screaming. You've never heard anything like that before, man."

"And you don't want to, boy," added Simon.

"No," agreed Austin. "No, I don't. I really don't."

They were all quiet for a moment. The story crossed the point at which *every* victim of an atrocity deserves a moment of silent respect and dignity just for being human if nothing else. Austin was drunk, and he wanted to be on the plane, 30,000 feet up, sleeping it all off. He wished he'd never left the airport.

Simon broke the silence. "What my friend here didn't tell you is that *he* was the poor bastard that had to take care of the body when it stopped burning."

Johannes was staring down at the floor. "That burnt-rubber taste was all over my tongue, man." He made a face like he was going to vomit, then took a long guzzle of his new beer.

Austin looked at his watch. Regardless of the time, he was out of there. He had heard enough. He was now totally terrified of going to Africa. Here he was still twelve hours away, and he was hearing horror stories. Maybe he *was* in over his head. After all, just about everyone he knew thought he was crazy for going. "Africa?" they would say. "Why are you going *there?*" Everyone but Johnny Long and his friend Marc, who was married to an Ethiopian woman, thought he was completely out of his gourd. On the other hand, both Marc and Johnny assured him that the trip would change his life. Austin had no doubt his life was about to change. For better or for worse, *that* was the question after hearing Johannes' story.

Austin announced that he had to be getting back to Heathrow. "There's just one thing," he said. "Why didn't you stop it?"

Johannes and Simon looked at each other and smiled. Johannes held up his shaking hands as if the answer was incredibly obvious. "They're savages, man."

Chapter 11

Austin was not looking forward to dealing with security all over again. Heathrow's checkpoint was relatively tight, and there would no doubt be a line. Thinking about the security checkpoint made Austin think about the two Afrikaners. They were actually deployed in their own country, and this shocked Austin. He couldn't imagine that ever happening in the U.S. During the New Orleans flood, the Army and National Guard were deployed to help and generally keep the peace, but it never seemed like a *military* operation. Whenever Austin flew he thought of September 11th. He couldn't help it. As he stood there waiting in line to pass through the security checkpoint, it occurred to Austin that September 11th was the closest thing to a military action in the United States for quite some time, maybe since the Civil War. Even in Heathrow, the cops were outfitted more like Marines than police officers – dark-blue jump pants, black helmets, face shields, Kevlar vests, automatic weapons. They looked prepared. Austin felt inconvenienced but reassured. He took off his shoes and piled his stuff in the grey plastic bucket to send through the X-ray. "If I knew what *they* knew," he thought, "I'd sure as hell be advocating a much larger show of force." This was a classic example of putting yourself in the other guy's shoes.

Austin still remembered where he was the morning of September 11th. How times had changed. Austin remembered his mother and his Aunt Diana asking, "Do you remember where you were during the Great Blackout?" There was no doubt about it - Those days were gone forever, man. By the time he was thirty or thirty-five, his entire generation would be telling their kids not about some blackout but about some lunatics flying jumbo jets into the World Trade Center, the Pentagon, and almost the White House, in the name of their God.

He called Johnny right after he switched on CNBC and saw the first tower engulfed in smoke. Austin knew immediately it was Bin Laden. He had heard the name thrown around on John Bachelor's talk-radio program a lot in the weeks leading up to the attack. First American Investors, Johnny's firm, had something like five floors and lost people. Johnny said he was inundated with calls from panicky clients who wanted to go to cash on everything, so he couldn't talk. On the 13th, Austin remembered crying when the news showed the thousands and thousands of pictures of the "missing" people popping up spontaneously all over the city.

Nevertheless, turbulent times followed for investors. And as Johnny said, savers didn't fare any better than usual. What was truly amazing, though, was how well Austin's portfolio did. Sure, the volatility was there. The problem with fraudulent earnings really concerned Austin. But as Johnny told him just the other day, there will *always* be those kind of problems. And if you look back over all the ups and downs in the history of the market, how on Earth would you know when to time things perfectly? One thing was for certain, the markets are a lot higher now than they were twenty-five years ago. No surprise to Johnny, the companies that posted better and better earnings over the years showed the highest gains. Conversely, when they finally stopped increasing earnings, those stocks began to drop in value over time. Even today, Austin couldn't believe how well he'd done in just seven years.

Johnny's Growth of Income Strategy worked much the same way. In preparation for his presentation to the Penn folks in Botswana, Austin poured over the back-testing and other research Johnny had. The numbers were there. It was fascinating – where growth stocks trend higher and lower over time with their earnings-estimate revisions (and their actual earnings, of course), so too do utility stocks with regard to their dividend increases. As an analyst raises yearly dividend estimates, and as actual dividends *do* increase, so too does the stock price over time. As estimates and earnings trend up, so do the growth stocks. Likewise, as yearly dividend estimates and dividends trend up, so do utility stock prices. It was so obvious and yet so brilliant, Austin could scarcely believe it.

In retrospect, choosing Johnny Long as his advisor was the best thing he'd ever done. And Johnny's importance in Austin's life went far beyond picking stocks. A day or two before he left for Botswana, Austin realized that, in sending him to Africa to talk to a client, Johnny was giving Austin an opportunity to find himself. It was then that Austin realized picking Johnny all those years back was so obvious and yet so brilliant. Johnny's success in investing Austin's money made Austin feel proud of himself. It made him feel good about himself.

After hanging out with those two Afrikaners, though, Austin felt somehow that he could "bring something to the table," to quote a phrase he heard over and over again on CNBC. Having taken his seat in first class, Austin felt like he had a *responsibility* to do something smart or responsible. Above all, Austin, like Johnny Long, felt responsible to *give opportunity* in the way that his father, through his legacy, gave to him. Austin felt the same way when he received his scholarship to Stanford; he felt that he owed the music community and Stanford in general his absolute best effort. Thus, if Austin felt he was slacking off, not giving his best in return for all he received from the world for no particular reason, he got depressed. This new project, yet another gift from his father and Johnny Long, rekindled that sense of duty.

He prepared for his presentation with the Penn administrative people like he prepared for his midterms and finals at Stanford -- he put in the work. In that way, he did his part. If he was special, his talents would become obvious; if he was average, he would at least be as *fully average* as possible, if that made sense. He felt he owed the world that much. In fact, he was so prepared for this trip (which seemed to almost everyone else he knew to be some kind of impulsive flight from reality) that he packed his carry-on as if he'd been making this trek for years. His aged Polo leather bag looked like a well thought-out survival kit. There were, among other items, a brand-new pair of XL mesh sweats, a cotton turtleneck, flip-flops, two new pairs of ankle-high sweat socks, toothbrush and paste, emergency contact lenses and a pair of prescription glasses, a flashlight, three oranges, two bottles of spring water, and an assortment of pens, pads, books, notes, and even some toilet paper. Funny, he had packed a similar bag (add a Swiss Army knife and filter masks) when he went down to Ground Zero just a day-and-a-half after the attack to help his friend retrieve vital hard drives from his office located just one-half block from a collapsed building. Naturally, the power was off in the building as well as in the surrounding area. He thought they might have to survive on their own in case they got trapped or something.

The more Austin worked on the Growth of Income Strategy, the more he realized how valuable a tool it was for letting people experience new challenges throughout their life. The interconnectedness of the two strategies did not elude Austin. The more he studied them, the more he discovered a beautiful symmetry, what Pickett might call "Polyphonic Duality." The Growth-Stock strategy built wealth like nothing else Austin had seen. The Growth of Income Strategy then secured a growing income so you could enjoy what life had to offer. The Growth of Income Strategy really impressed Austin. There was something about it he liked even more than the growth-stock strategy. In fact, Johnny said something that made an impact on Austin. The ability to *do good* by helping hospitals, not-for-profits, and such, brought to investing an added dimension unique to the capitalist system. By studying both strategies for several days, and then heading straight out to the middle of Africa to help out a hospital, Austin realized that money, at least in itself, is neither good nor bad. Rather, it *allows* you to *do* good or bad depending upon how you are inclined.

When Austin woke up, he was somewhere off the coast of Spain. He still had quite a way to go. The bathroom in first class was occupied, so he headed back to economy class. Most of the passengers were asleep. A few were watching the in-flight movie *Jarhead*. Others were reading. He poked his head through the curtain dividing the premier economy and business class cabins. Standing next to the large door on the port side of the plane were three jocular Brits yucking it up with two English girls in their late twenties. Austin ducked into the bathroom as one of the men guffawed and then broke out in a thick smoker's cough.

When Austin emerged from the bathroom, a flight attendant was handing the group a round of drinks. She turned to Austin and stuck a drink in his hand.

Austin was a bit startled. "Oh—thanks," he said.

She smiled, gave Austin a quick "cheers, love," and moved on about her business.

"Aye, look at that," said one of the man wearing a green and blue Oxford tie. "That's service for you, mate." He winked at Austin.

Austin joined their group next to the door and introduced himself. The best thing about long flights is the size of the jet. You had to get up and stretch your legs occasionally. The large cabin afforded some standing room here and there. Once those "fasten seatbelt" signs go off and the drinks are served, the British passengers come alive. Austin was happy to have the company. It seemed the three men were from Liverpool, although their accents weren't particularly strong. They were heading to Johannesburg on business. They were in security software. The two girls, Sofia and Heather, did not know each other before the flight. They just happened to be sitting next to each other. Both women were from South Africa and got along fabulously.

Austin felt he had begun an adventure. His brief encounter with Johannes and Simon assured him he was right. Thinking back over the events of the day, Austin felt he had done quite well actually. After all, so many people back home warn that Americans are absolutely loathed abroad, as if they are trying to convince their fellow Americans that they are bad or something. But Austin hadn't encountered any real prejudice. To the contrary, Johannes and Simon seemed to like him just fine. They felt comfortable both complimenting and criticizing him like it was no big deal. This made Austin feel more confident on the road. For a while there, he had been a bit worried.

Austin listened to the Brits discussing Tony Blair and his barrister wife, who just made over £130,000 representing the government in a dress-code case brought by an Islamic female high-school student. Labour heir apparent Gordon Brown sounded a lot like Howard Dean and Tony Blair sounded a lot like President Bush. So maybe, thought Austin, he wasn't so freakish after all. He realized that countries have very similar problems the world over. Austin did not feel any resentment or dislike for Johannes. He might not agree with the ex-soldier, but Austin did not *hate* the man for his views. This, in itself, made Austin feel self-confident and smart, for even when he was at Stanford, a school he loved, so many people around campus were quick to condemn whatever they didn't agree with. The faculty was no exception. This always made Austin feel uncomfortable. Now that he was out on his own little adventure, Austin adopted a more aloof perspective in order to remain more respectful and open-minded. After all, he really didn't know what cultural differences to expect once in a new territory.

Despite his wealth, Austin was politically naive. As a music major at Stanford, he didn't take many electives covering the political arena. Instead, he preferred to take a few art, literature, and psychology courses to round things out. He traveled Europe on several occasions, but he never really took much interest in the regional politics. He and Cathy mostly shopped, saw the sights, or went to the hotspots at night. He politely listened to the comments of the people he met in his travels – like the folks from Liverpool – but he never really launched into any political diatribes one way or the other. It wasn't his thing. Moreover, the two most important living men in his life, Tony Pickett and Johnny Long, were decidedly apolitical. That was *their* way.

Pickett came from a perfectly average middle-class family. His father was a fairly successful guitarist who played for numerous famous blues artists like Son Seals, Aretha Franklin, Muddy Waters, Buddy Guy, B.B. King., even Janice Joplin and some Jimi Hendrix studio sessions. Accordingly, he was not embraced by any political group around Palo Alto or even L.A., where he went to school at U.C.L.A. As a middle-class Black man with talent and a Ph.D., he fell through the cracks of the political world. His penchant for the Afro, multi-colored dreds, or anything George Clinton for that matter, made him unusable by conservatives back then. Because he didn't consider himself a victim of anything racist, classist, patriarchal, logocentric, phallocentric, or gender-biased (although he may well have been), he was of no use to the Left. He just taught music and played it. He felt he could take responsibility for each and every note he played. The rest was not his concern.

Johnny Long was the same way. His childhood and education were not as stellar as his present demeanor conveyed. Case in point, he was a military brat. When his father was reassigned, Johnny and his mother moved too. New school, new friends, new house, new base – this was a pattern to which Johnny had to adapt. Was he close to his parents? Did they nurture him? Was the world fair to him? You could never tell from looking at Johnny Long. It was as if those sort of questions never entered Johnny's mind. What was the use? For Tony Pickett, the beauty of music – a simple beauty in its purest form - was that it was totally apolitical. For Johnny Long, the beauty of capitalism was that it afforded people *opportunity* so long as they had the right information. Yes, achieving wealth was an information-driven game. So it seemed totally obvious to Johnny to make that information available to anyone who would let him... for a fee. That's how the system worked.

Johnny's great success – and his clients' success – was a three-stroke feat of genius. First, he was bright enough to understand that there was no legal way to control the stock market. Continually crossing ethical and legal lines by using inside information was not how Johnny wanted to build his business. More importantly, being a criminal was not how he wanted to live his life. Nevertheless, the "smart money" never just gambled as if stocks were nothing more than colored numbers on a table. For smart investors, there was something else going on.

For his part, Johnny made plenty of "stupid mistakes" when he first started out. He would recommend three or four stocks based on a *Barron's* article, some technical break-out point, some hot new product release or something like that. Once he told Austin, "I would bust my ass to impress the guy... color charts, articles, stuff like that. The funny thing was, if I got the account, I really didn't know what to do next!" Johnny and his client would pick a price above and below where they bought it and sell it accordingly. Sometimes he made money, sometimes he lost money. After about two years, Johnny realized that he lost money for his clients a lot more often. Even when he did well for his clients, he never really got the bulk of their assets. He got the "stock jockey" money as he called it that day in his office with Austin. Johnny Long quickly realized that successful advisors at First American Investors had something else going on. Johnny Long realized that he must be of *unique value* to his clients. He must have a *strategy*, a discipline, which he could present to his prospects and clients that differentiated him from other advisors.

First American Investors had a wonderful answer to this all-too-common dilemma of advisors picking stocks. They provided their clients an array of outside money managers who could manage client assets a whole lot better than Johnny. In this way, First American Investors advisors could focus on asset gathering and leave the investing to the "professionals." For many advisors, this was a wise idea, especially if they couldn't devise a successful strategy. Most couldn't even if they wanted to, and most did not want to. Every young advisor wanted the perfect "triple bagger" for their clients. One, make your client money. Two, charge a quarterly fee that would increase as the portfolio increased. Three, steadily bring in new clients while continuing to grow existing accounts. The perfect "triple bagger." In this way, clients' accounts would grow, fees would grow, and assets under management would grow. Everyone wins, most of all the client whose account is expertly tended by institutional money managers.

If you think about it, the Private Money Manager program was an ideal solution to a common problem – client turnover. The easiest way to lose a client was to make mistakes picking stocks. Moreover, if an advisor was focused on bringing in new clients and bringing in new assets, how were they to adequately tend the accounts they already had? First American Investors Private Money Manager program solved all this. A broker became an "advisor," offering a menu replete with expert money-managers to suit each client's individual risk tolerance. In this way, First American Investors advisors could allocate their clients' assets with the appropriate manager to ensure the client was properly invested. Then, the advisor was free to meet with new prospects and clients, get their accounts, pair them off with a money manager, and so on. This was done for a flat fee as opposed to commission, so the advisor and the client were "on the same side of the table" as they say.

First American Investors led the way in introducing such programs. Soon, all the large firms on Wall Street followed suit. When Johnny started out in the business some twenty-five years ago, he thought the best way to gain clients was to pick three or four stocks and go with it. If he did well, he would get a few thousand more to invest. If he did poorly, he would inevitably lose the account sooner or later. Johnny Long knew the name of the game when it came to investing was *growing assets*. Clients depended on that money for their retirement. Their investments had to grow if they were to meet their retirement goals. As for brokers, they had to continually grow their assets under management if they were to make a decent living, let alone retain their clients. Even with income-based accounts, *growth of income* was really the crux of the issue. Johnny realized from the get-go that he was under pressure to make money for his clients. Every young broker sweats this out every minute of every day. If the client didn't pound it into Johnny's head, his managers did... daily.

Picking a few "good" stocks and discussing them with suitable investors was a dead-end career path. You simply couldn't "beat" the market enough to satisfy clients, especially after taxes and commissions. It is the classic and somewhat tragic scenario of managing other people's money – the rat on the wheel, running his heart out, going... nowhere. It was classic because as long as there have been stocks and a market, brokers trying to make it, trying to please their clients, have focused only on price and securing more short-term gains than losses after taxes. Either that, or they just bought and held. In either case, they were victims of a fatal myopia. Like Oedipus, they may have been brilliant and able to solve the riddle of the Sphinx, or they may have scored in the 95th percentile on their corporate personality profile, but what good did it do them when confronted with one fatal flaw - *their own decision making itself.*

It was tragic because if they made decisions based solely on price or an analyst's opinion, there could be only more questions. What's worse, there could only be three results:

1) They sold for a short-term profit. But was the stock going higher? What good was a price target if the analysts kept raising it? Hell, why *did* they raise it to begin with? If the stock did, indeed, continue lower, why? Moreover, why didn't they short it?

2) They sold for a short-term loss. But would the stock recover or was it going lower? Again, why not short it? Options... sell calls, buy puts? How did they know what to do next? What if the stock ran up after they sold it off? Should they jump back in at a price higher than where they sold it? What if that was a short-term peak? Worse yet, what if they stayed out and the stock ended up five times higher two years later?

3) They sold for a sizable gain or loss only to be left anew with the problem of what to do with the proceeds, if any. Repeat process... see numbers 1 and 2.

What did you do with _____? Fill in the blank. You don't need dates, you don't need sectors, you don't even need a specific stock. *There is no escape from the above three scenarios.* And the mere fact that one can say "fill in the blank" underscores how true this is. Unless you have a *strategy* of some sort. You can't ever win when winning is always some form of *losing...* unless you have a strategy of some sort. In some ways, this is precisely what Oedipus discovered. He had it all figured out, right? He figured out why his kingdom was beleaguered by plague and pestilence. He had all the answers; after all, *he* solved the riddle of the Sphinx. But, the *real* answer to the riddle of the Sphinx was not "Man" as he claimed, but rather *himself*, or more specifically his own *self-ignorance*.

Like so many advisors faced with the challenge of "beating" the market (which is unbeatable if attempted legally), Oedipus didn't get the awful truth; namely, his own inability to provide absolute answers to questions that *have no answers.* You needed a *strategy* for doing things. But it's all a kind of sick joke from God. The joke is this -- all systems may be inherently flawed. What? Are you kidding me? Stop and think about it. God is a great comedian sometimes. Even *God Himself* requires a leap into the *unknown.* Believing in God requires *faith* precisely because we can't know the ultimate result otherwise. The stock market is a God term like so many others. Why you did what you did, when to stop doing it, and what to do next were never in doubt. *That* was the best you could hope for. *What to buy, when to sell, and what to do with the proceeds...* Johnny Long was a priest heralding another way.

Johnny realized early on that he had to do things differently. He had to have a strategy, and one that worked despite inevitable mistakes along the way. The problem was a bit more nuanced, however. If Johnny could claim brilliance, it was in this – *all* successful money managers had a strategy, had a plan. That's exactly what made them successful money managers. There was nothing perspicacious in that. No, what made Johnny Long brilliant was that he realized that an advisor's strategy must *also* set him or her *apart from the competition.*

Johnny was a frequent guest speaker at the prestigious First American Investors corporate training center in North Jersey. He loved addressing rookies. Their zeal for the business was always refreshing.

It was unadulterated and pure even if greedy. His presentation always started the same way. "Having a strategy is crucial. But it's not enough. Your strategy must also be *unique*. It must set you apart. It must say to the prospect, 'Hey, you can't get this from anyone else.'" First American Investors always put a high value on creating *unique value* as it was called. That was one reason why the company sought to maintain the best and largest team of analysts on Wall Street. First American Investors provided its people with valuable *information* with which to make decisions, with which to become *advisors* rather than brokers.

The problem with programs like the Private Money Manager was not so much the investments. Johnny was perfectly blunt about this. "If you're not going to have a strategy, then don't mess with people's money. You have no future as their investment decision maker." Instead, he suggested that they put their clients' money into Private Money Manager or some such program where internal or third-party managers invested money according to a strict discipline. Each manager had a clearly delineated *strategy*, and that was crucial. As Johnny would quickly point out, though, programs like First American Investors Private Money Manager were available at every investment firm. "What is there to differentiate you from your counterpart at any other firm?" Johnny always waited a moment or two for effect. The greenhorns would usually purse their lips and realize that things were going to be a bit more difficult than they were told. "There's nothing wrong with being just an asset gatherer," he would continue. "Just expect to take a number and get in a long, long line for assets. Oh, and look around… *nine out of ten* of you will not make your asset hurdles and will be gone within a year." Johnny found he usually got the room's full attention for the next hour.

Johnny used the next hour to acquaint class after class of trainees with his two strategies. He used the three-stroke engine analogy. To begin with, he *had* a strategy, a clearly-defined reason for buying, selling, and reinvesting. Moreover, it was unique to him and referral after referral came to him as his strategies proved successful. But more was needed. If the first stroke was having a strategy, the second stroke was developing a strategy that worked and worked *well*. It was one thing to have a strategy. If it didn't work, you would still not be successful. As Johnny said all along, the key was *information*.

Thus, the second stroke was far more complex than the first. The funny thing about Johnny, though, was that the need for a strategy and where to turn for vital information seemed perfectly obvious. He chose to work at First American Investors because they had the best research on Wall Street. It seemed obvious, then, to turn to the analysts for a strategy. After several years of research, Johnny devised his two strategies that were wholly based on First American Investors research, namely earning per share estimate changes and yearly dividend growth projections. And there it was. The third stroke was relatively simple. Get the word out. *Sell information.* Make First American Investors research – its most valuable commodity – available to the investing public at large. Take the power institutional investors had and disseminate it to his clients. *That's* how capitalism was supposed to work.

Chapter 12

Austin escorted Heather up to the First Class cabin. The appeal of free cocktails and tales of stock-market riches were too much for Heather to resist. She was single after all, and she was going to be on that plane for quite some time. She was tall at around 5 feet 9 inches. Her body was tight and thin, if somewhat pale. She had huge blue eyes. Her shoulders and back were well-defined from years of crew and swimming. Her short blonde hair still looked chlorine bleached and tousled as if she just got out of the pool. She was political without being argumentative. She never heard of Guy Ritchie before he married Madonna, and couldn't Madonna stop talking about the *kabbalah*? She drove a tri-colored Mini because it was cute *and* economical, loved wild animals, preferred Austin Powers to both Roger Moore and Timothy Dalton. Sean Connery had no equal. She still rowed when she could find the time.

Having rowed throughout high school, Austin recognized immediately that Heather was no average girl. They belonged to a special group of masochists. "After I go through a really hard workout," she told him, "I feel like I have emphysema of the body." Anyone who could get up at four in the morning and willingly put themselves through such intense, burning pain before having so much as a cup of coffee has a very particular definition of discipline and achievement. Austin was immediately attracted.

What really interested Austin, though, was Heather's profession. Heather was a wildlife biologist. She studied wildlife migration throughout South Africa, Botswana, and Zimbabwe with a particular focus on waterfowl. "Wildlife Biologist" was something of a career hat-rack. In her many travels – and travails -- Heather wore quite a few hats indeed. At times she was a biologist, chemist, and virologist; at other times, she was a conservationist, guide, hunter, and historian. Just as crew is far more than a sport, being a wildlife biologist was far more than just a job. Austin was impressed by her level of dedication, commitment, and spiritual satisfaction. Heather seemed to have the balance of things Austin so badly desired. More than that, she seemed to be making a difference in a world that seemed so huge to Austin at times.

Austin sat down in his luxurious First Class seat. Heather did likewise in the unoccupied, pod-like seat across from him to his left. Austin rang for the attendant and ordered two splits of South African red wine.

"Nobody's sitting there," he told Heather. "So looks like you won a free upgrade." Austin winked.

Heather sat back in her seat. "This is about the size of my first flat at Troy University," she said.

Austin leaned toward Heather. "Well, now you know way too much about what I am doing trekking out to Africa. Now it's *your* turn to tell me about what *you* are doing in London."

Heather squinted seductively and pouted her lips. "Wouldn't you like to know?" she teased. "Actually, I was attending a symposium at University College in London."

"Really? That must have been fun. Did you get to go out on the town at all?"

Heather smiled. "I spent most of my time attending seminars. But I did get to SoHo a bit. And Chinatown. I love to visit China Towns throughout the world. Mostly, though, I worked on my presentation."

Austin was impressed and a bit embarrassed. "I'm sorry. I just assumed you were there as part of the audience. How rude of me." He hoped his foot was out of his mouth.

Heather laughed. "Oh, stop it. It's impossible to offend me, love. I'm just letting you do your thing. You have so much energy."

Austin felt a wave of excitement come over him. "My God," he said. "I can't tell you the last time someone actually complimented me on my energy level. It's so nice that you can allow me that."

Heather tipped her wine. "I love South African reds. But who said I was complimenting you?" She held a dead-serious face for several seconds. Austin froze until Heather broke out in laughter. "Just breakin' your buttocks, hon." She held up her glass. "Cheers." They clinked glasses. "You know, Austin," she continued. "We South African girls are quite something."

"So I'm learning," he replied.

Heather nodded. "Yeah, I'm beautiful, smart, *and* I can drop a rhino dead in its tracks from one hundred and fifty meters in a crosswind."

Austin was beside himself. He felt young, self-confident, and attractive again. When he was with Cathy, he never felt like that. It was always about her rich guy friends (whom Austin never met) or her wanting to do this or that "fabulous" project (which, of course, she never actually did). But with Heather, Austin felt different. He felt like he could actually *believe in* Heather and vice-versa. This would be a totally new experience for him. Being so optimistic, it just slipped out. "That's so hot," he moaned.

"Bet your sweet arse it is," she shot back. "Things are always like that in Africa, Austin."

"How do you mean?"

"You get a little bit of everything, I should say. A good mix of everything, yes."

"Just like you?" he teased.

She held up her wine glass. "A rare and truly fine blend. I'm half Dutch, so you'd better take care. I'm brutally honest, *and* I'll knock your knickers off in bed." She winked at him.

Austin smiled. That was about the only response he could muster at that moment. She totally overwhelmed him. He remembered the golden rule of dating: When you're in trouble, ask her about herself!

"So wait, you study the wildlife?"

"Not *the* wild life," she answered. "That's for your fraternities. I study wildlife migration, especially in South Africa, Botswana, and Zimbabwe. It takes me about the continent."

"I'll say," replied Austin. "So tell me, what does that entail?"

She told Austin tale after tale of amazing interactions with a whole world of different animals. "I have the best job in the world, Austin. It's not even fair to call it a job. Imagine having these countries as your personal zoo!"

"I never thought of it that way. Damn, that's hot! But I always thought animal people were all into the 'this is not our land' sort of thing. It's funny to hear you call it 'your zoo.'"

Heather rolled her eyes. "Maybe the chickies back in the States, yeah? I'm South African. I have to survive just like the animals. We're in it together."

There was that phrase again. Simon and Johannes immediately jumped into Austin's head. He wasn't sure if he'd offended her or if she was teasing him again. She was a ball-buster, that was for sure. It was tough to tell.

Heather noticed Austin's blank look. "What are you thinking about, Austin?"

Austin squeezed his eyes closed and had some wine. "You know, no one ever asks me that?"

"What," said Heather, "what's on your mind, you mean?"

Austin half-nodded and half-shrugged. "Yeah. It's weird. No... I was just thinking about... you reminded me of these two guys from Johannesburg."

Heather made a visible gesture of being impressed. "Well now, I see you get around."

The ambiguity of her comment put Austin a bit on edge. Was she calling him a womanizer or world traveler? He decided to take a risk and tell her the gory story, even if it wasn't the most romantic of ways to meet a girl. She took in the story with genuine interest.

Like a good cup of hot tea, she found the tale both stimulating and familiar at the same time. Throughout his tale, Austin sensed that he was shocking her. Yet at the same time, he got the distinct feeling that such episodes were somewhat commonplace to her, like she was reading the newspaper or watching the news. He arrived at the finale of the story, the part when he asked Johannes why he didn't do anything to stop the murder. Johannes said something like "because they're savages, man."

He finished and waited for her response. He ordered another round. He didn't smoke cigarettes, but he wanted a cigar right about then.

Austin wondered why the hell he was so nervous. What was it about this girl that made him feel like a schoolboy? "And that's what he said," wrapped up Austin. "It was like he didn't care one bit."

Heather arched her eyebrows. "Very ironic, huh?"

Austin assumed she was talking about killing the baby. "You mean killing the baby as a way of ending the family?" he asked.

This hadn't occurred to her. "Oh," she said. "I hadn't thought of that. I was referring to the ending, the part where Johannes said he didn't help because they were savages. That's so ironic."

This hadn't occurred to Austin. "Oh," he said. "Well, I didn't think of *that*, so there you go." He threw up his hands. "What do you mean?"

"Well," continued Heather, "who's the real savage, yeah?"

Austin stroked his unshaven face. "Hmm... that's a great point. I think I like you. You said you can shoot a gun?"

Heather laughed out loud, almost spitting up her wine. "Austin, you're *adorable*."

Austin blushed bright red. "What? What did I say?" He held out his hands and shrugged.

Heather stared at him with those blue eyes of hers. She shook her head. "You didn't say a thing, luv. You're just adorable, that's all."

Austin was a bit surprised. "Wait, you don't find that to be a totally horrific story? It freaked me out for hours."

"But you have to understand something, luv... Everyone, in Africa has a death story."

Austin was struck by the words "death story." He grimaced. "Do *you* have a death story?"

She looked Austin square in the eyes. "*Everyone* has a death story."

"Man," said Austin, "it seems like you're talking about a newspaper article or something. But when you stop to think about it for real, it makes you sick." It suddenly dawned on Austin that he may have offended Heather just then. "Oh my God," he pled. "I didn't mean to offend you. I'm sorry."

"I already told you, it's impossible to offend me." Heather poured out another glass of wine for each of them. "It's horrible, Austin. Believe me, I know. But look at it from my perspective. Most people would say the part about the guy killing off the baby was the worst bit of your story, yeah?"

Austin nodded. "Uh huh." He sat back and listened. It was clearly her turn to talk.

Heather held up her index finger. "Would you be surprised if I told you that part made the most sense to me?"

Austin looked puzzled. "Really? I would think that, as a woman, you would find that horrible."

Heather shrugged. "I do find it horrible...brutally horrible." She held up her finger again. "But that's not what I said. I said it made the most sense to me."

Austin crossed his legs. "Humm... I'm not sure I follow you, but go ahead. I want to hear your thoughts on this."

"Well, let me put it into terms I deal with every day in my research. Let's see..." she paused to think. "OK... did you know that you mustn't kill a male lion less than five years old? Did you know that?"

Austin made a sarcastic face. "How am I supposed to know that?"

Heather laughed. "Right, right, sorry. But your story about killing off the baby reminded me of this rule of thumb – never kill a male lion less than five years old. Because..." she made herself more comfortable... "because if you do, that lion's *entire lineage* is put into jeopardy. Wherever that particular lion was in the hierarchy of things, there is now a void, right?"

Austin nodded. "I'm with you."

"Well, a literal *war* ensues in which competing male lions actually *kill off* all the other males lions in the lineage. Then they go on and sire their own in place of the adolescents they killed."

Austin grasped the parallel right off. "Wow, so other male lions actually destroy the entire family of their competitors if they can."

"*Exactly*," she said. "That's exactly right. Now think about your story. Isn't it amazing? It seems to me that you are most appalled by what is perhaps *most instinctive*. That's what I mean when I say everyone in Africa has a death story. It's a story because you can learn something from it, yeah?"

Austin was speechless for a moment. "You know...you're an amazing woman. I can't believe how you can look at things in that way... objectively."

"Well, I'm a scientist, aren't I? But it's true. Look at yourself. You haven't even been on the continent yet, and you already have a death story." She arched her eyebrows.

Austin thought about it for a second. He cocked his head. "You know, something...you're right again."

Heather threw up her hands. "All you had to do was meet two South African guys in a pub! If it wasn't so funny it would be sad."

"Well," responded Austin, "I'm not in Kansas anymore."

"Certainly not luv."

"Wait, you said you had a death story too?"

Heather nodded. "Yes, I do. I'll tell you another time. I don't want you to get the wrong idea about Africa. It is the *last wilderness*."

She had Austin hooked. "I absolutely love Westerns."

Heather's eyes lit up. "They're so sexy!" She put her hands on her knees. "I love the old America in Westerns. Now imagine being out in the middle of the Kalahari Desert all by yourself with just some old, green Land Rover with rust spots wearing through."

"Is it really like on TV?" Austin asked her. "I know that sounds hokey, but you know what I mean."

"No, no listen... Africa is vast. It's unbelievably big. You have no idea how good it feels to have all that *space*. I can grab my gear and head out to the bush... it's really more of a vacation than work. The sky! Austin, you should see the evening sky in the Kalahari Desert while you're lying on your back listening to the *Rolling Stones*."

Austin heard the needle slip on the record. He did a double take. "*The Rolling Stones*?" he asked incredulously.

Heather looked back at him as if he had three heads. She feigned offense. "Of course. What do you Yanks think, all we *'animal people'* as you called me just sit around smoking marijuana and eating *Ben and Jerry's Kalahari Safari* or *Chunky Monkey* from hollowed-out gourds?" She watched Austin's face turn to stone. Then she broke out laughing. "Well, what do you think we listen to while we're doing all that?" Austin laughed out loud. "Seriously though, you feel like an ant under those stars." She cleared her throat and got lost in a memory while staring at the floor.

"What are you thinking about?" he asked her.

Heather snapped out of it. "Huh, oh...sorry 'bout that, luv."

Austin crossed his legs again. "I've been dying to ask you something," he said. Heather nodded, "What do you want me to notice most about Africa?"

Heather smiled a warm, inviting smile. "Wow, thank you for asking. That was a lovely question." She thought for a moment. "I'd have to say... well, I already said you will see that everyone you meet has a death story. Also, I'd say you should notice that nothing is as simple as it seems. I've traveled all over the world, Austin, everywhere...you name it... and I can say without a doubt in my mind that *nowhere* is that more true than in Africa. Anywhere in Africa. It doesn't matter. Nothing is as simple as it seems."

"Huh, that sounds ironic. I just don't know why." He threw his head back and laughed. "Ha! I've actually been getting a lot *stupider* lately."

"Umm, the last time I checked, luv, 'stupider' was not a word."

Austin drooped his head and smiled. He was a little tipsy. He threw out his hand, palm up. "See what I mean!" He looked up. "Oh God, I'm drunk already."

"Oh," said Heather. "One more thing you ought to notice." Austin nodded for her to continue. "You will be drinking from now until you get on the plane to return to the States. But I digress... where was I? Oh God, I'm afraid I'm a bit pissed, too."

"And you don't even have a first class-." She cut him off sharply.

"Arse? Says who? I beg to differ." Austin was laughing so hard, he bent over.

"Oh yes," continued Heather, "Now I remember. Nothing about Africa is as simple as it seems. I learned that from the animals. Call it my wilderness rule of thumb."

Austin smirked. "Sure, I'll remember that the next time I'm way out in the bush somewhere in Zambia"

"Ah, Zambia," she replied. Her speech was faster now. "Have you been to Zambia? I love Zambia. Of course you haven't been, what am I saying?" She stopped and took a deep breath. "My wilderness rule of thumb. It is ironic because I can apply the same rule to *people*. Get it?"

Austin cocked his head. "Say that again. Did you say you can apply what you learn at work to your life as well? Why is *everybody* telling me that lately? How am I missing this while it's obvious to everybody else?"

Heather shrugged. "I don't know. It doesn't seem like anything super special to me. It just makes sense. I like to make things as simple as possible for myself. I like to reduce things to their lowest common denominator, know what I mean?"

"Sure," Austin agreed. "Who wouldn't?"

Heather held up her hands. "Well, there you go then! Find something that works for you and run with it. That's the first thing you learn working with animals out in the wild."

Austin couldn't help laughing. "What, running?"

"Very cute, Austin. What I mean is that animals just *do*. That's what I love about them. A group of lionesses in a pride don't sit around debating whether they should go on strike because they do all the hunting and the males never show enough gratitude."

Austin guffawed out loud and then hushed himself. Other passengers were sleeping. Heather smiled. "I'm serious. Think about it. I spend my days out in the bush or wherever witnessing first hand the immense power of *instinct*. It works, yeah? Then I come home and read the newspapers and think to myself, 'This all seems so *counter*-intuitive, yeah?'"

What Heather was saying reminded Austin of why he liked music, why he liked Tony Pickett. It reminded him of why he liked the two investment strategies, of why he liked Johnny Long. And it reminded him of what he was missing. "You know," he said, "I'm really glad I ran into you."

"A wild encounter, eh?"

"Cool. No, really, what you just said made me understand a few things about myself."

Heather smiled and finished off her glass of wine. "That's always nice, isn't it, Austin. I do spend a lot of time alone – well, with the animals, but you know what I mean. I wonder sometimes if I remember how to talk to *people*."

Austin guffawed again and covered his mouth. "I take it, then, that you talk to *animals*."

She smiled coyly, "Well naturally. You know Austin, what I love about working in the wild is the sheer..." she scrunched her face trying to find the right word, "yeah, the sheer *vastness* of Africa. It's absolutely *huge*. It's a continent, and yet people think of it as a single country. Most people have no idea where the boundaries are drawn, yeah? And I use that phrase intentionally, yeah?"

Austin held up his hands in a sign of surrender. "You caught me, man. I had no clue about boundaries and borders before I signed on for this trip."

Heather laughed at his choice of words. "Before you signed on... It sounds like you were one of those salty sailors in *Moby Dick.*"

"*Heart of Darkness,*" Austin chimed in simultaneously.

"Yes, yes!" said Heather. "You are on a journey into the Heart of Darkness." They touched glasses and toasted adventure. "You're certainly going to have an adventure, Austin."

They both smiled at each other and sat back. They both closed their eyes and had the same thought – it was nice to find someone with whom they could just be quiet. For her part, Heather was understating the size of Africa. Indeed, most Americans refer to "Africa" as if it is a huge nation state. In fact, Africa is three times the size of the United States. If pressed, most Americans probably won't know where it is located. Most of us know that it is far away, so to speak, the place where malnourished babies stare off in a torpor, the place *flies* go for vacation.

On the one hand, we are right to consider Africa the far-off "Dark Continent," the land of adventure, the last wilderness. As Heather said, "nowhere else in the world is instinct in its most basic, unadulterated form so powerful. In many instances, the people of Africa are *un-enlightened* in the best sense of the word – they are not subjugated by the intractable laws of logic and enlightenment. God? God could just as well be found in the cycle of rains and droughts as in a church. As varied as it is from country to country, from people to people, there is one common thread weaving together the cultural fabric that is Africa; namely, the boundary between life and death is far more eroded than anywhere else in the world. In this way, too, Africa is "dark." And yet, millions of vastly different people called "Africans" all seem to share a common quality – an instinctive knack for survival in a life which includes death as a daily occurrence. Just as Heather was saying, accepting death as a daily occurrence is an instinctive survival mechanism. Contrast this to, say, American's zealous worship not just of living, but of living *as comfortably* as possible. It is almost a single-minded obsession. "Whose is the better survival mechanism?" is a question Heather would often ask herself on those nights when she couldn't sleep because the wild dogs howling nearby were creeping her out.

On the other hand, seeing Africa as some sort of world populated by backward people with backward customs is somewhat myopic. After all, are Westerners – with all our logic, technology, and wealth – *closer to* or *further from* our instinctive selves? You can see it both ways. As Heather said, in Africa "things are not as simple as they seem." Working in the wild made Heather remarkably unjudgmental. That's why it was "almost impossible" to offend her. Judgmental and objectivity work inversely. They battle each other for dominance in the same way Freud saw the Id and the Super-Ego in constant struggle. And if one could learn this from spending time in Africa, how "dark" could it be? Perhaps there is a unique wisdom to each culture in the world just as there is a unique balance of survival to each ecosystem around the globe?

It is unavoidable that you will become a sort of anthropologist as soon as you step off the plane in Africa. You can't help but study *human beings*. It's a totally *different* sort of animal study. In this sense, too, Africa is far from darkness. On the contrary, we can learn quite a bit about ourselves, *precisely* the sort of intellectual endeavor the Enlightenment sought to catalyze, right? Yet, how many people know that the African continent is literally a stone's throw from southern Spain? True, North Africa is in our collective minds because of Islamic terrorism. But it stands to follow that there must be a southern Africa connected to it.

This is the land of Botswana, bordered to the south by South Africa, to the west by Namibia to the north by Angola (separated only by a thin strip of Namibia) and Zambia, and to the east by Zimbabwe. Eastern Botswana is also a short jaunt from Mozambique. Thus, Botswana lies in the heart of the most beautiful, precious game lands anywhere in the world. Accordingly, there was much Austin could learn about himself. Having been to Botswana on business in the past, Johnny Long knew Austin would greatly benefit from his journey. It was almost instinctive on Johnny's part, just like it was instinctive for Pickett to jump on board the benefit concert tour or Johnny to fly all the way out there to meet with the Princess Diana Hospital directors a year earlier. There was something about the chance to visit Africa that called out to the courageous. It wasn't so much a matter of danger per se, but rather the opportunity to compare and contrast oneself to a place and a people so radically different.

From the moment he ran into Johnannes, Simon, and now Heather, Austin sensed this himself. He was excited now for two reasons. First, he would recommend a new income strategy to a hospital that desperately needed financial guidance. He would make some money doing business with them, but he would also *make a noticeable difference* to the people of Botswana. Now on top of that, Austin knew he would be rekindling something that is lying dormant in most of us; namely, the ability to continually remake and better ourselves. Johnny Long was a master of this art and Austin welcomed with open arms the chance to become more like Johnny.

Chapter 13

Austin landed in Johannesburg, South Africa, and was swiftly escorted by signs on the wall to his next flight. He had to take a smaller plane to Gaborone, Botswana. After the thirty minute flight, Austin stepped off the fifteen-seat puddle jumper and onto the hot tarmac of the international airport in Gaborone, the capital of Botswana. Gaborone was widely heralded as *the* up-and-coming city of Africa. Gaborone, or "Gabs," as locals called it, was indeed a social magnet for people throughout southern Africa. Unlike so many African nations from which millions fled, Botswana – and Gabs in particular – was actually *growing* by leaps and bounds. Known as one of the staunchest anti-corruption governments on the continent and renowned for its attempts to provide quality education from early childhood *through* graduate school, the Botswana government stood with arms wide open to the people of Africa. Above all, Botswana was a haven of non-violence on a continent torn asunder by some of the most gruesome violence in the history of humankind. Whereas many other African flags incorporate black and red stripes to symbolize numerous wars for liberation, the Botswana flag boasts a beautiful light-blue background against which there runs a single, horizontal black stripe bordered by two thin white stripes, a symbol of racial harmony. For all intents and purposes, Gabs was a huge, never-ending *Grateful Dead* concert.

The capital had been booming for several years. It boasted an excellent British-style university that drew many well-educated Batswana *back home* to continue their studies (again, the people of Botswana are called Batswana). This was a distinct economic and social advantage compared to most lesser-developed countries like India, China, Russia, and Kenya which usually experience a "brain drain" when their brightest young people emigrate to countries in Western Europe or North America to study and work. Business investment grew accordingly as large international companies began developing operations in Gabs. Their new buildings stood out for miles against the empty background of the African plains. It was only a matter of time before an indigenous Botswana middle-class began to grow and grow. They spoke the Queen's English, dressed right out of a J. Crew ad, and took a taxi to the finest restaurants and cafes.

Apparently, though, the economic boom had thus far missed the airport facility. When Austin stepped onto the tarmac, he was immediately struck by how spread out everything was. The terminal building looked more like an old warehouse than a major transportation hub. His was the only plane around. There was some crabgrass with a flagpole between the tarmac and the terminal. That was about all. The terminal seemed so small to Austin. He was used to massive, expansive designs like Newark or Logan Airports. This terminal seemed so tiny, like it could blow away with the next monsoon.

Ironically though, things were inverted. In America, major urban airports dominated their surroundings. In Gaborone, the terminal looked miniscule against a massive, seemingly endless landscape. Austin felt dwarfed standing next to the plane, however small it was. When you're seated inside a plane, you have a sense of proportion that makes you feel in control. But when you stand outside next to a plane, it seems so much larger. Heather was right – Africa was huge. Looking past the plane, Austin saw the backdrop of a mountain range set against a vast radiant blue sky which seemed to stretch on to infinity. Standing there on the tarmac with the plane in front of him, the mountains behind the plane, and the sky behind the mountains, he felt like an ant.

Austin picked up his only bag and turned for the terminal building. He was surprised to see that everyone else had already gone into the terminal. He was alone. He hustled inside. Austin was incredibly relieved that everything was written in English. In fact, English was the official language of Botswana, and everyone spoke very well, better in fact than many urban Americans speak English. Everybody smiled, too. Contrary to what Austin felt after talking to Johannes and Simon, everybody was pleasant and looking to help out. This put Austin at ease despite his profuse sweating. He was beginning to enjoy himself again even if his jeans were wet with sweat and clinging in all the wrong places.

Following the signs to the security checkpoint, Austin noticed for the first time that there were more Chinese around than any other visiting ethnic group. He would have to find out if this was a trend. Each of the five Chinese passengers sent a ripple of confusion. The visitors did not speak English. It seemed each had violated several security protocols, but trying to explain this to them was proving both futile and comical. Eventually, the guards just pushed the Chinese through the gate, laughing and speaking to each other in their native language. Apparently, they were quite entertained and welcomed the distraction.

As an American, though, Austin was floored. If this was any indication of "airport security" throughout the lesser-developed world, terrorists would have a field day. Austin began taking off his shoes and emptying his pockets. The guards started laughing as if he were doing a clown routine. "No, no," they told him. "It's OK. American?"

Austin nodded. "Yes. How could you tell?" he asked jokingly.

The guards started laughing again. "Years of training," replied one.

Austin slipped his shoes back on. "After the World Trade Center disaster, I'm used to very strict security," said Austin.

The guards chuckled again. "Not here."

"No strict security?" asked Austin.

"No, no. No World Trade Center here in Botswana," said the guard who seemed to be in charge.

A woman chimed in. "We have crocodile and hippo attacks like you see on TV, only real."

Austin was not amused. "Hmm... We have bombings like you see on TV only real."

The third guard handed Austin his bag. "If you need a taxi," he said, "just ask at the information desk. Have a nice visit in Botswana, man." He guided Austin through the security doors and on his way. He could hear them laughing through the doors. But it was all good.

Following the advice of the Information Desk staff, Austin went out to the cab line for a ride. If you've ever been to JFK or Newark, you're used to seeing a kind of fast-paced chaos with horns honking, whistles blowing, and cops yelling. *Move it or lose it* is the rule in effect. Outside the terminal, things were just the opposite. People just sat around chatting or reading the paper... no horns, no whistles, no chaos. The first thing you learned in Gabs was that *everyone's* a cabbie. If you needed a ride, and you had twenty Pula (three dollars), any man with a car was your man. Just climb on in. And just as everyone with a car was a potential cabbie, every car -- taxi or otherwise -- seemed to be a white Toyota Cressida from 1982. They all had the same bucket seats, the same crushed-velour interior torn in various places, the same sun-bleached black dash with some sort of statue stuck to it.

The driver's name was Seretse. He was named after Seretse Khama, the famous Prince Regent who came to power as the first leader of the Botswana Democratic Party in 1962. Some fourteen years earlier, Seretse Khama had the audacity to marry an Englishwoman named Ruth Williams while he was living in London studying law. How ironic. Not only did Khama's uncle staunchly oppose the union as a violation of tribal law (a Ngwato chief must marry a Batswana woman chosen for him by tribal leaders), but British authorities also opposed the marriage for fear that both the Rhodesian and South African governments would be so appalled as to withdraw their offer to sell plutonium to the British. In a touching display of racial détente, the British conspired together with the Ngwato and Batswana to bar Khama from re-entering his own country. Five years later, Seretse Khama and his children renounced their claim to chieftainship and were allowed back into Botswana.

Throughout history, it was often said that freedom and democracy were *natural* human conditions. The story of Seretse Khama exemplifies just this. Free of his nepotistic constraints, Seretse Khama returned home and was free to advance freedom and democracy through the newly-founded Botswana Democratic party. It was no coincidence that in 1998, Gaborone – not Johannesburg, Riyadh or Dubai – was established as the first International Financial Services Center on mainland Africa.

In bearing the name Seretse, Austin's driver was a testament to the Batswana's ability to persevere. As a driver, however, Seretse was painfully slow. It was clear that Seretse was not worried about hustling up as many fares as possible that day. Austin got the point pretty quickly. Their slow pace gave him a great opportunity to check out the surroundings. The main road into town (the "Bypass") took Austin past the business district on his left. The new development was evident. Large buildings stuck out against the blue sky. They didn't fit the landscape at all. What's more, the architecture, like the cars, seemed out of the 80's even though the buildings were new. For modern construction, the office buildings seemed oddly out of place. Nevertheless, new money was pouring into Gaborone. Buildings were being built, jobs were being created, quality of life was improving. The roads were in excellent condition, and the radio station was great. As Seretse told Austin, everyone in Gabs absolutely loved the new television building. Life was good.

When Austin turned to his right, however, he saw quite a different scene. The juxtaposition was impossible to miss. For what the "Bypass" bypassed were the everyday people inhabiting Gaborone's outskirts. Running along side the Bypass was a wide, red dirt footpath the locals used for travel on foot. When you hear someone use the term "a well-beaten path"... well, this is the one they are talking about. The clay-red dirt was dry as a bone, and a cloud of dust puffed up with every step. Hundreds of barefoot people were walking about. This was clearly a major thoroughfare. Driving was a privilege. Hoofing it along one of these dirt paths was a more common means of transportation if you didn't want to spend the two Pula (thirty three cents) on the bus.

Interspersed along this path were numerous stalls ranging in stability from rickety to dilapidated to an abandoned pile of rubbish.

It took Austin only a minute or two to recognize that what we call "abandoned" and what they called "abandoned" was totally different. Indeed, the refrigerator box we might throw away would be considered a McMansion by these more rural Batswana, especially if it was made by GE or Frigidaire. Some corrugated metal structures also dotted the roadside. Austin asked Seretse if they were houses.

"Yes," he answered. "Sometimes workers sleep in them as well. Each is different."

"Hmm…" mumbled Austin. "That's interesting." Austin had seen shanty towns before in Mexico. But this scene was different. There was a kind of hustle and bustle to it all. Everyone seemed to be walking somewhere, intently moving from rural to urban, from one environment to the next. Unlike the new office buildings just across the Bypass, the masses of folks who moved along these dirt roads fit right in with the environment. They looked dry, dusty, and resourceful. This was their life. They were born to it, and they accepted it as such. At moments like these, you realized that being an American is like winning the birth lottery.

After passing by several stalls, Austin noticed that they all sold the same thing – roasted corn on the cob. Old ladies whose skin was made even darker from years sitting in the intense African sun sat tending their slowly roasting corn cobs for hours. He asked Seretse about this, too. "Oh yes, the corn," he said. "Everybody loves it. You can take it home or eat it while you are walking."

Austin was amused. "Yeah, we have that too. It's called fast food!" They both laughed.

"Ah, McDonald's," said Seretse. "Yes, we have that too… but no corn there." They drove through a jug handle and turned toward the Grand Palm Hotel and Casino. Grazing on the grass in the middle of the roundabout were about a dozen goats. Seemingly untended, the goats lazily chewed on grass, in no particular hurry to venture out into traffic. It was amazing… the traffic took the place of a herder. The goats were stuck in that spot until their owner retrieved them. An amazing display of ingenuity – what we might call "multitasking." The goat herder must have been off somewhere doing two things at once. Odds are, though, he was probably drinking in one of the corrugated shanties.

Heather was right about one thing - Gaborone was a city of dichotomies. Nowhere was this more evident than driving along the Bypass. Still, it was one of Africa's fastest-growing cities. As recently as the early 60's, Gaborone was merely an obscure village. Now home to over 200,000 people, Gabs had seen some of the greatest economic growth in the *world*. As soon as he pulled into the long, tree-lined drive of the Grand Palm Hotel and Casino, Austin realized that people with money visited Gaborone. Austin paid Seretse his 20 Pula. Seretse gave Austin his cell number in case he ever needed a ride. That's right, Seretse had a cell phone. As Austin would discover, it seemed everyone had a cell phone in Gabs. Of course, there were few landlines. Why bother? Batswana simply bought airtime cards at the local market – an organized-crime racket – and that was that. They never had a bill. If their card ran out of time, they bought a new one. Modernity was in their hands.

Austin checked in and went up to his room. The Grand Palm Hotel and Casino was probably the best hotel in the city, but it was far from the palatial accommodations he was accustomed to when traveling throughout America and Europe. To the contrary, his room was quite average. But the view from his window... well, that was spectacular. It occurred to Austin that the middle-of-the-road design of his "upgraded" room told him everything he would need to know to properly experience Gaborone. In typically understated fashion, his Gabs accommodations said – Why are you inside? Get out with the people, man! Indeed, below Austin's window was the pool area, accented by a large, rectangular tiki bar. Austin noticed right off that the bar had a real thatched roof. Thick, billowy white clouds filled the horizon, making a picturesque backdrop for the numerous thatch-covered tables dotting the poolside lawn.

Looking down from his window, Austin could see several groups of people sitting around enjoying lunch and cocktails under the crystal-blue sky. "Hmph," he said to himself out loud. He found it interesting that he saw only a handful of white people taking in the rays. Most of the people were black Africans on holiday. Most of what Austin read in the papers made it seem like all Africans are dirt poor and living in huts. And of course, there were all those people along the dirt road. But the guidebooks Austin read were right – Gaborone was home to well-off Africans.

Austin felt more at home, more comfortable. He laughed to himself. It never occurred to him that black Africans would visit parts of Africa on vacation. Why not, though? Surely there were many wondrous sights throughout the continent. How about Victoria's Falls or the Kalahari Desert in a small plane flying at 1,500 feet? It occurred to him that Victoria Falls was just like the Grand Canyon in the States – of course Africans who could afford it would want to see the Falls. Even the Okavango Delta was a bustling hub of tourist activity.

Austin leaned back in the window, grabbed his presentation notes from the desk, and headed down to the pool. But first, he changed. Before he left the States, he tried to get an inside scoop on what the locals wore. He got a good fix on the weather patterns but nothing really specific on clothing. However, there did seem to be two fashion rules of thumb, both rather hip. Middle-class blacks sported the J. Crew line – sporty yet causal, clean, unimposing... all very well-behaved. White Africans, mostly South African, were somewhat more idyllic and adventurous in their choice of attire – khaki or white right down to their socks, clothes seemingly right out of the Banana Republic catalogue ten years ago. All that was missing was a pith helmet, a weathered map, and a beat-up old Land Cruiser to complete the 5th Avenue window display. As for the many Chinese, they all wore government-issue gray flannel slacks and white shirts... with pocket protectors.

None of this was what Austin expected. Thankfully, Austin guessed right when he went shopping back in Philly -- Banana Republic. Stick with khaki, white, and rustic accent colors. He would fit right in. That was important to him. He pulled up a chair at the tiki bar and breathed in the fresh air. Not a hint of smoke or over-spritzed perfume. It had been a whole three hours since his last drink. He was coming dangerously close to violating the minimum blood-alcohol level for African adventurers. He ordered a Johnny Black and Coke. The liquor was pre-measured in *gils* just as in Great Britain. But the Coke was not dispensed out of a soda gun as it was in the States. Instead, he was given, and charged for, an entire can. Austin ponied up twenty-seven Pula. After doing a quick calculation in his head, he was amazed. The Johnny Black cost him about $2, while the Coke cost him a little over $3. Austin poured the soda over the scotch and ice. "No wonder everyone drinks so much," he thought to himself. Halfway through his drink, Austin realized he had been using ice cubes made with Batswana water. He was horrified, imagining the African equivalent to Montezuma's Revenge. He could feel his bowels grumbling already. Not wanting to seem ignorant, Austin opted for the indigenous cure for malaria – more alcohol. He ordered another round and began looking over his notes.

A couple of things about Johnny's Growth of Income Strategy still confused him a bit. He wanted to get it straight in his head before his meeting the next day. His first concern was risk. He knew Dr. Stone and his colleagues would be most concerned with risk. Most fixed-income buyers are. Dr. Stone originally called Johnny because their UPenn endowment income was rapidly dwindling, and they needed Johnny's guidance before they started eating up their principal. This money was precious to the hospital. Without it, hundreds of thousands of people could go without proper HIV care, not to mention care for the other ailments that afflicted the population. Austin did not take this lightly. He spent hours prepping because he felt it was his responsibility to protect this money. After talking it over with Johnny, however, Austin realized the best way to serve the hospital was to *increase* both its income *and* principal using Johnny's Growth of Income Strategy. He just had to convince Stone…

Austin scribbled a note. *Growth is protection. Bonds are guaranteed.* Johnny stressed to Austin a number of times before he left that his Growth of Income Strategy was *not* less risky than a guaranteed tax-free bond. Of course it wasn't. It wasn't even close. However, was Johnny's income strategy worth the increased risk? Of course it was. Austin was a believer. He had seen the results himself. Moreover, he was *invested* in the Growth of Income Strategy. He put his money where his mouth was. He figured people would find that important. Was he advocating a strategy he used for himself, or his grandmother, so to speak. Austin realized from the outset, though, that the 'Saver' in fixed income is not necessarily "better." This was particularly important, and he was careful to demonstrate his point.

Like many fixed-income savers, the Princess Diana Hospital had no choice but to become more aggressive. Its income had dwindled below acceptable levels. Johnny called this the Saver versus the Investor scenario. Austin saw it a bit differently. For him, it was a matter of fixed income versus growing income. That's where Austin would start his presentation. A fixed income saver was trading rate-of-return for the security of a guarantee. An Investor, on the other hand, sought to increase his income *and* principal alike. Austin sipped his drink and racked his brain for a way to depict this. He could have used one of Johnny's many colorful elaborations – he had a closet full of freshly pressed similes, metaphors, analogies, and illustrations he could bring out to elucidate just about *any* point. What made Johnny so trustworthy to his clients was that they *understood* him even when he was unpacking rather complex concepts such as derivatives and options. Born with a tongue of gold, Johnny built his financial house to match. Austin was not as colorful with words as he was with music, however. He did see the similarities between the two. And having been trained by the impeccable Tony Pickett, he wanted to get it just right on his own. This was part of his adventure, too. In recommending his proposal, Austin would try to be like a storyteller. Like a writer, a storyteller searches for the perfect words, even when telling another person's story. It's not only part of his craft, it's also part of his distinct self, what sets him apart.

Suddenly it came to him. Austin scribbled furiously, scrawling hieroglyphs all over the paper. Imagine you lent your brother-in-law Herb fifty grand. In return, he guaranteed to pay you back the whole amount (and was good for it), and he would also pay you interest every six months for your troubles. Hey, it's all in the family, right? You have some extra money around. It's making *absolutely nothing* sitting in your checking account. This sounds pretty good. After all, Herb is good for it. He runs a big company.

But there's a catch. With in-laws, there always is. Being your brother-in-law *and* the head of a big company, Herb decides to stick it to you just a bit. This is part of who Herb is, so you just have to deal with it if you want to make a few bucks off him. He made enough money as it was, so why shouldn't you get yours off him? Ah, but the catch is this – Herb reserves the right to pay you back at *anytime* and walk away from his interest obligations to you.

"What was that last bit there, Herb?"

"Oh, nothing important," he says.

You wonder, did Herb's lawyer write this or what? Damned straight he did. Along with his accountant, his comptroller, and his board of directors. "Boy," you say to Herb. "That's a fine 'thank you.'"

Herb doesn't get it, though. This all seems smart on his part. But you figure, hey you'll make a buck or two. No harm, no foul. So you agree to lend Herb the money at 8% interest, and things are going great. Every six months, he sends you a crisp, clean check and a lovely letter about how thankful he is for your loan and so on. After a couple of years, though, you get a call from Herb's office. A nasal-voiced woman asks you, "Remember that bit about Herb paying off your loan early?"

You look puzzled. "Hello? Who is this?" It's not even Herb! It's someone from Herb's company. Huh, how's them apples?

Well, it seems Herb is paying off your loan, thank you very much. Oh, and by the way, Herb would like to borrow another $50,000 from you. Is that OK?

You look puzzled again. "Well, why did he pay me back if he needs the money?" you ask. This seems to the point enough, right?

"Well," says Herb's employee, "Herb was talking to his friends at the country club, and it seems *they* are only paying *their* brothers-in-law 5%."

"OK. What does that have to do with me?" you say.

"As I said, Herb is going to pay you back immediately."

"Then he wants to borrow the money again?"

"That's correct. But this time he's only going to pay you 5% with the same guarantee and conditions."

You are startled. "What? Why only 5% this time?"

"Obviously," she explains, "Herb is very upset that you would take advantage of him like this. Imagine him paying you 8% when all his friends at the club are only paying *their* in-laws 5%. And after all he's done for you! Shame on you! Boooooo! Booooo!"

You imagine the uneasiness at Christmas and Thanksgiving. "Oh my," you cry. "I didn't mean to do that. It was just the offer he made me."

After a long silence she says, "Hmm... well you *did* accept it, didn't you?"

144

After a moment you realize that you have no choice. Well, that's not exactly true. You *can* leave the money in your checking account. But what good would that do? It certainly wouldn't help family relations any. You think about it for a second... it's not like he's paying you *nothing* for the new loan. And where else are you going to turn? Herb was friends with everybody at the club. Once they found out he would only pay you 5%, they would follow suit and put the rest toward their bar and dining bills.

You accept the deal. What else are you going to do? You get your Christmas shopping list out and scratch off that surprise vacation to Mexico you were planning to spring on the family. Ah... all the Mexicans are moving to the U.S. anyhow. So much for that. You plop down on the couch and flip on the tube, wondering what else Herb has up his sleeve. The *Sopranos* is on. In a flash, a chill puckers your skin. You realize Herb is just like Tony Soprano. He runs everything around you, controls everything within your reach. You are subject to his will. You don't want either as your partner. Once they get their foot in the door, they will cut your income and eventually eat up your principal while you live on less and less.

Chapter 14

Thank God Johnny's Growth of Income Strategy broke the fixed-income paradigm. Dr. Stone and the Princess Diana Hospital were victims of Herb and his buddies. Their endowment income had shrunk while their needs grew. Worse yet, their needs would continue to grow. So too *must* their principal. They had no choice in the matter. But so long as they had the right research and focused on utilities that were expected to increase their dividends – and actually *did* – the three-year result was awesome. It made your jaw drop. Austin scribbled something down – *Johnny never had a utility portfolio under-perform a bond portfolio.*

For Austin, the real risk was *not* being in the Growth of Income Strategy. Opportunity cost was the kiss of death for Savers. To assure investors, Johnny would ask them, "What is your utility bill today? What was it five years ago? What is your telephone bill? What was it five years ago." Did rates go down? Of course they didn't. Nevertheless, one had to be *extremely* careful when it came down to actual stock selection, even with utilities. As Austin would point out even before an objection was raised – in the 80's alone, many utilities either ceased to exist, cut their dividend, or canceled their dividend altogether because of new construction cost overruns on nuclear projects. As Austin would stress with Dr. Stone again and again, it's one thing to understand that some utilities increased their dividends on a regular basis, and it is very, very different from knowing which companies they were.

Austin coined a phrase – "Rent-A-Nerd." That was his way of saying "at First American Investors, you are buying information, analysts' research." Austin never heard anyone approach prospects in that way before Johnny. Of the advisors he interviewed before meeting Johnny some seven or eight years ago, not a single one mentioned research. In profiling Stone before leaving the States, Austin noticed that Dr. Stone never once mentioned his advisor. This smelled like the usual scenario to Austin. It smelled like opportunity. When asked exactly why the hospital's advisor buys, sells, and re-invests, Stone said "Uh, right then... and tell me, sir, where exactly is the *tensor faciola* muscle." Austin got the point. Stone didn't know because it wasn't his job to know. It was his advisor's job. However, as fiduciary for the hospital's endowment fund, it *was* Stone's legal responsibility to ensure that the money was judiciously managed. Austin would focus on this, too. Stone was very worried about his fiduciary responsibilities.

It was no joke to either of them. Just as Austin profiled Stone to set up his argument for how important it was to select the correct money manager, Stone was busy profiling Austin. Being a pragmatic Englishman, Stone knew his next financial advisor would be his last. Stone's last choice of an advisor, a middle-aged man named Sterling Holliday, worked in the Gaborone office of Peabody Lineham, a large international firm based in England. A referral from Stone's brother-in-law, the relationship with Holliday was close to becoming a disaster. During Stone's tenure over the past eleven years, the hospital's laddered portfolio of high-quality U.S. bonds returned less and less income. Each time a bond matured, rates seemed lower than what they used to be. On top of that, the hospital was paying a 1.25% management fee. By the time all was said and done, the Princess Diana Hospital was making maybe 3%. And the hospital was lucky to net this much. Their favorable tax status made things a bit better. Of course, an individual investor would be even worse off.

When Stone took over as Associate Director eleven years ago, the endowment fund topped out at a little over seventy-five million. For a hospital in Africa, this was sizable. A senior doctor made about sixty thousand dollars U.S., a nurse about thirty thousand. Even today, it would cost only five million dollars to build an entire five-story extension for the hospital. As operating expenses increased – due greatly to the astronomical cost of HIV medications – the income from the endowment fund continued to decrease, satisfying fewer and fewer of the hospital's obligations. Before long, they were spending principal to cover operating expenses, thereby guaranteeing an even smaller income. If not for the steady flow of amazing volunteer physicians from the University of Pennsylvania and a grant from the Bill and Melinda Gates Foundation, things would be even worse.

When the hospital's account hit fifty million a few months ago, Stone was in a panic and with good reason. People were beginning to question his relationship with Sterling Holliday. Back in England, this would never have been the case. One's sense of professional etiquette would value facts over accusations. For all the daily haranguing and impunity slung through the hallowed halls of Parliament, charges of fraud and embezzlement are still considered a matter of personal honor. Not so throughout Africa where corruption was more commonplace than using the ATM. Stone knew very well that all eyes were upon him. It's not everyday that an African hospital amasses fifty million dollars. That's close to *three hundred million Pula*. The government spent great time and effort working with countless agencies, corporate givers, and so on. Even Botswana's President, Dr. Ketumile Masire, mentioned something to Stone's boss, the hospital director, William Khutse.

Again, when large amounts of money went missing in Africa, the worst was always suspected first. In the States, a hospital administrator might be answerable to a board of directors or some such bureaucracy. In Botswana, things were very, very different. William Khutse was not a doctor. Running the medical side of things was Stone's responsibility. In fact, running the entire hospital was Stone's responsibility. No, Khutse worked directly for the *government*. Thus, Stone was answerable directly to the government, and that was a bit scary. You don't expect sympathy, and you don't expect due process. If something doesn't pass the smell test, that was trial enough. Khutse may have occupied the top of the pyramid at the hospital, but he was quite low on the government hierarchy. If Stone did something wrong, it was Khutse's ass, too. He would have no problems throwing Stone under the bus to save his own hide. No problem at all. And he made this quite clear to Stone on a weekly basis.

This certainly didn't help matters. Now it goes without saying that no fiduciary likes to be at the helm of a losing portfolio. The amount of pressure is unbelievable, especially when trying to explain to your superiors the completely unexplainable... namely, the market's caprice. Dr. Stone was not in danger of being sued. Litigation in Botswana simply is nowhere as extensive as it is in the States or even Europe for that matter. No, it was Stone's reputation as a senior administrator that was at stake... as well as his job, of course. If the government really suspected him of wrongdoing, it would just throw him in jail until his case came up for review. The British Parliamentary system was in effect, but privileges like the American *habeus corpus* were not. It's pretty easy to figure out that you don't want to go to jail *anywhere* in Africa. It's something you just... try to avoid. Not to mention the fact that Stone's wife, Jill, was not particularly anxious to visit her husband in jail on a regular basis.

Jill Stone worked at the hospital. She administered the Penn program at Princess Diana. She saw firsthand how distracted from his daily work her husband became. Usually mild-mannered, witty, and patient, Jill Stone saw her husband becoming more and more frustrated by seemingly insignificant daily trifles. On days when the markets were down, he would lose his temper with subordinates for nothing at all. He was constantly *worried* – worried about money, worried about payroll, worried about the world economy, worried about terrorism, worried about paying for expensive HIV drugs, worried about spending money on upgraded equipment, worried about staffing.

Jill Stone had been with Tony Stone far too long not to see how losing twenty-five million dollars was tearing her husband apart inside. He was just angry all the time. At times, usually when they were sitting out back on their lanai taking in a beautiful, fiery-orange sunset, Jill would try to coax him into talking about it. One time, tears actually welled up in his eyes. "Nausea" was how he described it. He felt sick all the time, out of control, frustrated and afraid of what might happen. That's when Jill decided to step in and take a more active role with the account, for the hospital's money was not the only thing of value at stake. Her marriage was deteriorating as well. Once a warm and caring spouse, her husband was no longer happy. Jill started networking back through Penn in search of a new advisor, someone who could turn things around. If not, then at least someone who could get Stone to loosen his white-knuckled grip.

He was close to his breaking point. He couldn't take it anymore. He knew he was being consumed by that damned account, but he couldn't help trying to *control it* more and more. He knew that only made matters worse, but he simply couldn't help himself. He didn't know what else to do. He felt paralyzed. If you've ever been beaten up by the market, you know how totally manipulated you can feel. People will respond differently to this feeling of being out of control. Some people may laugh and worry about it later. Some people may scream at their brokers or their wives. Still others may cry. Everyone is faced with the same three questions – Why did they buy what they bought? When should they sell? What should they do with the proceeds? And if their professional so-called "advisors" didn't know the answers, how the hell should they?

Stone was not a professional money manager. He was a doctor, and his work as a doctor was suffering due to his responsibilities as a financial administrator. Naturally, he tried to handle the problem like a doctor. He tried to cure the problem, right? He performed numerous inspections of the portfolio... maturity dates, coupon rates, ratings, etc. Where mutual funds were concerned, he tried to get an up-to-date list of the hundreds of holdings. None of this made any difference. None of these things was the *cause* of the portfolio's poor performance. They were just symptoms. That's the thing about being responsible for a losing account, especially when you don't even know *why* you own what you own. You're never focusing on what really matters where performance is concerned. Johnny's Big Three questions loom large here. Sterling Holliday *was* a financial professional, but he could not present Stone with a coherent strategy tailor made for the hospital's situation. This only made the doctor more irate. He felt like a patient dying from something but no one could deduce what it was. Was the patient supposed to diagnose himself? That made no damned sense at all.

Working with an advisor like Johnny Long alleviated much of this, however. That was the overwhelming response Jill got from the Penn people. It turned out that Dr. Stone was not alone in his suffering. Indeed, many fiduciaries and individual investors alike were going through the same personal hell as Stone. When you're having money problems, it's so important to know you're not alone. It changes your perspective on things. You don't feel so closed in, claustrophobic. Indeed, when Jill told him about Johnny Long and the work he had performed in the past, Dr. Stone *breathed* for the first time in a long time. He knew Jill was trying to help him. That evening when she told him, he remembered how much they loved each other. If not for her, he didn't know how on earth he would manage to take the appropriate action.

It would be easy for Austin to attack Sterling Holliday and get some wind in his sails. Johnny stressed to Austin *not* to criticize the hospital's advisor. Sterling Holliday had no way of knowing that HIV would infect hundreds of thousands of Batswana. Nor could he be impugned for laddering the hospital's portfolio. That was standard operating procedure. As a financial professional, he *should* have been more sensitive to Stone's political situation, but it was too late for that now. Holliday and his clients were simply caught in a prolonged period of rate reductions. The squeeze was on everyone. Well, everyone except Johnny's clients. That was what Austin would try to show Stone. Rather than attack Holliday's performance directly, Austin decided to focus on the positive; namely, Johnny's amazing track record with his Growth of Income Strategy. "Let the returns speak for themselves," instructed Johnny. "Illustrate don't implicate." Focus on the positive.

Stone was not angry with Holliday so much as he was just plain angry at the markets. Nevertheless, he had to be pragmatic and make a change before it was too late. He had to be proactive. His back was up against the wall. If projections were correct, the hospital would run out of money in less than twelve years. That was no legacy for him to leave. Like so many other bond savers, Stone needed Johnny Long. It would be up to Johnny to save the hospital's endowment, thus keeping the place running smoothly. Disease was not projected to abate. HIV infection was not expected to diminish. The birth rate was not anticipated to go down. The Batswana people *needed* the Princess Diana Hospital in the worst way. Literally, hundreds of thousands of lives depended on it. There was a *moral imperative* at work here, one that Sterling Holliday may have recognized but could do nothing about. He had no strategy, no plan of action. He was ill prepared to handle what Johnny called "life money," money upon which lives depended.

This was precisely why Johnny liked working with hospitals, charities, and the like. At this point in his career, Johnny sought more than just financial security. He had achieved that long ago. He was working for something more, something spiritually gratifying. Johnny sought accounts where life money was at stake so he could *make a difference*, so to speak. In a strange way, then, Johnny Long needed people like Stone. Johnny always said that success in business meant success with people. Life money exemplified this better than anything else. Johnny managed money using two incredibly successful strategies. But he needed people in need to fulfill his spiritual destiny. He needed people to help.

That was something special that differentiated Johnny from other advisors, and he valued it very highly. Too many advisors used their clients as a means to and end. That's why "broker" is so often equated with "commission." Johnny broke that mold by "selling information," but he differed in another crucial way. You see, Johnny's two strategies were really an extension of a greater plan. Johnny believed in compassion. For Johnny, devising a successful investment strategy really meant doing everything to lead the *client* to a better way of life. This is not so simple as making his clients a lot of money. His clients were free to do with their money what they wanted. The point was that they *had choices* they didn't have before. Johnny's clients were *empowered* because of his strategies. And to a larger extent, Johnny was himself empowered by his principle of compassion. It trickled down to everything he did.

Sending Austin to Botswana as his surrogate was no different. When Austin first came to him years ago, Johnny saw sitting in front of him a special young man. Like all people, Austin was experiencing both great loss (in the death of his mother) and great gain (in his father's legacy). Like Austin's father before him, Johnny undertook teaching Austin how to appreciate this duality, to show the young man that things were not so simple as they seemed. Everything Austin had to do to satisfy his father's challenge embodied this principal. On the one hand, he received a lot of money, more than he ever had dreamed of. On the other hand, if he wanted more, he had to risk losing it. He could simply do nothing and keep the million. Ah, but that entailed *losing* the opportunity to get another *five million* and so on. When he didn't have any money, he was quite satisfied just playing his sax and going to class. Now, Austin had everything, and yet he felt a tremendous *lack*. Good God, even the very nature of a lack is paradoxical – you know for sure something is missing, but you don't know what the hell it is! So what do you really know at all?

By sending Austin to Botswana, Johnny was satisfying two needs. First, somebody needed to meet face-to-face with Stone. Even over the phone Johnny could tell he was a wreck. Problem was, Johnny was too busy to go himself. Sending Austin solved that problem. Second, Austin needed something to fill the void. Remember, Johnny needed people to help as much as those people needed Johnny. Again, Johnny's strategies were applicable to life and to his greater sense of compassion in general. In sending Austin out to see Stone -- who was in trouble himself -- to discuss an account consisting of life money, Johnny felt he was doing a multiple good. That was a rule of efficiency that satisfied him spiritually. In the same way that he bought only stocks that had increasing earnings or increasing dividends, Johnny helped people raise their own stock, so to speak.

Chapter 15

Jill Stone walked out onto the lanai holding a silver cocktail tray with a nice assortment of cheese, some crudité, and two glasses of gin. She put the tray down and dropped some ice cubes into their drinks. Dr. Stone always loved the sound of ice cubes tinkling against fine crystal. For some reason light resonance reminded him of what Africa must have been like 100 years ago. Jill squeezed some lime into their drinks and sat down next to her husband. Spread out across the sky in front of them was a searing sunset working its way below the tree line which surrounded their backyard.

The doctor took a healthy sip. "Ahhhh. Nice and cold, yeah?"

Jill sat quietly next to him. She took his hand in hers and kissed it. "I'll be so happy when this is all over," she said.

Dr. Stone nodded ever so slightly. He was off someplace else just then. "You know," he said, "I can just imagine what the plains must have been like when Livingstone first got here. Can you imagine sitting in front of a big canvas tent looking at the same sunset? That must have been something else indeed."

Jill imagined the scene for a moment. Her father was the first mayor of Gaborone. He came over as a missionary with his young daughter Jill and wound up playing a quintessential part in shaping

Botswana as we know it today. "Imagine seeing the Okavango Delta region for the first time. Unspoiled. It reminds me so much of when I was growing up. It was as if nothing was here except what God Himself put here."

Dr. Stone sipped his drink. "I tell people you had a magnificent sandbox to play in growing up."

"Hmm... indeed. We've come quite a long way, haven't we?"

The doctor looked at his wife. "You mean as a country?"

Jill turned to him. "No, no. I was thinking more of you and me. We've come quite a long way together. That's what I thought of when you imagined that canvas tent sitting out in the middle of plains like that. I saw the two of us sitting there, totally immersed in our surroundings, and thinking... we've come a long way together." Her husband laughed. "What?" she demanded coyly.

"I was thinking of lion hunting."

"Yes. Well, you would, wouldn't you, Great White Hunter that you are." She chuckled. "Can't even bring yourself to step on a scorpion now can you?"

"Perhaps, my dear. But remember, I am a healer. It's not in my nature to be aggressive."

Jill turned serious. "Speaking of which, you've been a bit of a brat at work this week. A few of the staff have mentioned it."

Stone was a bit annoyed. "To you?"

"I suppose they feel safe talking to me."

"Well if they want to bloody well bitch about me, they can bloody well bitch *to* me." He put his drink down and stretched his arms out over his head. "Or whatever. I wish I could get back to medicine one of these days. If I knew I was going to be a stockbroker, I would have asked my parents to drop me on my head a few times as a child. I'd be better at the job. Sterling Holliday my arse. It's more like a trip to hell. That wanker."

Jill stood up to go inside for a moment. "Yes, well... that should change very shortly."

"Well, I bloody well hope so. I'll be sacked soon enough.

And I'll really have Khutse up my arse like a sadistic proctologist, yeah."

Jill came back out and started massaging his shoulders from behind. She leaned in and kissed him on the ear. "Such language. This Austin fellow can't get here soon enough."

Stone turned around and put his arm around Jill's waist. "Well," he said pulling her closer, "maybe he can wait just a bit longer."

While Stone and his wife were busy unwinding, Austin headed out on the town. Well, that was a bit of an overstatement. For a new "city," Gabs was very, very spread out. You needed a taxi to get from one place to another. Gabs is sprawling, but not in the way Los Angeles is sprawling. From a rooftop you can see the countless neighborhoods of Los Angeles melting one into another as far as the eye can see (smog allowing, of course). You can almost hear the different music, smell the different foods, and see the different cars as your eye moves from neighborhood to neighborhood. In Los Angeles, you're dead without a car to get from point A to point Z, but at least there are points B through Y in between. Things were quite different in Gaborone. From high atop the Orange telecom tower, one could see from the mountains to the plains. Dotted sporadically all about were developed urban areas, but there was virtually nothing between. Points A and Z buzzed with activity; points B through Y were as yet still imaginary.

When deciding where to go in Gabs, the word "outposts" comes to mind. Indeed, the commerce areas were just that – outposts, oases of modernity in a land where the wilderness still ruled. Austin found this awesome, adventurous, exciting. He was used to walking out his door and quite literally having the world at his feet. His breakfast was even cooked and waiting for him every morning. In Gabs, things were different... very different. Just going out for a cocktail was an act of adventure. No wonder Livingstone's name was everywhere in Gaborone. The great missionary left his mark on everything. He came from another world entirely, and yet his message was universal. Even back then, the Batswana were more than willing to listen with aplomb. They were not threatened by what strangers had to offer. No, the Batswana were quite comfortable with who they were. This was still the case. From the moment he stepped off the plane in Gaborone, Austin recognized that the Batswana were very special people, for they were completely uninhibited by Father Freud and his great Anglo-European crisis of Self. Even their views toward Christianity – Livingstone's greatest legacy – were devoid of guilt, shame, and obligation. It was as if Christ were simply another piece in the nature of things. If there were ever a people before The Fall, they were Batswana. The Batswana were a *natural* people.

When Austin stepped out of the taxi and into the Bull and Bush, perhaps the most famous drinking hole in Gabs, it was like stepping back in time. No matter where you are in the world, ask anyone who has ever been to Gaborone about the Bull and Bush. Odds are you will be regaled with a story right out of Kipling, it was that much a part of where the bush met the blacktop, so to speak. It had everything but pygmies and Bushmen. The twenty-minute drive from the Grand Palm brought him to the threshold of this popular outpost. It was the last two-hundred yards or so that reminded Austin he was in another world. For despite its great popularity with anyone who has *ever* been to Gaborone, the Bull and Bush was almost inaccessible by car unless you had a truck or an SUV. Well off the main road, the B&B was some two hundred yards down a treacherous dirt road riddled with potholes so numerous and so deep one wondered if it was recently carpetbombed.

Despite Gaborone's tenacious growth, there was no pork-barrel Department of Public Works to eat up a month filling and paving the road as we would have done in the States. Evidently there was also no local politician whom the B&B owners could bribe in order to get the road paved. The local cabbies would not dare exceed five miles an hour for fear of cracking an axle, thereby guaranteeing themselves a destitute future. At that pace, it took Austin almost ten minutes to reach the Bull and Bush from the main road. This only added to the overall authenticity of his first little expedition into the city. He was in no rush, and a good thing for that. Austin recognized from the get-go that not a soul *hurried* in the least, let alone *rushed* anywhere. Gabs ran on African time, and moved to a pace all its own. There was no resisting it, either. Africa Time slowly sucked you in until, comfortably tucked away in its bosom, you recognized the needlessness of rushing anywhere at all. The people living in the dilapidated shacks lining the dirt road leading to the B&B had sat watching countless cars bounce by over the years.

As soon as he stepped out of the taxi, Austin realized he was far off the beaten path. The surroundings appalled him. Nobody else seemed to notice, however. Bordering the left of the stone pathway leading to the front door was a stone patio with about a dozen tables. The patio was separated from the rest of the community by a large black wrought-iron fence. This kept the local population safely *outside* and the more affluent patrons safely *inside*. Inside was a "fancy" bar (the stools had real leather) and a large dining room which was always empty except for the staff who used it to hide out and smoke cigarettes for a while before dropping their order. Off the fancy bar was the real appeal of the Bull and Bush – a *real* thatch-roofed bar area. There was nothing like enjoying a cocktail in the middle of Africa listening to the thunder and rain beat out rhythms overhead with not a drop coming through. Far be it for something as commonplace as pouring rain to interrupt the city's imbibing.

You could lose track of time drinking under that big thatched structure. It was like an African bigtop. Your problems completely disappeared, were completely forgotten. In fact, you could lose track of the *century* sitting there watching the sun set across the plains. Yet it was Austin's *American past* that seemed so oddly out of phase with the world. Everything and everyone catered to being lost in time. The result was a warm sense of well being and carelessness. Perhaps this was a sort of Jungian state of mass-denial, a neurotic response to a country immersed in death and disease, a country looking *forward* and seeing half of its population dying of AIDS. Then again, maybe it was a whimsical response to the grand order of things, an indigenous wisdom that, like a Phoenix, immolates itself only to be reborn from the ashes. In Botswana, as in much of Africa, the famous Baobab is the symbolic tree of life. Stunted, salty, and grotesque, yet deeply rooted and seemingly made of iron, the Baobab is beautiful as only pure irony can be. When contemplating the Baobab as a symbol of the Batswana self, you don't know whether to laugh or cry. Then you realize you have glimpsed the essence of the trope, the essential Baobab and the Batswana alike. For if there is such a thing as a timeless human struggle for survival, it is certainly suspended in each tear that falls to the parched Botswana earth. And if there is wisdom in laughter, the riotous Botswana sense of humor is pregnant with the sagacity of the millennia.

Like Heather said, nothing is as easy as it seems in Africa. Educated in the ivory tower of Stanford University, Austin half-expected to see radicals handing out pamphlets and calling for mass equality. But he soon realized that pontification and political wrangling was a privilege of the elite. This duality between life and death, between hope and despair, between bravado and fear was not nearly as important to the average Batswana as just getting up and going to work. Living another day with AIDS was all the philosophy and politics necessary for the time being. African Time. Being a wealthy American visiting on business, Austin was a bit anxious about all this. How on earth was he going to talk flat-out, bottom line in a world so focused on *needs* rather than *wants*?

He was reassured by Johnny's parting advice. "You are on a mission of good," Johnny told him.

"But what if I mess it up?" Austin replied.

Austin remembered Johnny laughing out loud. He always did this before delivering a sermon. "Austin, how the hell can you mess it up? You are bringing them a truth. You are bringing them an alternative when they thought there was none. You are bringing them *choices* when they thought they didn't have any. You are on a mission. You're a missionary. Just deliver the good word. Anyway, their accounts are so messed up anyway, how much worse can we do?" He smiled and was silent. The sermon was over.

When Sebele, his waitress, took his order, she could see the anxiety written across Austin's face. He was so out of place. It was so obvious. Here he was sitting at a large table all by himself scribbling notes on index cards. Clearly, he was not from around there. Austin ordered his usual Johnny Black with a can of Coke on the side. That was the last he'd see of Sebele for twenty minutes. You see, prompt service in the American sense was not seen as vital at the Bull and Bush. African Time was the rule of thumb. If you waited twenty minutes for your whiskey to arrive, so much the better for your liver. Where were you rushing to anyway? In this way, the B&B was a refuge and provided exactly what one would want in a frontier oasis – plenty of cheap booze (to kill the malaria and any liver working properly), over-cooked food (to kill the parasites and any semblance of taste), potable water (to kill your thirst and the hot pepper singeing your tongue from dinner), and half-naked women who would have unprotected sex with almost anyone who asked (to kill the boredom if not most of the population). As an added delight, as icing on the cake for the weary adventurer, the Bull and Bush boasted "the best ribs in Africa." Of course, exactly what animal once used those ribs remained undisclosed. It was probably best that way.

One reason the men of Gaborone didn't worry much about anything was the abundance of eligible women. Austin noticed the women right away. He couldn't *not* notice them. The American saying "baby got back" described Batswana women perfectly. Flo-Jo had nothing on these girls. Austin was accustomed to the snobby girls of Olde City, Philadelphia, and Palo Alto, girls who would size you up at a glance rather than take the time to get to know you regardless of your gender, frail bleached-out girls who starved themselves to the point that their bodies started consuming their brains. Compared to the European girls he had already met, Austin found American women immature. But these African women were something else again. Austin expected to see frail, emaciated women carrying baskets on their heads. And maybe they were out there somewhere walking along some dirt footpath. Not the women at the Bull and Bush, though. They were big. They were strong. They were outgoing. They were on you like white on rice.

If cheap liquor was a cultural necessity, so was an ample supply of free sex. The women *ran* Gabs. Despite their lack of legal standing, despite a suspected 1,000 rapes a month nationally, despite HIV running rampant among pregnant women, the women called the shots. It was amazing. In contrast, the men were short, thin, and far less amiable. More obvious, they were subject to the women's constant ballbusting. Of course, this was all part of the mating game, just not according to the usual power dynamic. Your average American woman would never be able to keep up with the pace of sex in Gabs. Some may say "good thing," but that would be seen as unnatural by the same sort of standards.

Needless to say, Austin was the *American d'jour* that evening. The chicks were on him one after the other. They shot in like diving birds. Each wanting her share, her piece of the action, her piece of Austin. At the same time, though, these women were willing to hang out and listen to him with the same sort of fascination as if he'd just stepped out of the bush. They found his stories absolutely amazing.

Austin was shocked. Back in the States, guys had to ease their way in – mostly wallet first – if they wanted to get a date with an attractive woman. They were attracted to him for who he was. This seemed like a more natural order of things. Compared to Europe or the United States, Botswana had a more natural and *instinctive* order of things. If you want to talk - talk. If you want to drink – drink. If you want to have sex – have sex. That was that. This was not a Puritanical country, nor was it gasping beneath the weight of Western-style feminism that had men and women alike running around in circles trying to cover their asses. Africa was *wild, not counter-intuitive.*

Unrestrained by Western mores, Austin took creative liberties. The girls were really enjoying him, so why not enthrall them as much as his imagination allowed. Anyway, he wasn't so much interested in sex as he was enjoying the *power of storytelling*, the power to literally *re-create* the American experience as he saw fit. He was, after all, a missionary. He could redefine reality. Like Johnny said, he was "on a mission." So Austin decided to run with it as far as he could. He would perform a little experiment for his own edification. He would see if he could derive the truth about certain things -- the natural order of certain things – before returning to the States, just as he did when Johnny taught him about the Growth of Income Strategy and capitalism in general.

Before he left, Austin was a little afraid of being an American abroad. Actually, he was scared shitless. Day after day, the American press pounded home how awful Americans were, how myopic, violent, and destructive they were, how wasteful, greedy, and colonialist they were. But Austin was on a mission. He could not falter, not in front of Johnny Long. Austin had to carry the flag for Johnny. More importantly, there were lives at stake. His mission, pure and simple, was to do whatever he could to get Johnny's hands on the hospital's life money. So much depended on it. Johnny made it clear to Austin – America was the bastion of capitalism and democracy in the modern world. And despite any drawbacks these two systems may have, they embodied a *natural order of things* that could not be denied, at least as far as Johnny knew. Austin, then, was to carry with him a beacon of life, hope, prosperity, and equality. Little did he know it at the time, but the blue and black Botswana flag symbolized the calm nature of the people (the stability of living a natural, intuitive life), racial harmony (the power of enfranchisement and democracy), and prosperity (the bounty of capitalism). Thus Johnny's Growth of Income Strategy and the hospital's dire financial state were two larger forces waiting to collide, and Austin was the lynchpin.

It was no question to Johnny that his strategy would turn things around for the hospital. He had done this too many times before to have any doubts. For his part, Austin, a neophyte, was filled with a spirit of purpose he hadn't felt in quite a long time. His positive energy alone was enough to attract a crowd at the Bull and Bush. If there was ever such a thing as the Great White Hope, he was it at that moment in time. This was no joke. Austin was a hero to the people there by virtue of his proposed work with the Princess Diana Hospital. Why? Well, he could actually make a difference. And despite what people may or may not have thought about Americans, *helping people* was as much a part of the American way as anything else. Austin's experiment was to test the assumption that "American" was synonymous with "Ugly American." Austin told embellished tales of stock-market riches he generated, covert CIA operations of which he was a part, and the development of the Third World which he would someday undertake. He pondered founding health-information organizations and media outlets, nightclubs, and private-investigation firms. All to the delight of men and women alike. The answer to his experiment was conclusive. Everybody *loved* America so long as they could be wrapped up in the U.S. flag and enjoy the trickle-down benefits of the greatest country in the world. Exclude them, however, and you have *Al-Qaeda*.

By the time Austin started talking about the Princess Diana Hospital, there were some ten or eleven middle-class, educated, and employed Batswana sitting at his table. The men were not feeling threatened by his airs, nor were the woman pawing him just then (they were, however, buying him round after round of drinks). Austin relished this feeling of power and control. For the first time in his life, he felt perfectly at ease talking to complete strangers. He felt confident and worldly, like he actually had something of value to put out there for public consumption. Where he was at first afraid of what he might encounter, Austin now felt an odd sense of dichotomy – was he *really* bright, attractive, and valuable? Or was he simply full of shit and blowing hot air at a bunch of people who didn't know their toes from their elbows? As he was laying out his fantastical plans to build a rural clinic in *Hukuntsi* in the western *Kgalagadi*

District, he realized… what difference did it really make? He was enjoying himself. His new friends were enjoying themselves. Why bear the weight of the world on his shoulders all the time. Did it really make any difference in the long run? Without knowing it, Austin had changed over to African Time.

Austin accidentally let the news of the hospital's financial problems slip out. His new friends were distraught, to say the least. They were well aware of the HIV epidemic, and it wasn't slowing down. Indeed, how many of them sitting at that table were HIV positive? If there were ten of them sitting there with Austin, odds are *four or five* of them were positive. Being well educated, they would probably be on meds. You could not say the same for the general population. Austin was relishing his popularity, especially among all these exotic women who would strip down at his command. Then it suddenly dawned on him that pulling out his manhood was exactly the same as playing Russian Roulette. Wait… stick to Russian Roulette. At least with Russian Roulette, Austin had an 83% chance of survival; with HIV, it was only 50%. It's a no-brainer. If you live in Botswana and you're horny, learn to get your thrills by putting a gun to your head and pulling the trigger… it's safer.

So Austin's mission was of great interest to these young people. People weren't going to stop having sex, nor were they just going to start using condoms. HIV/AIDS was still very, very taboo. The human animal is hard-wired with an insatiable drive to reproduce *and* pleasure itself. It is deeply instinctive and intuitive. And if you believe Darwin in the least, it is *not* a coincidence that sex satisfies *both* of these drives at once. How's that for efficiency? Yee-ha! So you could bet the house that folks are not just gonna stop screwing. Moreover, if you believe Freud, you know that we humans are encoded with as much of a *death* instinct as a *survival* instinct. That is, we are attracted to what is *both* good and bad for us. It is also no coincidence that sex in the modern age brings us right to this border (not to mention to the cusp of the Madonna-Whore complex which is timeless). So you could *also* bet the house that people were not always gonna use condoms… how boring… how bourgeois… how completely civilized! Where's the thrill in that?

The prospect of a fiscal crisis at the hospital catalyzed visions of untreated AIDS patients wandering the streets. The idea that

Austin could turn things around for the hospital made him something of a savior. It was very real money affecting very real lives, including those of the unborn. When Austin explained to them what the basics of the Growth of Income Strategy were, they caught on immediately. Not only were they well-educated, they had *common sense* as well. What Austin was proposing was common sense, it was obvious. In a world where things only get more and more expensive, why wouldn't one find a way to increase one's income. My God, especially for a hospital operating at the epicenter of the African HIV epidemic! Was one supposed to make do with the same income year after year? Only to the Western mind would this make sense because rarely was life money at stake. In actuality, even these "unsophisticated" folks sitting around the table with Austin knew that was an absurd premise.

Now, buying a bunch of fixed-rate bonds or CDs and crossing your fingers didn't even make sense to a bunch of doctors, yet according to mainstream modern portfolio theory, they were entirely uninformed. As both Johnny and Austin knew, they were right *precisely because* they were uninformed. They had not been indoctrinated – as had Sterling – in the hermetic logic of modern portfolio theory which extolled the virtues of asset allocation and laddered portfolios above all else. Ironically, Adam Mortensen, a famous finance professor at Penn, gave a well-publicized seminar about two weeks prior to Austin's departure. The event was attended by many affluent alumni in the Philadelphia area as part of a development drive for an extension to the Wharton School of Business library. Johnny was, of course, invited to attend. Mortensen's mathematics were at times complex and the historical documentation precise. Algorithms were placed as cornerstones upon which were built hegemonic pie charts. Exotic hedging strategies, straddles, leaps, collars... all fell victim to a single conclusion which was always the same: For growth of principal, buy the commission-free S&P 500 Index; for income, build a laddered portfolio of fixed-income vehicles like bonds or CDs.

Johnny has heard similar presentations countless times. The ending was always the same - a *fixed* ending for fixed income. In years of attending seminars, reading articles, and researching mutual funds, Johnny had yet to find a proponent of *pure income growth*. Almost without exception, modern portfolio theorists used "total return" to account for either decreasing rates (declining income) or increasing need (growing expenses). Thus, there was nothing unusual in what

Mortensen was saying. That was *precisely* the problem. Counting on total return rather than income growth was simply a way of hiding behind polemical mathematics. It was self-protective, a means for money managers to cover their asses by either over-allocating or playing it *too* safe. As even Johnny was quick to admit, bond savers would not lose money on their investments by following a strategy like that which Mortensen advocated. However, Johnny had long believed that such a client was nevertheless at greater risk when trying to meet his *income* needs. For Johnny, the gambit was miscast from the start. As he told Austin, "What good is protecting principal one hundred percent if you must then turn around and spend some of that principal because the income your investment generated is insufficient?"

In contrast, modern portfolio theorists like Mortensen always – *always* – put protection of principal ahead of growth of income. Any growth in principal came from growth investments. The fixed-income portion of the allocation was strictly *fixed income.* Johnny always saw "total return" as a sort of red herring. Simply put, any principal growth an investor captured in fixed income was completely random and could never be promised or predicted. So how was a bond saver to reconcile his budget. Under these circumstances, what income you received was both fixed and determined by the degree of safety. There was never much emphasis placed on the client's actual needs. Indeed, Johnny would inevitably chuckle every time a famous finance professor like Mortensen would simply espouse the rule of thumb that your percentage in fixed income should be the same as your age at any given time. It was as if the client – institutional or otherwise – existed in a vacuum. Prevailing asset-allocation and financial-planning models got it entirely backward. The tail wagged the dog. Instead of growing income to meet the client's needs, total income was *pre-established* by multiplying principal times the rate available. Thus, your laddered portfolio was built *without regard toward the client's income needs.*

To see how inadequate this method was, Austin needed only to look at the Princess Diana Hospital. A proponent of modern portfolio theory, Sterling Holliday culled the market for the best rates available in AAA bonds and that was that. He *never took into account* the hospital's growing income needs. How could he? Like all the others, Holliday did not know how to *grow* income. It was so obviously a problem, Austin was astounded when Johnny told him there was not a single major asset manager who focused on pure income growth. Even Austin's new African friends saw the absurdity of Holliday's approach. You see, when you're on African Time, you can slow down enough to see the obvious. When you operate at this speed, you are no longer "informed" by hyperkinetic Western assumptions. To the contrary, you are thoroughly *uninformed*, as Professor Mortensen would say. One young man seated at Austin's table actually asked him point blank – "How was the hospital supposed to cover its five-year projections on a fixed income that was too little to begin with?" Obviously, they couldn't. They were heading toward dire straights, Austin explained. That's why he was there, that was his mission. And he knew that Stone would have never heard of anything so thoroughly "uninformed" as investing for growth of income.

However, not everyone was enthralled by Austin's big talk. Also sitting conspicuously at his table were seven Norwegian nursing students doing a three-month rotation at Livingstone Hospital, a facility far more rural and underdeveloped than Princess Diana. Their shining blonde hair stood out like stars against a sky of black African heads. Back home, the Norwegians worked within a convoluted and bureaucratic medical system stricken by what they described in broken English as "too much talking." For the Norwegians, there was a time and a place for everything, and that evening was neither the time nor the place for a haughty American. For the young women, the time was right for mourning. They kept toasting *skől*, drinking themselves silly, and ordered drinks faster than the waitress could bring them.

As with Austin earlier in the evening, the Norwegians looked worried about something. They were getting too much education too fast. Compared to the artificial, processed, homogenized, and pasteurized world of socialized medicine, Africa was overrunning them with a poisonous dose of reality. It seemed that before departing, no one told them that in Africa, everyone had a death story. Within one day, they each had their own, and they hadn't planned for this. Well, of course they planned to see someone die. That happened everywhere. But they hadn't prepared themselves for all the dead babies that came in over the past three days. How could they? A bureaucratic socialist medical system was one thing. Dozens of babies dying from something as "simple" as an outbreak of dysentery and resulting dehydration was quite another. How could such a thing happen? Why did the parents wait so long before bringing the babies to the hospital? To the Norwegians, each dead, dehydrated baby represented the unthinkable. No, literally. There was absolutely no way the Norwegians could get their arms around such a thing. Symptom... cause... treatment... recovery. This was the order of things for them. Their rotation at Livingstone was a crash course in reality; namely, even "medicine," that hallowed Western totem, must inevitably succumb to the forces of the wild. Worse yet for the girls was that many of the babies came in with crosses painted on their heads. *That* was the initial treatment their parents administered to their sick children. Excuse me? What?

All human totems fail in the shadow of nature. And Batswana women are supposed to worry about being seen as sluts? The nurses would later meet many Batswana who believed it was *condoms* that caused AIDS. At one point, the brashest of the young girls, a sinewy, charismatic, tobacco-dipping nurse whose name translated into something like *Go-Katrina*, simply yelled out in the middle of the ward. Roughly translated, she screamed, "What the hell?" It was not so much a question as a declaration, a declaration of anger and frustration over the futility of it all. She was so resentful, this beautiful *Go-Katrina*. But how haughty was she to think that she was more upset than the infant's mother? Just embarking upon her career, *Go-Kat* had yet to learn the *real* life lessons of Africa. But at least she was there trying. That had to count for something.

Chapter 16

Austin woke up the next morning feeling like a prune. He was so dehydrated his calves cramped if he pointed his feet too far. Intense sunlight burst through the unshaded window. Austin could see the billowy clouds puffed up against the azure sky. His second day in Botswana was as gorgeous as his first. Austin rubbed his eyes and for a brief second, completely forgot about the young Batswana woman lying naked next to him. Palessa... that was her name. It meant rose in Botswana, and apparently Austin had taken hers. She was a vibrant young girl who just graduated from the University of Botswana. She had big energized eyes and a crisp British accent. Austin remembered they had hit it off from the start at the Bull and Bush, but Palessa was there with her boyfriend and Austin had his sights set on Freya, the tallest of the Norwegian nursing students who just so happened to dislike Austin the most. Anyway, there was no way Palessa, a self-respecting Botswana woman, was going to be outmaneuvered by some European nursing student.

Palessa snuggled closer to Austin and mumbled, "Good morning, luv." She clung to him like her savior had arrived.

"Palessa?"

"Yes, luv?"

"Where's your boyfriend?"

Palessa seemed nonplussed. "How should I know? Didn't we leave him pissed drunk in the casino?"

Austin thought for a moment. He remembered the casino in the hotel lobby. It was a sordid place out of the Twilight Zone. There were no ritzy tourists or high-profile players. Instead, the place was filled with local Batswana who had no business gambling away the little money they had. Worse yet for Austin, as one of the only white people playing, he was an instant target for the numerous drifters. These ugly, middle-aged women shod in old floral dresses circled the tables like sharks. Austin was completely taken aback. As with the airport, security was nothing like it was back in the States. Back home, these women would never have lasted more than fifteen minutes. In Gabs, however, they were as much a part of the casino experience as liquor, cigars, and hundred Pula chips. Were they hookers? Probably... the cheap and toothless sort. Were they HIV positive? Maybe... flip a coin. Were they annoying and right up in Austin's bubble? Absolutely... and nobody cared.

While Palessa was busy trying to prop up her alcoholic English boyfriend, Jim-Paul, Austin tried to play some black jack. But no sooner had he played his third hand than two drifters sat down. They each made Flip Wilson's Geraldine look like a supermodel. Austin could barely play these two women were so annoying. Between complimenting his sharp gambling mind, they repeatedly asked him for money under their breath. Austin kept looking at the *croupier* for help, but he was clearly not going to say a word. It was as if they were all playing their roles. Austin tried to show his discomfort by sighing and looking as annoyed as possible, but what did his discomfort matter to these woman. Really, they were no different than cold callers. It wasn't personal, it was efficient. It was all about the bottom line. So when Austin stopped coughing up ten Pula chips for the women to play, they quickly and efficiently moved on to Plan B... prostitution.

Between hands, both women got up and left as if on cue. One put her hand on Austin's shoulder, leaned in, and whispered something to him. The whiff of foul cigarette breath, gingivitis, and spiced curried goat engulfed Austin's face. He had no idea what she said to him. He figured it out soon enough, though, when she returned arm-in-arm with a tall, beefy woman in a light blue dress. "This is my cousin," the woman said as she pushed the other forward.

Austin wasn't really sure how to react. He really just wanted to play cards, but he certainly didn't want to lodge a formal complaint with the casino manager. After all, who knew how many "cousins" were around or even working for the hotel? Plus he was drunk, down $300, and wondering what Freya and her Norwegian friends were up to.

Austin eyed the woman in blue. He hadn't noticed her name, but he noticed her missing tooth. She was very broad, big even. She sat down next to him and put her large hand on his thigh. "Can I play?" she whined. Austin scratched his head and flipped her a chip. He didn't want to make a scene or insult her when he didn't know how connected she was. She rubbed his leg. "Thank you, baby," she said.

The older drifter walked up behind Austin and started mumbling in his ear. Austin could smell her breath again. "Do you like my cousin?" she asked.

Austin nodded. "Oh yes, she's very nice." The girl smiled at the compliment revealing a gold tooth opposite the missing one. "Yes, very nice."

"She will make a good wife," the woman said. "She knows how to take care of a man."

Austin looked the girl over. She seemed to be about twenty-eight, but who could tell. She was weathered. She was not emaciated or anything like that. But she was sickly, nevertheless. Unlike Palessa's eyes, this girl's were somewhat yellowed. If one ran a fifty-fifty chance having unprotected sex with your random Batswana off the street, God only knew the odds in play here. Sitting there in that smoky, soiled casino with the stained red carpet, what could be more fitting than gambling with your life, Austin thought.

He cleared his throat. Unable to help himself, he asked the girl, "and how many men have you pleased?"

The girl didn't say a word. It was as if she wasn't allowed to speak. Instead, she worked her hand up Austin's thigh as if to give him a physical demonstration of her skills. The older woman spoke up. "She is waiting."

"Waiting?" repeated Austin. "Waiting for what? For me?"

The girl laughed and the woman smiled. "Yes, yes! She has been waiting to go to America with a gentleman like you. It is not without reward that you would take her as your own."

Austin cocked his head. "To America?"

The woman nodded. "She will make a fine wife. And you will be..." she turned to the girl and said something in Setswana.

The girl looked at Austin and said in broken English, "Taken care of."

The woman poked Austin in the arm. "Yes! Taken care of!"

This was exactly the *opposite* of what Austin expected to hear. He pulled his bets and put all his chips in his blazer pocket. "Wait a minute," he said. "Let me get this straight. *You* want to pay *me* to take you to America."

The woman nodded. "To make a marriage. Yes. Fifty thousand Pula." By that time, the girl's hand had crept far enough up Austin's leg to solidify their friendship.

Austin was tempted to continue the conversation. But Palessa put a stop to all that. She stepped in between Austin and the woman and brusquely redirected the girl's hand. She said something obviously condescending in Setswana because the girl stood up and started giving Palessa a little how's your father in return. Austin was rather enjoying having three women fight over him. Where a woman might feel like an object or a piece of meat, a man feels like quite the Adonis. Moreover, he relished the irony of it all. Here he was, a rich white American guy being *fought over* by three poor African women trying to hitch their wagons to his. How outraged the Philly Police would be back in the States! But how primal, how base instinct it was! Hey, Austin thought to himself, who was *he* to pass judgment?

Palessa took Austin by the arm and led him over to the bar. "Are *they* your type of women?"

Austin was about to make a joke when he sensed that Palessa was actually offended. "Who, them?" he said. "I had no idea what the hell they were talking about. They kept bothering the hell out of me while I was trying to play."

"Well, stay away from women like that. They're dirty." Austin could see it affected her viscerally.

"No, no. I actually think they wanted to *pay* me to take them to America or marry them or something." He shrugged it off.

Palessa laughed. Perhaps it was her huge, innocent black eyes that sunk the hook in Austin. "But first you would want to sample the goods, yeah. For a fee, of course. Then after you pay them, you will never hear from them again. Oh, and your manhood will fall off." Apparently, though, Palessa posed no such threat, at least not in her own mind. She had no problems providing Austin with a suitable alternative to the pack of she-devil drifters that was trailing him around the gaming floor. What's more, her boyfriend, Jim-Paul, was once again too drunk to walk (a nightly occurrence) or do much else for that matter. For all her naiveté and kindheartedness, she felt she owed the wanker one. And here was Austin fresh off the boat, presumably disease free, and rather exotic. It seemed to her as if he was sent gift wrapped to her doorstep.

The only other thing Austin remembered about the end of the night was the short walk along the garden path that connected the casino with the hotel. Dozens and dozens of dogs were howling in the darkness. Some seemed quite distant; others seemed just beyond the brush. A cold chill ran through Austin. Were they wild? Did they ever attack? Were they even dogs? There was no doubt in his mind that they would choose to devour *him* rather than his indigenous sidekick. Palessa got quite a laugh out of the whole thing. As it turned out, they were your usual run-of-the-mill domestic pets, man's best friend. Austin objected – where do, like, fifty dogs howl in your neighborhood all night? Normal? Hardly. Austin's objections only added to his foreign charm for Palessa. She squeezed his arm, made like a wild dog and bit him, and pushed him off toward his room. The dogs howled through the night.

Chapter 17

Austin got out of bed and went over to the window. He was buck naked. That was so unlike him. He rarely slept in the nude even though his girlfriends almost always did. Even Palessa, his latest *bete d'amour,* was nude beneath the crisp white sheets. She rolled over onto her side and moaned with the sort of contentment a twenty-three year old co-ed has when she has found the romantic love of her life. Austin looked back over his shoulder. He remembered that neither of them had a condom last night. He cursed under his breath. If there was such a big problem, you'd think they'd put them in a big jar on top of the bar for Christ's sake. He looked down... at least it hadn't fallen off yet.

Austin squinted into the sun. "What time is it?" he asked.

Palessa stretched out her arms and moaned with contentment again. "How should I know, luv?"

There were no clocks in the room. Guests were presumed to be running on internal African Time. Judging from the crowd assembling around the poolside bar, it was nearing lunch time. "I have to be at the hospital by 1:30. Shit, I don't even know where it is. I'm such an idiot. Can you imagine coming more than halfway across the world for a meeting and not even knowing where the meeting is? How's that for planning?"

Palessa sat up in bed and threw the sheets off herself. Her naked black body seemed to actually glow against the sheets. "It's right off Notwane and the North Ring Road. All the High Commission buildings are there, too. And the Mall is across the street. My cousin owns a really cool café there. We can take a taxi together and then have lunch at his place. Maybe he'll be there. I can introduce you." Austin just stared out the window. Palessa continued, "What's the big deal? I'm here, aren't I? Everyone knows where the hospital is anyway. All you have to do is ask anyone." She yawned loudly as if to remind Austin of the pace of things in Gabs. "Someone will just point their finger in the right direction."

Austin turned around abruptly. "Hey now... you've been busting my balls about being an opinionated American all night. I think I've earned my street cred." He winked at her and then realized he was standing in front of her completely naked.

Palessa raised an eyebrow. "I'd say I busted them." She shot up and headed into the bathroom to freshen up.

Austin grabbed the first article of clothing he saw. "Thanks for offering to show me where the hospital is. I should be able to find it on my own though."

"Well let's have lunch together." She ran the shower to the right temperature.

Austin already had a shirt and linen pants on. "Um... why don't you take a shower and I'll call you later to meet up?"

Palessa stuck her head out of the shower. "What? I can't hear you, luv." Austin went into the bathroom and fiddled with his hair. Palessa looked at him in the mirror. "You're dressed already? Is that how things are in the States. Boy, you Yanks *really* don't like having your balls busted, do you?" She ducked back in the shower. No worries. Jim-Paul would be looking for her. Anyway, she would track Austin down at the Bull and Bush later that night. And she knew where his hotel room was. Where else was he going to go?

Austin was a bit embarrassed. "So I'll call you later then?"

Palessa didn't answer. When she got out of the shower, she was alone in the room. While she put on her lipstick, she smiled to herself in the mirror. Good thing she copied down Austin's address in the States while he was asleep… just in case she was pregnant. A girl can't be too sure. And wouldn't it be lovely to live in Philly!

Down in the lobby, Austin felt split in half. Part of him felt indoctrinated, initiated, accredited, *real*. He had a sense of power and control. But he also felt like everyone was looking at him, like he had just pillaged an ancient village or done something totally colonialist. He honestly didn't know which way to lean. For a second there in the elevator, he actually imagined *living* in Gabs! What was up with that? In fact, a lot of visitors felt like Austin did, but an *emotional* tourist's guide had yet to be written. Botswana had only gained its independence from Britain in 1966. It was a veritable teenager, and you felt as if you could romp roughshod right over the people, places, and things. Indeed, Austin felt a bit guilty for behaving like this with Palessa. Then again, thinking the Batswana were so submissive and helpless was to greatly underestimate what made them such a strong people. Like the *Baobab*, Botswana was deeply rooted. Their somewhat grotesque beauty was intended to be intertwined but not to be attacked. Trying to run over the Batswana would be as foolish as head butting a Rhino. Not only would you lose, *why* would you want to do it in the first place? To prove your worth somehow? To prove how tough you were? After seeing the drifters in the casino, Austin knew full well that he was playing an away game, and *they* had home-field advantage. The answer, then, was to just go with the flow. Switch to African Time and *everybody* wins. Let nature run its course.

Austin figured this out about halfway to the hospital. The taxi was taking him south along *Julius Nyerere Drive,* taking him right past the Gaborone Golf Course. Perhaps it was that epitome of civility – the golf club – that set Austin back at ease. At any rate, he was totally refocused on his meeting with Dr. Stone. His intense preparation – combined with his rekindled inspiration – was paying off. He had been very, very distracted for the last couple of days. Austin felt as if the long flights, the partying, and the general novelty of things had dulled his edge. As the taxi turned west on *Notwane* bringing Austin through a rather impoverished neighborhood, he remembered that there was a far greater purpose to his visit than just hanging out and drinking with the locals. He remembered that the country was dying. He remembered that he was not there on vacation.

The taxi stopped, Austin paid, got out, and there he was… in the middle of Africa standing in front of *the hospital*. He had his leather-bound presentation book under his arm. Following Johnny's advice, the focus of Austin's presentation was to inform Dr. Stone that there was in fact another way. In Austin's mind were the treasures of modernity; within the hospital walls were the ravages of nature and time. You couldn't go anywhere without seeing or hearing something about David Livingstone. In 1841, he arrived in Botswana (then simply the land of the *Bakwena*) and set about his mission of bringing Christianity to Africa. In fact, in front of the main entrance to the primary-care facility at the hospital was a large bronze statue of Livingstone. He had a book – probably the Holy Bible – under one arm while he pointed to the sky with his other hand. It looked as if Livingstone was addressing Divinity and how to live life another way. The parallel did not escape Austin. To the contrary, he drew strength from it. However haughty the comparison, if it helped him persuade Stone to take the necessary action it would change the doctor's life and provide a beacon of light for Botswana.

There were three large buildings on the grounds. Off to his left and back a ways was a relatively tall brick edifice built by Harvard University. The university's name was emblazoned proudly in metallic letters above the seventh floor for all to see. The building would have gone unnoticed were it to stand on Harvard's idyllic Camridge campus. But here, juxtaposed against the dusty streets of the adjacent *Boitsoko* and *Phologlo* neighborhoods, it stood out like a true ivory tower. Within its hallowed walls was conducted the continent's most ambitious HIV and AIDS research. It was the epicenter for the urban and rural outreach programs within Botswana that garnered a majority of the relatively little press coverage afforded to the African AIDS epidemic. Prestigious guest lecturers from Europe and the States made their way through whenever their respective causes were in need of positive press. Visiting physicians enjoyed tropical bungalow-style housing along President's Drive or elsewhere in the *Badiri* district. The Harvard building was not so much a theater of human pain and suffering as it was a stage for controlling world opinion.

Off to the right and behind the main building was Baylor University's contribution to solving the HIV/AIDS puzzle. It was a beautiful low-rise kidney-shaped building replete with gardens, wrought iron accents, mosaic inlays, and sitting areas for quiet repose.

The architecture befit the purpose. The doctors and researchers at the Baylor facility focused solely on children with HIV. Unlike the Harvard building, the Baylor building seemed more lighthearted, less serious... more *African*. Inside, hundreds of children waited daily to be seen. To pass time during their wait, they played with puzzles and other toys while their HIV positive mothers sat beside them. Because the Baylor team only treated *children*, these mothers had to seek treatment at either the Harvard facility or the main hospital building of Princess Diana. Either way, tens of thousands of men, woman, and children alike passed through the doors of the Princess Diana Hospital as they traveled down their truncated road of life.

Directly in front of Austin was the main building on the Princess Diana Hospital. This was the general in-patient facility. This was UPenn's milieu. The operation was typical for the UPenn folks... it was a monumental challenge. Whereas Harvard and Baylor swept in with an airplane full of cash and set up shop according to their own demands, the medical staff from Penn had to function according to African Time. Austin noticed this right off the bat. The Penn folks had their work cut out for them. The building looked like your typical junior high from the outside – bricks, wide windows, breezeways. Everything seemed more or less gray. Austin paid the driver and went inside.

The ground floor was empty. There wasn't a soul around. The security desk – one of those gunmetal gray jobs Austin's elementary school teachers had – was unoccupied. People were basically free to come and go as they pleased. There was no semblance of security at all, not even a sign-in sheet. The cinder-block walls were covered with posters and announcements for various public health programs - HIV, hepatitis, prenatal care, and so on. It read like a primer in public health. There was a phone sitting on the security desk, some stairs off to his right, and an elevator in front of him.

Austin walked up to the second floor. The sun was shining intensely. Even the short walk up the flight of steps made Austin sweat a little. Then he realized how accustomed he was to a frigid, air-conditioned environment. He stopped for a moment... there was *no* air conditioning. In fact, one of the front doors on the ground floor was propped open. This really surprised Austin. Not only did he keep his apartment cold enough to keep Walt Disney from thawing out, he was an avid worshipper of the ice cube, both of which seemed the stuff of fairy tales so far in his trip. From the moment he had stepped foot on the tacky tarmac, Austin had wondered how the Batswana lived with such intense heat. He felt like a lizard desperately in need of shade. Did everyone feel this way? The funny thing was, no one seemed to sweat, at least no one he had met thus far. How could that be? Austin chalked it up to being in the wrong race in the wrong environment.

Back at the hotel, Austin was surprised to see that the guests were much like up-scale hotel guests anywhere. Now that he was out in the wild, so to speak, he realized that wealthy people are more likely to move between *facades*. It was like visiting a zoo for rich people. Imagine it for a moment... money can be a sort of *insulation* from life's underbelly. Not that being poor is any more "keeping it real" than being rich, or being a crack-addicted prostitute is any more "down to earth" than being a stock trader who drinks. Everyone has their own way of insulating themselves from the elements life hurls at them. And when you had as much money as Austin did – and made it as quickly – you might gravitate toward controlled environments, a sort of World Zoo in which the very best and the very worst of life is placed on display for your perusal. Standing there on the second-floor landing, sweating, wearing linen pants and a button-down shirt, and carrying a laptop, Austin felt like a polar bear who suddenly found himself in the middle of a tropical rain forest. He had ventured outside the zoo.

It would be simplistic to leave it at this, though. Life is far more complex. For, like his neighbors at Harvard and Baylor, Stone was indeed trying to build the finest medical zoo in Botswana. The irony struck Austin as soon as he passed through the double doors into the first-floor hallway. The dark hallway was a stark contrast to the bright, windowed stairway. Immediately, Austin noticed the distinct lack of any hustle-and-bustle. Before he departed the States, Austin was prepared for the worst. Actually, he prepared himself to be stoic in the face of untold death, disease, and filth. And of course, during his flight his imagination ran wild contemplating all the "death stories" he would hear (and perhaps have one of his own?). But again, when he checked into the hotel, he felt embarrassed more than anything else. He felt like one of those Ugly Americans that callers are always complaining about on National Public Radio, someone who deemed anything not found at an American drive-through chain store as disgusting, ignorant, or primitive. So he changed his opinion and concluded that he would meet Dr. Stone amidst something like the set of *ER*... constant beeps and pings, phones ringing off the hook, sirens blaring, energetic young doctors rushing to and from solving the latest medical conundrum.

Standing there in the hallway, dripping with sweat, neck stiff from carrying his laptop, he felt like an idiot once more. That's what he deserved for deriving his self-worth from the celery-munching tree huggers who call in to NPR. For Austin quickly realized that not a single one of them would want to get sick in Gaborone. Granted, this was only an administrative floor. Nevertheless, things were eerily quiet. Echoing down the hallway were two voices discussing something indiscernible. Other than that, all was silent. There was a heavy sense about the place. Something seemed wrong. Austin headed toward the voices.

Chapter 18

Stone sat behind a mountain of folders, files, and paperwork. His desk was the embodiment of bureaucracy. When Austin entered, Stone was talking on the phone. From the conversation Austin deduced that there was a funding shortage of some sort. Stone seemed like he dealt with this sort of thing everyday. Austin had no doubt that every issue coming across Stone's desk eventually resided somewhere in those stacks of files and papers. He also had no doubt that all that paperwork was as much a part of AIDS in Botswana as anything else in the hospital.

Stone motioned for Austin to sit down in the torn leather chair in front of his desk. Shortly thereafter, Stone hung up the phone and extended his hand to Austin.

"Tony Stone." They shook warmly. Stone's handshake matched his British accent – refined, neither too strong nor too light. Austin sensed something compassionate in Stone's touch. Aside from all the paper pushing, this man was a healer.

"It's a pleasure to meet you," said Austin.

Stone straightened one of the stacks on his desk. He was tall and thin, the embodiment of British moderation. His gray hair was parted on one side but tousled. His tie was knotted in a double

Windsor but hung lose with the collar of his blue shirt open, and his sleeves were rolled up.

"Well, I must say," said Stone, "You've come a long way just for an account. It's quite considerate of you, but you know the Board will have to approve any recommendations you make."

Austin smiled. Things started off exactly as they always did with institutional clients. The great specter of the Board revealed itself right from the get-go. It provided a convenient way out if the decision maker got cold feet come crunch time. Austin was a pro at handling such caveats. He was prepared for it. But if things started out as planned for Austin, they quickly took a turn. In Botswana, life, love, business – whatever – did not move in straight lines; they meandered. Things always turned this way or that. African time. If there was one thing Austin came to expect about living or working in Africa it was this: Your point of departure had little if anything to do with your final destination. You just go with the flow, and reset your internal mechanisms to African Time.

Stone sighed. "I'm afraid I quite forgot you were coming today, Mr. Montgomery."

Austin was thrown for a loop but tried to stay cool. He held up his hand. "Please, call me Austin."

"We really should have rung you at the hotel, but things happened quite unexpectedly."

Austin tried to keep things positive. That was the first rule of sales Johnny taught him – stay positive. "No problem. It was just a short bus ride from the States."

Stone laughed but seemed sad nonetheless. "Yes, well, I'm afraid we've had a bit of a tragedy." This did not bode well for Austin. Whenever a Brit refers to a "bit" of something, it is always far worse as in Churchill saying London was in for "a bit of a challenge" during the German bombings. The classic British understatement. The air of casual concern. Austin rolled with it as best he could.

"They're out of coffee in the commissary?" Austin suddenly felt really hot. What a stupid comeback. God only knows what had happened, and he's talking about coffee.

"I'm afraid not," said Stone. "We lost one of our doctors this weekend."

Austin caught on right away and felt even more ridiculous for his coffee comment. "Oh my, what happened?"

"We had a lovely man, Dr. Benton, visit from the States. He was a brilliant man. Started the virology department at Penn. He was working in Oregon, but he still kept us in his heart. He and his wife came out to lecture for three months. A lovely man, a really gifted teacher. We were quite fortunate to have him."

Nothing could surprise Austin any more. He flew eighteen hours for a meeting only to be forgotten about. But what was worse was that something *much worse* had actually happened. What was he supposed to do? He had to roll with it. What do you say at this point? He just nodded and gestured for Stone to continue.

"The Penn folks went up to the Okavango Delta region for a weekend. Naturally, Dr. Benton and his wife joined them. They had only been here for three weeks or so and were determined to see the country. Are you familiar with the Okavango Delta region?"

"No," said Austin. "Except that it's supposed to be fascinating."

"The Okavango Delta region is in the north of Botswana. If there is a microcosm of African wildlife, this is it. You've no doubt seen pictures of it if you've read anything on Botswana."

"I have done some reading up, yes."

"Right then. Have you seen any pictures of tourists in little boats that look like canoes?"

Austin was relieved that he could finally add something of substance. "Oh, sure. It looks amazing. I would love to do that. What an amazing trip." Indeed, the tour guides were replete with pictures of the Okavango Delta region. It was the center of Botswana's ecotourism and for good reason. The Okavango Delta was the heartland of African wildlife and just about all Western adventurers made their way into its grassy swamps to catch a glimpse of wildlife up close and personal. The little boats were about ten feet long and held two tourists plus one guide who stood in back and directed the boat with a long wood pole. The guides were usually from Jedibe Island or somewhere else in the northwestern reaches of the delta where poling around was the only form of transportation.

"Those boats are called *mokoro,*" explained Stone in a somber voice. "Once upon a time, they were actually dug out from hardwood trees. Nowadays, they're manufactured from synthetic materials and shipped in from China."

"It's really cool how close to the water you are when you're sitting in one of those things," said Austin enthusiastically. From the pictures he'd seen, it looked as if you were maybe six inches off the water.

Stone sighed. Austin sensed he'd said something wrong, although Stone didn't seem angry. He seemed genuinely sad about something. Stone looked Austin straight in the eye and said in a firm British tone, "Yes, but what people don't understand about wildlife is that it's bloody dangerous. It's not like on the BBC where you watch lovely pictures from the comfort of your living room. That's the first thing I tell the Penn people when they arrive. Africa is dangerous."

Austin sat still and silent. There was a story developing here. Yet another fascinating twist in his journey was about to reveal itself. If only he could write, what a book this would make. At this point, though, he just gave himself over to Stone's narration. It was the only proper thing to do, for it was evident that something really terrible had happened, and it was no laughing matter. Moreover, he was acutely aware that a wrong word here would surely sink his chances with the "Board."

Stone rubbed his eyes. Now that Austin looked a bit closer, the doctor looked tired. The hospital's financial woes surely couldn't be helping. "Anyway, a bunch of the Penn folks went up to the Okavango, as I was saying. Dr. Benson was in a *mokovo* with his wife."

"So what happened?" prompted Austin.

"Dr. Benson and his wife were just canoeing along when a six-meter croc shot up out of the water and locked on to Dr. Benson."

It was so absurd Austin almost laughed out loud. He managed to check himself. The incident was really funny like a comedian is funny. In fact, it was a terrible story but completely absurd as reflected in Austin's blank look. Could you imagine something like that happening back in the States? The thought was completely alien to Austin. He really didn't know what to say. He couldn't really get his imagination around it. "Six meters?" was what he managed to utter.

The doctor nodded. "Ah right, about eighteen feet," said Stone.

Austin shook his head in bewilderment. He couldn't decide what was more startling, the size of the croc or the matter-of-fact way Stone said "18 feet" as if this sort of thing was commonplace. Then again, he was just as bewildered that his eighteen hour trek for an account was about to be derailed by some prehistoric, pea-brained reptile out of some animal show like *The Crocodile Hunter.* Austin reeled his jaw back in and said "and… this is the sort of thing that happens all the time?"

Again, Stone seemed unphased. "Actually the hippos are the leading cause of tourist deaths. They run along the bottom and rush up at the *mokovo.*"

At first, Austin thought Stone was joking. But then he thought about who was speaking and realized the doctor was serious… dead serious. "Are you kidding me? Wait… so *hippos* are the leading cause of death for tourists? That's what you're telling me?"

"Of course. But in this case, the circumstances were quite similar. It's very sad. Right in front of his wife.

Austin slid forward in his seat. "Did the boat tip over?"

"No. It was similar to a hippo attack in that the croc came up from out of nowhere. The guide saw him at the very last second and yelled "Croc!" But that was it. It was over in a second."

"Really?"

"The croc shot up from under the water like a missile, grabbed the doctor by the head, and plucked him clean off the boat. I'm told it was almost silent. The doctor was taken under and never seen again." Stone snapped his fingers. "Gone just like that. One second he and his wife were chatting, and then… all that was left was his shoe which landed in his wife's lap. Can you imagine that?

The thought of losing the account was no longer on Austin's mind, and he simply blurted out "amazing." An American through and through, he said, "Didn't anyone have a damned gun? Isn't this *Africa*? Please excuse my French, but this is terrible."

Stone brushed Austin's slip of the tongue aside with his hand. "Man, there has been many a time when those very words flew from my lips, believe you me. I can tell you this, almost every visitor we get experiences some moment of shock as you just did. It's nothing to be ashamed of. Ten years later and I think I've just about seen it all, and I *still* get a bit of a 'how's your father' from time to time. Like this weekend."

Austin was fixated on the firearms issue. "But again, didn't anyone shoot the damned thing."

Stone smiled. "If it were only that easy, Austin. Things are not that simple in Africa. Remember, they were in a wildlife preserve. You may carry a rifle, but you're prohibited from shooting any animal without prior government approval."

"What? Did anyone send that memo to the crocodile?"

"They did, in fact, call for approval and received it that evening, but by then, the croc probably moved on from all the diving and dredging in search of the body. Actually, they usually find a good portion of the remains because crocodiles store their kill for a day or two to let it putrefy a bit."

Austin just shook his head. "Is that right."

"I do hope they find the body. Mrs. Benson was very concerned that they find his wedding band. Apparently it was something very special."

"Where is she now?"

"She's on a plane heading back to Oregon."

Austin thought for a moment about what the 30-hour flight to the Pacific Northwest must be like for that woman. When her trip started, she would have had absolutely no idea where she would end up. No idea whatsoever. No clue, no hint… just the trip itself. African Time had made itself known to her. It had snatched her beloved husband away in what seemed like a second. But one could not ignore the irony that crocodiles had been doing just that – in exactly the same fashion – for millions and millions of years. For a crocodile, African

Time was simply the pace of survival. Austin would later learn that Dr. Benson had nursed his first wife on her death bed for three years until she finally succumbed to the cancer that made her insides look like blue cheese. Worse yet, he was married to his second wife – his travel companion – for less than a year. The honeymoon period had no sooner ended then she was a widow. And the thing that struck Austin most of all – the thing that had grabbed him since he met Simon and Johannes – was that Africa had no particular concern for people, places, or things. For all its apparent simplicity, the neutrality of nature was complex and often confusing.

Chapter 19

To Austin's surprise, Stone adeptly changed topics. "You see Austin, I encounter death all day, every day. But I also see amazing life-saving efforts such as new HIV treatments and so on. So I am able to deal with things as they come and move on when it's time. And now I suppose it's time to address the financial issues. All of the board members are not required to be present for your presentation. There are three of us who have a say over financial matters. But of course, I have been subject to intense scrutiny about the performance of our portfolio. I may have the say about the investments, but other people – government people – have the say about my job."

Austin felt more comfortable now that things were back on track. He was prepared for this part of the encounter. He became a professional advisor again. Like a good lawyer on cross-examination, he began asking questions he already knew the answers to. "Let me ask you something, Dr. Stone. Are you feeling a lot of pressure from having to manage the hospital's portfolio?"

Stone took a deep breath. It was as if a weight was being lifted off his soul. "Austin, I'm a doctor. Well, I'm an administrator as well. But I came to Botswana to practice medicine and manage the practice of medicine. And quite frankly, you wouldn't believe the changes we've made not just in medical practices but in medical resource management." Austin sat back and let Stone continue. The doctor was well on his way to selling *himself* on Johnny's services.

Stone sat back in his chair. He groaned methodically as he did. He suddenly sounded much more business-like than Austin imagined he would be. "As a businessman, he continued, "you couldn't imagine doing your job without performance metrics, could you?" He didn't wait for Austin to answer. "Now imagine that this hospital had *no...no* system for monitoring performance, services, efficacy, anything. And in fact, a significant benefit of having so much pharma research going on here is that they create *systems* in their wake." Austin nodded. "As I'm sure you have seen, Austin, things can spiral into chaos here quite quickly. I recognized directly when I started as a physician here that a strict and disciplined system of processes and procedures was needed."

Austin crossed his leg over his knee. He recognized this as an opportunity to draw parallels between Johnny's Growth of Income Strategy and Stone's own personal history. "Oh, so you basically have a strategy for approaching every situation."

Stone held up a finger. "Well," he cautioned, "you simply can't plan for everything. Nevertheless, if you have a strategy for how to go about things on a daily basis, a reason why you do whatever you do and you try to stay consistent to it, you have that to fall back on at all times. Nothing can take *that away.*"

Austin was delighted with that response. "Medicine is like that?"

"Of course. We have a clearly delineated strategy for approaching each and every patient that comes through our doors."

Austin nodded. His question was, of course, methodical. "I'm happy you said that because, as you will see, we take the very same approach to portfolio management."

Stone seemed not to hear Austin. Or he didn't care very much. It was clear he was looking for something else. "For me, Austin, I am a physician. I've dedicated my entire life to healing. Over the last five years, as the Director of Hospital Operations, I've worked intensely on making healing more systematic." He leaned forward and looked Austin square in the eyes. "Do you understand what I'm saying."

Austin noticed the slight tremble in his voice right away. Stone was actually sweating just a bit. "Austin, I can't remember a day when I *haven't* worried about this bloody portfolio. I *do not* want to manage a bloody bond portfolio."

"Is it adversely affecting your work as a physician?" asked Austin.

Now Stone seemed as incredulous as did Austin during the crocodile story. "Is it affecting my work? For God's sake man, I'm getting buggered and there's nothing I can do about it."

"What about your current advisor?"

"Well, obviously he is not doing satisfactorily. I do not blame the man for what he has done. The problem is that *I* get blamed for what he has done. What makes it God awful is that I can never explain to the Board what is going on. I have no idea. He just buys stuff and some of it goes up and some of it goes down."

Austin had the good doctor right where he wanted him. "Would you run your hospital that way?"

"Would I run my hospital that way? Of course not. That's why you are here. I was referred to Johnny Long precisely because he is 'a man with a strategy' or so I'm told. Well, he is or he isn't. My job will be lost or won according to his performance."

"Really?" asked Austin. It seemed as if the deal was a foregone conclusion.

"Of course. You did not think you flew out here for the hell of it, did you? You're here to save my bloody job. You have to understand Austin, that this hospital was nothing like it is now. If I were to be removed – and I am not the boastful type – but if I'm removed, there is going to be a problem. Keep in mind that we have tried to place an indigenous person in my role for several years now. That was always part of the plan, and I accepted it as a natural evolution. But we have yet to find a qualified candidate at all, let alone one willing to work for what I'm paid. The pressure belongs on your Mr. Long, my friend, not on me. I'm done. I'm out, and that's that."

Stone arranged another stack on his desk and stood up. "Ah yes. Shall we meet the rest of the decision makers, so to speak?"

Austin was a bit surprised. "Oh, right now? Are they waiting for us?"

Stone laughed. "Austin, scheduling is quite different here than it is in the States. The other two blokes are on the premises tending to their work. We'll just gather them and you can make your presentation."

"Well, OK, then." Austin was somewhat relieved actually. He was a bit worried about giving a formal presentation to a large board of directors seated around a huge table.

Stone led the way down the hallway. Things were still pretty quiet. He spoke to Austin over his shoulder. "This part of the facility houses mostly administrative offices. Naturally, things are a bit more active where the patients are."

"I would like to see that."

"I was planning on taking you around after your presentation if you have scheduled the time for it."

Austin laughed to himself. Had he scheduled the time for it? What else was he going to do? He was eighteen hours from home. His schedule was pretty wide open. He looked at his watch with mock exaggeration. "Hmm... I *was* going to take a *mokovo* ride, but I suppose that can wait now."

"Indeed," replied Stone as he passed through a set of double doors and headed up a dingy set of stairs.

Chapter 20

Dr. Stone showed Austin a seat in a small conference room before leaving to find his colleagues. Austin intended to do a Power Point presentation on his laptop. But as he surveyed the room, he could not find a screen or projector. He took it for granted that the hospital's board room would have all the necessary A/V equipment, but he was quite wrong. The laptop he had been lugging around all day would be largely useless. Thank God he thought ahead and made printed color copies of the presentation for distribution. The room had an old white board and some pictures of various historical leaders. Most notable was a reproduction of a famous Livingstone portrait by F. Havill. It was the sort of painting that hung in the National Portrait Gallery. The dark-haired, mustached Livingstone looked off in the distance to his left, as if he was setting his sights on his next mission. With a broad chin, nose, and forehead, he looked staunch and resolute, the epitome of Scottish determination.

No sooner had Austin stepped foot on Botswana soil than he noticed the omnipresence of Livingstone. He was as much a part of Botswana – Gaborone in particular – as anything else. In a way that was completely inexplicable by modern post-colonial theory, Livingstone was a *part* of Botswana in a way that no Botswana would do without. And that was that. And on this point, it was no coincidence that Jill Stone's father was the last surviving missionary from Livingstone's missionary organization. Tony Stone may have been under the gun for his role in the hospital's losing portfolio, but he was extremely well-connected. And in Botswana, like anywhere else, that mattered.

While Austin was booting up his laptop, he heard Stone and his colleagues coming down the hallway. The most senior, Stone entered first followed by a man and a woman. Stone introduced Austin, and they all took a seat around the scratched wooden table. The man and woman were both full-time staff at the hospital and, therefore, unaffiliated with Penn. Dr. Robert Silvia was the Director of Inpatient Operations. This meant that he played a crucial role not just in day-to-day delivery of services but in the politics of HIV as well. For it was Silvia who ruled over the historical record keeping – the classification, the documentation, the administration, in short, the politicization – of HIV as a medical record, as a *historical fact*. Accordingly, Silvia carried himself with importance. In reality, Stone ran the hospital and delivered quality services to a destitute, AIDS-racked population. On the other hand, Silvia lorded over hospital records with the ambition of a man determined to write history. What made Silvia such a valuable asset, however, was that his "figures" generated an immense amount of publicity and, most importantly, grant money. If Stone *ran* the hospital, Silvia funded it. And so Silvia and Stone were growing increasingly at odds over the performance of the account.

In Silvia's mind, that money belonged *to him*. It was only some organizational snafu that put Stone in charge of the investment decisions. It was true, a large portion of the endowment came from AIDS treatment programs and research grants. That meant that the money flowed through Silvia. But people mostly humored him to avoid confrontation. Everyone knew Stone had tremendous influence because of his father-in-law's history with Livingstone. In fact, Stone's father-in-law was the first mayor of Gaborone. More importantly though, Stone's work turning the hospital around did not go unnoticed. He was something of a legend around Gaborone, and more and more hospital administrators from around Africa were contacting him regularly about including him in conferences around the world.

Stone's growing renown among his worldwide colleagues did not make matters any better where Silvia was concerned. Stone could live with Silvia's snide remarks circulated via e-mail. Roughly each fiscal quarter, Silvia would shoot something out on e-mail largely to distance and exculpate himself from the losses. In this regard, Silvia was of little consequence. But truth be told, the performance of the endowment fund *was* eating into Stone's stack of chips and IOUs with government higher-ups who *really* called the shots at the hospital. Stone was just about out of favors. If things didn't change, he would surely be dismissed and his reputation besmirched with whispers of fraud and embezzlement.

As it was with any institutional account, Austin would have to discern these politics very quickly indeed. Moreover, he would have to negotiate this delicate terrain in such a way as to bring everyone *together* under a common system. The strategy – Johnny's or otherwise – had to be agreeable to everyone and could not be perceived as accommodating a single person's agenda. Johnny had a simple way of dealing with such challenges. His three questions were designed, in part, to level the playing field, so to speak, for more often than not, *all* the prospects he addressed were *exactly* the same in one way; namely, they could not answer at least one of the questions – What do you buy, when do you sell, and what do you do with the proceeds? Once everyone recognized that they were suffering from the same insufficiency of information, individual politics succumbed to self-interest because everyone was vulnerable in exactly the same way.

This accomplished, Austin would have to bring Stone and Silvia closer together in order to circumvent the growing divide between the two men. However, the third board member, Dr. Hylia Pantelia, would be a far greater challenge. She had earned both an MBA and an M.D. from Harvard and often oscillated between professional identities. Around the hospital, Pantelia earned her colleagues respect daily. Her work with HIV-positive children was the sort of hands-on care not spawned from personal ambition. To the contrary, Pantelia went about her business with a sense of stubborn determination so characteristic of her ancient Greek ancestors.

Despite her prestigious degrees, Pantelia had little concern for money. Hers was the sort of disdain for money that came from having too much of it her entire life. She chose to work in Botswana because AIDS infuriated her, especially when children were at risk. For Pantelia, money was a necessary evil and could very well be used for the good of the world. Thus, the hospital's endowment represented potential... the potential for healing. Any significant drop in the portfolio would result in a barrage of questions which Stone simply could not answer. It was no surprise, then, that she had a long list of questions prepared for Austin. She was neither against him nor for him; she just wanted the bleeding to stop, and she would support anyone who could do that.

After brief introductions, everyone took their seat. Not having a projector or any other technology, Austin had to rough it. He started in as planned, just like he discussed with Johnny.

He leaned in, cleared his throat, and dug in. "I know in my career, I have more than I can handle sometimes just tending to the daily demands of my job." He paused and waited for the nods of approval from the doctors. He knew they would come around. "So I don't know *how* you can focus on the overwhelming medical responsibilities you all have here and *still* worry about the performance of the endowment account." The three doctors laughed out loud. Austin started rolling. Now that he had them all in agreement with each other and all on the same side of the table, he set about presenting the need for his services.

"It seems to me that a hospital like this depends on every single penny it has for daily operations. As I understand it, there are several problems here." Austin caught the look Silvia gave to Stone and took action. "But I have to say," said Austin, "this is nothing that cannot be addressed pretty easily. Easier than you think, in fact."

Silvia cleared his throat. "Believe me Mr. Montgomery, we've been *addressing* the problem for some time now." He made quotes around the word "addressing."

Pantelia jumped in. "So Mr. Montgomery, you believe we can *correct* the problem? I think that's what Dr. Silvia is saying."

Silvia smiled – he had that way about himself – and responded, "Hylia, you know very well that we *talk* about this all the time. Do you know what I had to do to bring that money in?"

Pantelia laughed. "Yes, yes, Bob" – she was the only one who didn't call him Robert – "and we all love you for it. That's why we're here."

Stone spoke up. "I suggest we all focus on the future and spare Mr. Montgomery our prattling." He turned to Austin. "Please continue."

Austin sought once more to establish unity among the group. He turned to Silvia. "True, past performance is important to understanding your *tendencies* as investors and also in assessing whether or not your needs were met." Then he looked at Pantelia. "Other than that, though, we need to focus on what to do *going forward*, and here I would start off by stating simply..." He paused for effect. "I do not believe your portfolio to be an *investor's* portfolio."

"Really?" said Silvia almost immediately.

Stone spoke. "Interesting. Please explain."

Things were going just as Johnny said they would. Austin was really enjoying himself. He missed that feeling, that buzz of excitement that comes when you light a fire and people come. "Well, I think you folks are *savers*, not investors. There's a huge difference." Pantelia nodded her head and seemed to have one of those ah-ha moments. "A saver is someone who places safety of principal above all else."

Dr. Silvia looked puzzled. "Well, isn't that our goal?"

"Yes and no," replied Austin. "You see," He scratched his head and appeared to look puzzled. "It's just not that simple. Yes, protection of principal is an important goal, but not *the only goal*. Do you see the difference?"

"We have several needs for the money," said Pantelia.

Austin nodded. "That's *exactly right*, doctor." Austin tapped his finger against the table for emphasis. "In your case, you need to protect principal as much as possible. But you *also* need *income* to cover expenses. *This* is the problem, right? *This* is where the rubber meets the road, so to speak, with fixed-income."

"Isn't that the trade off, though?" asked Silvia.

Austin turned to Stone. "Dr. Stone, maybe you can help me out." Stone smiled. "OK then, tell me - over the last, say, fifteen years, has the cost of medicine gone down?" Everyone laughed. Austin didn't wait for an answer. "Of course, it hasn't. More importantly, though, did it go up more than eight percent a year to stay even with your fixed-income interest?"

"I wish it only went up eight percent a year."

"Or you had a bond yielding twenty percent, right?" said Austin. They all laughed. He had them going a bit now. "And in general, is it safe to assume that the overall costs of treating a patient has increased at a rate far, far greater than the interest rate on your fixed-income portfolio?"

"My goodness yes," replied Stone.

"Increasing cost of services is something that will never change," added Pantelia.

"Sure," said Austin. "Now, think about this. You are really no different than any person buying fixed-income. You want protection of principal *and* you want income. But it has *never* ceased to amaze me that fixed-income buyers – *savers* – don't first assess what they actually *require* for income. It's as if they just sort of buy the highest yield offered with the rating they're looking for." Austin turned to Dr. Stone. "Sound familiar?" Stone smiled.

Silvia was getting a bit antsy. He asked Stone, "Doesn't our investment person know this?"

"I don't know that it has anything to do with him, though, Bob," said Pantelia. Stone just sort of shrugged.

"It doesn't," said Austin. "Now, don't get me wrong, *who* you choose as your investment advisor has *everything* to do with how your money is invested. But it seems to me that you probably just told the guy to protect the money."

"That's more or less correct," said Stone.

Silvia needed some clarification. "So what you are saying, Mr. Montgomery, is that we based our investment decisions – or rather, Dr. Stone based his investment decisions – on protection of principal rather than income needs."

"I can't answer for Dr. Stone or your advisor. What I *can* say, however, is that *by definition* a bond *saver* always subordinates return to safety of principal, which in and of itself is fine. The problem – the serious problem – occurs when your income falls short of your needs. Then you have a problem."

That's what's happening right, Tony?" Pantelia asked Stone.

"Exactly," he replied.

"But this is what *always* happens with bond savers," said Austin for re-emphasis. "Again, you are no different from the person who switches everything into fixed income and retires. You have whatever sources of income you may have. After that, what do you do when you need money?"

This was something Stone knew all too well. "Unfortunately, you have to dip into the principal."

"Of course you do. This is where the trouble begins. It's like a downward spiral. First, you exhaust what income you have. But your needs are in excess. So you sell off some of your fixed income investments to cover the shortfall. Now your principal is less, we know your operational needs, or retirement needs, or whatever certainly aren't going down... but guess what. You have less now invested in fixed income so your *income goes down*. Sure you can live on a budget, but what if you need more money? Then what? You, the bond saver, have a big problem. You might even be selling off at a *loss* prior to maturity."

"This doesn't sound very promising," said Pantelia. Silvia let out a sarcastic snort.

"Promising?" said Austin. "Well, I can *promise* you this. Most bond savers find that their financial needs increase steadily over the years while their rates stay fixed."

"I guess that's why they call it fixed income, isn't it Mr. Montgomery?" stated Dr. Pantelia.

Austin smiled at Pantelia. "Yes indeed, Dr. Pantelia. Yes indeed. Only your interest stays fixed. Nothing else stays fixed, does it Dr. Stone?"

"I'm afraid not," responded the doctor.

"Most bond savers ladder their portfolio. Are you all familiar with that term?" They all nodded. Nevertheless, Pantelia asked "Is that when you have different maturities for the bonds and CDs?"

"Sort of. A laddered portfolio of fixed income means that your bonds and CDs mature one after the other at different times so that there is always money available. You then go on and reinvest the money. Well, this works OK if rates are constant or higher when you reinvest. But what if they're not? What then?"

Stone leaned in closer and got ready to take notes. "Can you please expand on that."

"Sure," said Austin. "Let's say that you had a million dollars in fixed income ten years ago. If you built a so-called laddered portfolio, you would divide the money into ten different investments each with a different maturity date. Some would come due in, say, two years, others in five, others in ten, twenty, thirty. It depends on your cash-flow needs. But of course, if you don't take your *income needs* as paramount or if you simply don't know when you're going to need money, this may not necessarily work for you."

"This is what we have currently," said Stone.

"That is not your fault or your advisor's fault. It is nobody's fault. This is how ninety percent of bond savers invest their money. And like I said, it's not investing at all. You see, as time went on, you saw rates do what, Dr. Stone?" asked Austin.

The doctor shook his head. "Rates kept going lower over the years."

Silvia jumped in here. "That's not entirely true. Rates moved up sometimes."

Austin came to the director's defense. "You are both correct. The point is, however, that those fluctuations in interest rates are nothing when compared to the long-term decline in rates over the last twenty years."

"Really," said Pantelia.

"And now stop and think how many people, institutions, and the like own a laddered maturity bond portfolio. Just think about that. Millions of people just like you folks saw their income sinking lower and lower each time they reinvested their money at lower and lower rates. And remember too, that every time you dip into principal to cover shortfalls, you have less to invest. So that's *less and less* to invest at *lower and lower* rates." Austin paused a moment. "Dr. Silvia, how does that sound to you?"

Silvia snorted again. "It sounds bloody awful, that's how it sounds."

"Let me tell you," said Stone. "It has been terrible for me. Hylia, you know that. You talk to Jill. There was really nothing I could do."

Austin looked at Hylia. "That's totally correct. The problem is that you were savers, not investors. Success is not possible under these circumstances. In fact, savers by definition cannot be successful *investors* because they are always constrained by the fixed nature of fixed income." As if on cue, a woman appeared with tea service. Her timing was impeccable as it allowed time for Austin's comments to sink in. He already knew where he was going next, but it was always better for clients to make the leap themselves. He was waiting for a collective ah-ha moment.

Pantelia dipped a biscuit in her milky tea. "So according to your analogy, it's like a downward spiral because when it comes time to reinvest, rates are lower, so your income keeps declining. Is that it?" She nibbled her biscuit where the Earl Grey soaked in. "So... this isn't really going to change, is it?"

"Fixed income is fixed income," replied Austin. "That's the problem. It doesn't change. Only your needs do."

Pantelia actually seemed a bit relieved. She was the type of person who worried most about what she didn't know. Now that she knew the mechanisms of the game, so to speak, she knew what had to be overcome. She liked having a certain order of things. Her Greek ancestors would have referred to her as Apollinian in nature, the embodiment of order, structure, knowledge. Interestingly, the Apollinian spirit is the spirit of music. Born of form and structure, music adheres to certain laws, certain... strategies. For the Greeks, as for Tony Pickett, music always gestured toward something beyond itself, something unobtainable and pure, something infinite. This was the Dionysian, the spirit of chaos and destruction, the *uncontrollable*. And precisely because chaos cannot be controlled or understood, the Greeks felt compelled to worship just as equally an order of things, systems, strategies. This is, after all, the essence of irony as the

Greeks understood it. And if the markets represented a type of chaos, then Johnny's strategies represented order. They were not guarantees. But they were a means of understanding and capitalizing on the uncontrollable.

Robert Silvia was not so well-balanced, however. He could be set off by something or nothing. That's why his colleagues walked on eggshells around him. They were as likely to offend him as please him. Both Austin and Stone saw the twitch in Silvia's left eye getting more pronounced. Seemingly out of the blue, though, Silvia cocked his head and seemed to have an epiphany. Like Pantelia, he actually seemed more relaxed.

He cleared his throat and straightened up in his chair. He was clearly on to something. "Please correct me if I am mistaken, Mr. Montgomery. What you're saying here is that we have been getting a fixed income over all these years, and that income has been steadily decreasing because the interest rates on the new investments are *lower*. Is that correct?" Pantelia nodded her head in agreement with Silvia's assessment.

Austin nodded as well. "Umm... yes that's exactly right."

Silvia turned to Stone. "Tony, were you aware of this?"

"Yes, of course," he replied. "But one can only purchase what is available at the time."

"If rates are low, rates are low," added Pantelia.

Silvia nodded his head slowly as if he were contemplating something much deeper than the obvious fact that fixed income – bonds, CDs, whatever – will pay only as much as rates indicate. "So... you're saying there was nothing paying any higher interest whenever you went to invest some money," continued Silvia.

Stone knew the answer, but he waited for Austin to give him a reassuring nod. "If you recall," said Stone, "our primary concern is *protection of principal*."

Silvia seemed to miss Stone's point. "Well that didn't work out too well," he responded.

Austin jumped back in at this point. "Well, we need to understand something here. I reviewed the performance of your portfolio over the last several years. It's important to understand that you didn't *lose* any money, you *spent* it. It was a kind of double whammy. While you spent principal to cover rising expenses, you had less and less to reinvest. That, coupled with consistently decreasing rates is why your account has gone down in value so much. But remember," Austin waited until he had everyone's full attention. "Remember... your fixed-income investments were very, very safe. In fact, in most cases you were guaranteed to get your money back upon maturity. A big problem is that rates were generally *half* of what they were when you first invested. So when your bonds and CDs started coming due, you got all your money back, but you were forced to reinvest the money at much lower rates. Do you understand?" Austin looked at everyone. They nodded, but he still felt he needed to reinforce the point.

"Look, you could have gotten much higher rates. But you would have had to sacrifice safety of principal. It's that simple. Rates and safety work inversely."

Pantelia scratched her head. "This is all very frustrating," she said sardonically. "It's enough to drive you mad."

"So if we want to assume more risk," added Stone, "we may actually have to forfeit the guarantee of getting our money back or even getting the interest payment we're entitled to."

"Really?" said Pantelia.

"That's right," answered Austin. "Many, many companies – high-yield companies – default on their interest payments. And then where are you? You can lose everything."

"What about preferred stocks. Don't they generate income?" asked Stone.

"Is that an option?" added Pantelia.

"Not for you," answered Austin. "Again, it's a very rational concept. You cannot get more income from equally safe or more safe fixed income vehicles. For the most part, it's going to be six in one hand, half a dozen in the other. If you want triple-A insured paper, you will get X percent for the most part. If you're willing to take B+ paper, you will get Y percent interest for the most part. There are some exceptions, but believe me, the markets are very, very efficient in this regard. Now remember this... CDs and bonds have a *maturity date.*"

"That's the guarantee?" asked Pantelia.

"Well," replied Austin, "it's a guarantee that at a certain date in the future, you will get your principal back. You are essentially lending money to the bond issuer, and they are going to pay you back at a specified time in the future. The higher the quality of the bond, that is, the stronger the company borrowing money from you, the higher the investment grade. Sometimes you can even buy bonds that are actually *insured*. This is *much, much* safer than preferred stocks which have *no maturity date at all*." Austin pounded his finger on the table for emphasis. "Let me repeat that," he continued. "Preferred stocks do *not* have a maturity date and are much riskier. They could literally go to zero." He looked at Pantelia to make sure she got his point.

The doctor nodded. "So you can get a higher rate, but you are taking a lot more risk, yeah?"

Austin smiled. "That's exactly right. And keep this in mind as well... preferred stocks are *still* a form of fixed income, right?" The three doctors each had blank stares.

"I thought it's a stock?" asked Dr. Pantelia.

"OK, OK... when a new preferred stock is issued, it is issued with a *predetermined dividend* rate. The stock is priced at, say twenty dollars with a ten percent dividend rate."

"That rate is not guaranteed?" asked Silvia.

"Ah... only if you bought the stock at the original issue price, or twenty dollars. It's a stock and the price can fluctuate dramatically. If you bought that same preferred stock at twenty-three dollars, your effective rate would be *lower*. Conversely, if you bought that preferred issue when the price was lower, you would get a rate higher than ten percent. It works inversely. The lower that preferred sinks, the higher the dividend yield."

Stone spoke up. "But I have seen bonds move up and down in price as well."

Austin nodded. "True, bonds move around in value, sometimes substantially, as interest rates fluctuate. But again, if you buy high-quality fixed income, it is fairly certain and sometimes even insured that you will get your money back. There are no such guarantees with preferred stocks, and even using the word 'guarantee' is somewhat inappropriate. The higher the rate, the greater the risk. It really is that simple."

"The higher the rate, the greater the risk," repeated Pantelia.

"Yes," confirmed Austin. "So let's get this straight. Fixed income will pay a rate *inversely* to its level of safety. You can't get blood from a stone."

Stone spoke up again. "Mr. Montgomery, this is no less reassuring. I was rather hoping for a viable alternative to stem the bleeding."

"Indeed," said Silvia.

Austin smiled. "Doctors... doctors... do you really think I flew all the way out here to offer you more fixed income? Come now," he said jokingly. "I have far greater ambitions for you folks. After all, the work you do here as doctors is something I could never do. But I can certainly do my part to ensure that you have the financial opportunity to continue doing it."

"That is exactly what I was hoping," said Pantelia.

"Indeed," added Stone, "it would be a much welcomed change if you could turn things around and let me be a doctor again."

"We all came to Botswana, Mr. Montgomery, because we felt a certain calling. Regardless of what that calling was for each of us, we all came here to practice medicine," said Pantelia. She looked at Stone before she continued. "As Dr. Stone knows, I too deal with finance all day, more so than I deal with patients these days. That's not my calling. The point is this. I am not a professional money manager, and I really don't care to be. That's not why I up and moved to Africa."

Stone followed up. "Yes, Mr. Montgomery. I think Dr. Pantelia speaks for us all, eh?"

This was the part Austin relished, the big revelation, the sort of moment Johnny Long was all about. "In that case, I am happy to say that *there is another way.*" He paused to let his declaration sink in. "Your situation is all too common for fixed-income buyers. You are *all* in the same boat. So this is not about playing the blame game or living in the past."

"It was so much money, Mr. Montgomery," said Pantelia.

"Of course, I don't mean to belittle your losses. I was once in a similar situation, or at least had to make similar decisions. That was when *I* found Johnny Long. Now it is your time. He used to tell me this about losses. I always felt better afterward. He used to say that knowing when *to sell...* when *to sell* is the key to successful investing. You can sit on your portfolio indefinitely, that doesn't mean your needs will be met or that things will come back. Indeed, I dare say they will not on both accounts. What you have to invest – your investable assets – is what you have to invest at any given time. It makes absolutely *no* difference what you had yesterday or the day before. The only thing that matters is what you will have in the future. Yesterday's losses are irrelevant. What you do with today's money is the issue."

Austin finished off his Earl Grey and cleared his throat. "So, what was lost in the past was lost in the past. It is gone, it's never coming back. Time to move on. But here is the mistake most fixed-income buyers make. They do *the exact same thing as they did in the past.* Expecting different results is crazy."

Dr. Stone nodded. "I know exactly what you mean, Mr. Montgomery."

Austin smiled. "I mean if you were treating patients for some unknown disease, but they kept dying year after year, would you continue to employ the same treatment, use the same strategy in the future?" He looked to Silvia. "Would you Doctor?"

"Of course not."

"You would search for a better treatment plan, right."

Silvia nodded. "Of course."

"Well it's no different here. I dare say, physician heal thyself, right? Employing the same fixed-income strategy – if we can even call it a strategy – is simply *not* going to give you different results. How can that be? Nevertheless, all fixed-income buyers continue to make the same mistake again and again. But I don't really think it's a mistake per se." Austin paused again for dramatic effect. This was a major point in his presentation. "I think it is a *lack of knowledge.* Specifically, I think fixed-income buyers simply don't know any alternative exists."

"Without assuming any more risk? How can that be?" asked Silvia.

"It can't be. Like I said earlier, you can't get blood from a stone. Unfortunately, you've been bleeding to death and need a transfusion immediately. That means taking more risk, but *not*... I repeat *not* haphazardly."

Well," said Stone, "we are in something of a quandary. Your medical analogy is correct. We are bleeding to death, and the treatment we have been using is ineffective in meeting our needs, so to speak. So please continue."

"Johnny Long is brilliant in his simplicity. He is also a master of analogy. Before I came here, he told me to think of you as a patient. He said you would understand that very easily. Think of it as if you were dying of thirst. What you need is water. Similarly, you need a certain degree of safety with your principal. Without it, you will die. At the same time, however, if you drink *too much* water, your electrolytes actually become *too* diluted and you can die. This happens to marathoners quite often."

"So you're saying that too much safety will kill us just the same, right?" asked Silvia.

"Essentially, that is correct. But there *is* another way. And once people find out about this alternative, their lives take a turn for the better."

Silvia grimaced. "I'm confused, Mr. Montgomery. On the one hand, you've told us that we have to have safety of principal. On the other hand, though, you are saying that we are too safe."

Austin smiled and pointed straight at Silvia. "That's the conundrum, isn't it. *Everyone* who buys fixed-income faces that same problem. That's what I was trying to say. Safe is not safe when it can't return what you need. In fact, that's very, very risky... as you have seen firsthand. The question you should be asking, the question *all* fixed-income savers should be asking, is this: Based on the amount of principal I have, what rate of return do I need to maintain my needs, budget projections, lifestyle, plans, or whatever."

Stone looked concerned. "So what you're saying is that we have been going about it backward?" He rubbed his face in exasperation.

"Is that what you're saying?" asked Pantelia.

Johnny always made it a point not to attack other financial advisors, and Austin was not about to start now. Things were going quite well. And anyway, this problem is symptomatic of fixed-income buyers in general. "First... yes you were going about it exactly backward. Second, this is not unique to you. This is almost automatic unless you happen to catch an upswing in rates. It's usually short lived though."

Stone cleared his throat. "So then what is this 'other way' you mentioned?"

Silvia snorted. "Yes, I certainly would like to know."

Austin loved this part of the presentation. He followed Johnny's road map, and it always brought clients to the point where they *want* to know more. Johnny taught Austin how to let clients do the hard work for him. "OK, so we've established that you need to protect your principal but that the *income itself* is just as important if not more so. In this scenario, fixed income will not help you reach your goals. In fact, as you have all seen, it may actually *prohibit* you from attaining them. And this has absolutely nothing... *nothing* to do with your advisor, or the quality of the bonds, or Dr. Stone, or anything else for that matter. It is simply the nature of the beast." Austin turned to Dr. Stone and smiled. "No offense intended, doctor."

Stone smiled. "None taken. But please continue. It sounds as if you are working up to something interesting."

"Well, I was saying that fixed income is very limited in its upside because the end result is determined and, in many cases, guaranteed. Come the maturity date, you will get your initial investment back having earned so much interest income. Aside from price shifts while the bond or CD ages toward maturity, there is little market activity as compared to the stock market. With high-quality fixed income, there is very little if any speculation. That's why returns are so low."

Silvia cocked his head. "Are you suggesting we put some of the money in stocks instead of bonds?"

"We need to play catch up?" asked Stone.

"That sounds a little dangerous," responded Pantelia. "After all, we still have… what… fifty million dollars in the account."

"A little over fifty million," answered Stone.

Austin waited for everyone to settle back down. "I am not suggesting that you put some of the money in stocks just like that." Austin made quotes with his fingers. "A 'growth of income portfolio' as that would be called is not what I'm talking about. Nor am I advocating a 'total return' approach. If your stocks do well, your returns are often diminished by the bonds. Your bonds generate very little income because you have money in stocks. So where are you in the end? Your total return is often below the S&P 500 Index, and your income does not total anywhere near what you need."

Dr. Pantelia nodded her head. "I see… it sounds almost counterproductive."

Austin didn't answer her. Instead he let her comments speak for themselves. Johnny Long always believed that leading clients to one of those Ah-Ha moments and then watching the look on their faces when they make the final connection is what teaching was all about. Johnny always saw himself as a teacher. He imparted this to Austin. He taught Austin to teach himself; then he taught him to teach others.

Hylia Pantelia had that look on her face. "Yes, I get it now." She looked at Stone and nodded. The knot Stone had growing in his gut for the past year suddenly started to unwind. He smiled back at her. "All these mutual funds and glitzy money managers do quite a bit to dress up the fact that fixed income can't really do the trick."

Stone jumped in. "Or else they use fixed income to stabilize stocks. But like you said, Hylia—"

Silvia actually finished Stone's sentence. "It seems counterproductive. Bloody hell this really steams me."

Pantelia laughed. "Why Dr. Silvia, I do believe we are seeing a new you? And I didn't put it quite that way, love."

Now that Austin felt everyone was on the same page, he continued. "You see, you can't get sucked into the marketing game. Of course, every product has marketing. I suppose what I mean to say is something I learned from Mr. Long a few years ago.

In his years as a financial advisor, Johnny Long never ceased to be amazed at how little his prospects knew about other investment options available to them. For Johnny, making a prospect into a client is an *educational* process akin to a spiritual conversion." Austin underwent this conversion himself. He became a believer the moment he realized that there was *"another way,"* to use Johnny's phrase. Johnny saw himself as more than just a man with a plan. He saw himself as a *teacher* opening up new possibilities. Long a student of psychology, Johnny knew that he could not bully people into following his strategy; they had to see the benefits *themselves*, they had to convert, become believers. Johnny's clients – Austin among them – had tremendous *faith* in him not because he had a better way for them to follow blindly. Instead, they came to see things for *themselves,* and this made all the difference.

But Johnny did not see it as "faith" per se. Instead, he believed his clients gave him great *trust* and belief. This is very, very different from faith, a distinction that, ironically, Austin was never able to completely sort out for himself. Faith involves a trust and belief in something one *will never see for oneself.* Thus, faith is eschatological. One can have faith in God, one can have faith in wisdom, the soul, and so on. All faith involves trust and belief. But not all trust and belief involves faith. There exist forces of *reason* – equally a matter of trust and belief – to counterbalance faith. Johnny's clients were self-interested; they wanted to make as much money as possible. But they were not just going to fork over all their money to Johnny. Instead, Johnny had to earn their trust by showing them another way. His clients had to believe in Johnny's strategies by experiencing firsthand the returns Johnny generated. Indeed in most cases, Johnny's clients started him out with a small percentage of their investable assets and kept feeding him more as their returns grew. They had to see *proof* first. This is not faith.

And so Austin explained to the three doctors that there was, in fact, another way and that for the first time, they would learn of a cure for their financial ailment. "You have to understand," he told them, "that very few people ever see past this or that mutual fund, bond, or CD." The doctors nodded. "I dare say, very few *advisors* ever develop beyond this cursory level of sales and asset gathering. They just focus on bringing in as much money as they can and hand it over to the so-called 'real professionals' running the mutual funds.

Either that, or they'll buy some bonds. How has that worked for you? It's killing you."

Stone let out an enormous sigh. "Yes lad, but why?"

Austin smiled. It was the perfect transition. "Well... and you all need to pay careful attention to what I am about to tell you... according to your desired goal of meeting your fiscal needs over the years to come, you have simply been putting your money where it doesn't belong."

Pantelia look surprised. "Really?"

"Yes, please explain," said Dr. Stone.

"Well, it's quite simple actually. Your income needs *increase* over time, right?"

"Correct," replied Silvia.

"Well then... *fixed income* – emphasis on *fixed* – is inadequate for meeting that goal."

Before Austin could jump into the details of Johnny's Growth of Income Strategy, there came a timid knock at the door. In walked a young Batswana dressed in green scrubs. Austin assumed she was a nurse. She was maybe 5'3 with zitty skin, the signature perfect body possessed by so many Batswana women, and very close-cropped hair. She couldn't be more than 18 or 19 years old. Her buzz cut made her large eyes seem even larger and more solemn, as if she had grown quite accustomed to seeing what she would prefer not to see.

She lowered her head when she approached Dr. Stone. "I am sorry to interrupt you, Doctor," she said in a hushed tone. "You asked for this report right away, so Chief Nurse Masire told me to bring it right to you." She handed Stone some papers and left without further comment.

"Ah yes. Excuse me a moment, Mr. Montgomery." Stone thumbed through the papers shaking his head from time to time.

"Was she a nurse?" asked Austin.

"I think she is a junior nurse," replied Silvia. Stone nodded as he thumbed through the report.

"They can do quite well for themselves as nurses," added Pantelia. "They come in from the country because they can make, what..." she looked at Silvia.

" I'd have to say around thirty-five thousand U.S. for a senior nurse. A senior physician is making around eighty-five thousand."

"That's an enormous amount of money for this area, isn't it?" asked Austin.

"Yes, it is. Welcome to our overhead," answered Silvia.

Pantelia had to interject, "Although a flat in the city will run them over half of their income."

"Still," retorted Silvia, "they share a flat and do quite nicely."

"Nevertheless," Pantelia came back, "many of the junior nurses like her commute from the countryside."

Dr. Stone interrupted them. "Well-" he looked at Silvia. "Looks like another thirty thousand lost in expired drugs."

Silvia turned beat red. "What the hell is going on with the inventory in the dispensary? Can't they count?" He looked at Austin. "At this rate, we'll *never* be able to meet increasing costs. This is ridiculous. Last month we spent, Mr. Montgomery, two hundred thousand on new equipment that half of the native staff *still* can't use."

Austin seized the opportunity to get back on track with his presentation. "I am certain that a degree of cost cutting will help make ends meet. Cutting waste and making the business lean, as they say, is always wise. What I focus on is the income side of things. Like I was saying, you really need a portfolio that provides growth of income rather than just income. Do you see the difference? I am talking about buying investments that actually pay out *a higher and higher dividend over time.*"

Now that the doctors were once again focused on Austin, they all looked rather startled. "Really?" asked Pantelia.

"Honestly, Mr. Montgomery, I didn't know there was such a thing."

For a moment, however fleeting, Silvia wasn't sure if he was angry at Stone for his investment ignorance or elated with Austin for his perspicacity. Pantelia caught it right away. "Why Dr. Silvia, are you actually smiling?"

"Absolutely not," he replied. To cover up his momentary sign of weakness, he chided Stone. "I honestly don't understand how this is all new to you, doctor. Is this fellow really so unique in his ways?"

"It is for me," answered Stone.

"The important point is that you are starting to see that there is another way, right? It is very important for you to understand that there is another way. Most people never get this privilege. Once again, I am talking about investing – not saving – investing in income vehicles that actually pay *increasing* dividends over time."

Dr. Silvia jumped in. "Then this Growth-of-Income Strategy you're recommending consists of stocks? "

"Yes, that's right," answered Austin.

Silvia made one of his sour faces now famous around the corridors of Princess Diana Hospital. "*Entirely* of stocks? Are you sure that's wise?"

Austin smirked just a bit. He always got a kick out of clients who questioned Johnny's methods as if they actually knew what they were talking about. "That's a great question, doctor. Excellent, excellent." The other doctors nodded. "As I said earlier, I am very concerned with risk. But remember… *risk* is very, very different from volatility."

Silvia caught Austin's eyes as he spoke. "Like you said, Mr. Montgomery, bonds can be both volatile *and* you can lose a lot of money."

"Really?" asked Pantelia. "How so?"

"No matter how volatile the bond market over the duration of your bond, you are guaranteed your principal back – plus interest – at a certain point in the future."

"Provided you buy high-quality bonds," added Stone again.

"Correct again," replied Austin. "So you see, Dr. Silvia, there is volatility and then there is risk of loss. They are two very different concepts when looking for income." Austin pressed forward before Silvia could backtrack on him again. "The strategy that I am proposing for the hospital does not utilize any sort of fixed-income vehicles. I want to make this very clear from the outset. OK?" Stone and Pantelia nodded; Silvia withheld response. "Good, because it's important that you realize there *are no* maturity dates in play here. Your portfolio will consist of utility stocks with a certain future of dividend increases, *not... not* utility bonds."

Johnny instructed Austin very carefully on this point. It was imperative that clients understood the increased volatility and risk they were taking on when they used Johnny's Growth-of-Income Strategy. "There are no guarantees," Austin told them. "Just like with a bond, you could conceivably lose money. But unlike the AAA-rated bonds and CDs you have now, you are not assured of either a fixed rate of return or principal protection."

Silvia couldn't hold back. "So why would we want to sign up for that? Haven't we lost enough already?"

Austin clapped his hands together. "Ah-ha! Think about what you just said."

Silvia looked around the room. "What? Why would we want to do that?"

"No... the other thing."

"You mean, haven't we lost enough already?"

Austin pointed with both hands. "That's right! Think about what you just said. As safe as your portfolio supposedly is, you've been losing quite a bit of money. How can that be?"

Stone jumped in and answered this one. "Well, it wasn't so much the investments as the hospital's growing financial needs."

"Sure," replied Austin. "You had to sell down to meet your cash needs. But I ask you again – isn't this incredibly risky?"

Silvia puffed out loud. "Well sure, but at least we paid the bills with the money. It's not like the money just evaporated into thin air as it would if a stock went down."

"That's true," added Pantelia.

"I understand that," answered Austin. "And that's why the Growth of Income Strategy provides not just intense growth of income but growth of principal too. I haven't told you that part yet. Otherwise, Dr. Silvia, you'd be entirely right. As it stands, however, you couldn't be more wrong. Let me explain."

"First, your portfolio will consist of about ten utility stocks based on a list kept by Johnny Long. Keep in mind that literally hundreds of advisors at First American Investors follow Johnny's every move in the portfolios they manage for their own clients. Now, this list is based solely upon First American Investors research. It's the best research on Wall Street. These analysts know the ins and outs of the companies they cover like nobody else. With utility stocks, their focus falls acutely on *dividends*. Years of research tell us that the rise and fall of utility-stock prices is directly related to their dividends. What the research tells us is not complex or particularly erudite. First American Investors analysts are in constant communication with these companies and make many adjustments to their dividend estimates, changes which the general public – you folks sitting right here – never see."

"OK, Mr. Montgomery. Allow me to put this in context for a moment," said Silvia.

"Certainly. Go right ahead."

"Thank you. Obviously, we have lost money for a variety of reasons, one of which is our increasing need for income. Because our income from investments was too small to meet our growing needs, we had to sell off and use principal. At the same time, when we reinvested the remainder of the proceeds from the sell-off, we got lower and lower interest rates, thus ensuring even less return going forward, and so on. What you referred to as 'a double whammy.'" Silvia looked as if he had a chicken bone caught in his throat. His face was turning a bright scarlet as he went through the gory details of the account's demise. "Lovely, Stone. Bloody lovely."

Austin took control again. "But as I was saying, the strategy I am proposing offers *growth* of income. Earlier I said that owning utility stocks is significantly more volatile than owning bonds or CDs because there is no maturity date, no guarantee that you'll get your principal back in the future as you would if you owned high-quality paper – you know, like AAA bonds or something like that. But, I can guarantee one thing which is crucially important, OK?" He waited until they were all transfixed. "I can assure you that each of the ten or so utility stocks you own will have a future of *dividend increases.*"

"Who keeps track of all that?" asked Pantelia.

"Well, like I was saying, Johnny Long uses First American Investors research exclusively. It's the best on the Street. That's why Johnny's there and has been there for so many years. First American Investors analysts are constantly revising their dividend estimates, remember that. You're never going to get this information by reading the newspaper until the company actually announces a change. But in the meantime, they are guiding analysts behind the scenes."

"Is that legal?" asked Pantelia. "Really?"

Austin laughed. "Of course it's legal. This is not inside information. This sort of communication between First American Investors analysts and the companies they cover takes place all the time. Johnny's people track these changes on a daily basis so as to ensure that the stocks you own are always trending *up* in dividends."

"Mr. Montgomery," asked Silvia, "can you elaborate a bit on the, I guess the *mechanics* of your strategy?"

"Yes," added Stone. "Please explain the day-to-day operations so we know what to expect."

This was exactly the sort of question Austin was waiting for. The prospect was taking initiative and actively learning. "OK. Out of the thousands of dividend-paying companies out there, only a few hundred, say, are utilities. So from thousands, we are down to hundreds."

"Why utilities?" asked Silvia.

"Good question. The easiest way to explain it is that in America, utilities are like mini monopolies. When my electric company sets rates, there's little I can do about it. Who else can I go to? Utility companies have more or less unchallenged price control. Moreover, there is little if any competition for a region. For the most part, one single company controls an entire region. There is virtually no market competition. This makes utilities unique investments in significant ways. There's a more subtle reason as well. Utilities have tremendous pricing power in that they can control their rates. Electric utilities through their subsidiaries engage in the generation, transmission, distribution, and sale of electricity. Many serve residential, commercial and industrial customers. Utility companies also engage in the construction, acquisition, and management of generation assets, digital communications services, and optic fiber solutions to telecommunication providers. Also many companies hold investments in synthetic fuels. And before I forget, utility companies generate power from oil, nuclear, hydro, wind, coal, natural gas, and solar. In other words, they are all over the power field. They are often highly leveraged, but they pay out almost all of their net income to shareholders. That's dividends to you.

"Now imagine that out of the hundred or so utilities that First American Investors covers, Johnny Long ranks them according to certain criteria." Austin looked around the room. "I wish I had a white board. There's a little math involved."

Pantelia laughed. "I think we can handle it."

"OK. First you rank the utilities by the current dividend yield. Next, by the increase in next year's dividend."

"Is the current yield how much the stock is paying in a dividend?" asked Stone.

"Sort of. It's the dollar amount per share in dividends in relation to the current stock price. This is found by dividing the dividend by the stock price. So then you have the current yield. It's the yield as a percent of the stock price. After that, you determine the dividend growth rate. Obviously, qualifying stocks have to have a higher dividend expected next year than they are paying currently. In this way, we are assuring you that, based on current research, you will be receiving higher income than you are getting now from that stock. So you find out what the expected growth rate is. Finally, you take the current yield and *add it* to the dividend growth rate. That gives you a score. All qualifying stocks are ranked according to this score."

Stone scratched his head. "So then this is how you decide which ten stocks to buy?"

"The top ten stocks are purchased in your portfolio, and that's all. So what you have is a portfolio of only those utility stocks that have the highest dividend yield and the highest dividend growth combination. Think about that for a second. Think about how fundamentally different this is from what you are doing now. At *all times* you have a portfolio stacked for income *growth.*"

Stone seemed in awe. "This is so very different from buying *fixed* income. I see it now."

"Yes," said Pantelia. "Everything we would own in this strategy of yours delivers a growing income stream."

"That's all well and good," said Silvia. "But what happens when one of these companies reduces their dividend? Won't we lose our money then?"

"That's a very good question. You will only own utility stocks that are expected to increase their dividends next year. It is highly unlikely that they will cut their dividend. Our research is good. And even if they did cut the dividend you will be diversified. The likely outcome, over time, is your income and principal will grow. The income growth is what you need in order for you to keep up with your growing expenses.

"I see," replied Silvia. "But how do we know when to sell a stock and replace it with a better investment? Just like your three question investing rule."

"Naturally, that's Johnny Long's job. Remember, guys, you're no longer managing your own portfolio. You can go back to being doctors again. Leave the other stuff to Johnny. That's *his* job. Every month, Johnny reviews First American Investors research and records every dividend estimate projection. *Every single utility stock* First American Investors covers is rescored and reranked. But your portfolio is rebalanced every quarter so that you own the top ten stocks once more."

Stone looked at Silvia to make sure he understood. "So in other words, Mr. Montgomery, every quarter, Mr. Long automatically updates our portfolio to ensure that we have the current top ten utility stocks in our portfolio. Is that correct?" Austin nodded. "Is that clear to you two?" Stone asked of Pantelia and Silvia.

Silvia scratched his head. "My question for you, Mr. Montgomery, is why do we have to wait until the end of three months. Why aren't the changes made as soon as there is a change?"

"Well, research has shown that many utility stock dividends tend to increase over time. The important fact to remember is that a series of repeated dividend increases will definitely pull a utility stock price up over time. So relying on First American Investors research is key because that's what clues us in."

"No one's perfect, Mr. Montgomery" said Pantelia.

"I know. Even First American Investors analysts make mistakes. They can only go by the numbers they have. But you need to remember something. As doctors, you follow a certain system when diagnosing a patient, right?" They all nodded. "Now, you don't necessarily know what's wrong with that patient at first, so you follow your system until you get a conclusive symptom and then you fix it, right?"

Silvia grimaced. "In a matter of speaking, but I see where you're going."

"Go on," instructed Stone.

"The parallel is pretty simple. The analyst is like a doctor. He constantly reviews the health of each company he follows. By using only the best utility stocks over time, your portfolio will grow in value. This method of only owning the best utility companies keeps your portfolio healthy and growing. This is a great sign of a healthy patient."

Pantelia laughed. "Hey, so we always have a bunch of nice, healthy utility stocks!"

"If it were only so easy with our patients," added Silvia.

Pantelia jerked her head up. "Dr. Silvia, did I sense a moment of acquiescence?"

Stone cleared his throat and tried to move things along a bit. "So, Mr. Montgomery, what else do we need to know about this strategy?"

Austin threw his hands up. "My God, I could go on forever."

"Um – please keep it this side of eternity, Mr. Montgomery," chided Silvia.

"It *is* almost tea time," said Pantelia. "A bit of cake would do just beautifully."

Austin clapped his hands. "OK then."

Chapter 21

Stone walked Austin out to the breezeway. Now that the meeting was over, the doctor began to revert back to the nervous, overworked administrator Austin had met. Austin noticed the sweat stains beginning to reappear under Stone's arms. The doctor bid Austin a hasty farewell and disappeared down the dim gray hallway. Alone now except for some random staff members walking across the breezeway, Austin took a moment to reflect on the day's events.

He felt quite confident about his presentation. There was little doubt he would win the account for Johnny. Ordinarily, he would be elated. Austin lived for the rush of success. Had he been back in the States, he would have hired a limo, rung up a few girls and some of his friends, and hit the town hard. Austin loved to revel in his own success from time to time. Oddly though, he felt different this time. Austin bit his lip and stared out into the vast azure sky that stretched on for infinity. The sky sucked him into its depths leaving Austin feeling insignificant rather than cocky. He was struck with an overwhelming feeling that nothing people did was really so significant after all.

Austin decided to mark the occasion by doing something really special, something he would remember for the rest of his life. Wouldn't it be amazing to fly over the Okavango Delta? When he arrived at the Gaborone Airport, he noticed a sign advertising sightseeing flights as well as plane rentals for qualified pilots. That was the ticket ... take up a Cessna 172 Skyhawk and see Botswana from yet another unique perspective. The meeting at the hospital was in and of itself something Austin would remember forever. But that was work and would no doubt lack the vividness and vibrancy of an aerial excursion over one of the most famous wildlife preserves on the Dark Continent. Never one to miss an opportunity to try something unique and exciting, Austin jumped in a ubiquitous white taxi and made for the airport.

Austin's rapid success at First American Investors invigorated him in ways he never would have associated with "work." Nevertheless, nothing made Austin happier than the feeling of flying a plane. For him, flying his own plane was both dangerous and liberating at one and the same time. Maybe that was the attraction? Anything could go wrong without notice and yet he was in total control of his own destiny – just the way he liked it. Oddly enough, there was something very... liberating in that precariousness. What's more, there was something forbidden about visiting the skies. They were not meant for people to claim as their own and history was filled with foreboding tales of man's demise amidst the clouds.

Of course, he wouldn't have been able to afford such caprice if it were not for work. But the freedom of flight always represented the ultimate reward for him. As he was signing all the requisite paperwork, it occurred to Austin how truly fortunate he was. Moments like this were not often afforded to the common man. Going through his pre-flight routine before taxing to runway 08, he took a moment to reflect on all his good fortune.

His thoughts were interrupted by the control tower clearing him for takeoff. Austin's adrenaline kicked in. This was the thrill of a lifetime. Austin pushed the throttle forward. The engine roared to life and the propeller strained against the thin, hot air. Climbing out from runway 08, he turned left sharply and headed 348 degrees northwest towards the Okavango Delta. Viewed from above, the grand scope of the terrain revealed itself. There was an ancient, unending dynamic at work, one that could not be fully appreciated from ground level. The recent rains had turned the normally dry, dusty landscape into a lush patchwork of greens and browns. The ebb and flow of life filled the panorama. Austin continued climbing, exchanging the Gaborone

Airport for visages of the Kapong and Molepolole villages beyond which lay the Ghanzi District including the renown Central Kalahari Game Preserve. To the west, the flat expanse of the Kalahari Desert ran seemingly forever into the horizon until it met the azure sky.

This was the best Austin felt in months. It was totally liberating this feeling of transporting into an ancient cycle. As he flew over the preserve drawing closer to the Ngwanalekau Hills that bordered the Okavango Delta to the south, he began to catch sight of the wildlife he had only seen on TV. As he passed over a pride of lions, Austin realized that the trials and tribulations of the people whom he met on his amazing journey into Africa – each with their own death story – were really extensions of this enigmatic landscape. It may sound trite to someone who had never been, but the people of Botswana were truly players on an ancient and unforgiving stage.

An hour in, Austin dialed in the Maun radio frequency and heard voices clatter away. On the southern tip of the Okavango, Maun was the hub for adventurers seeking safari camps otherwise unreachable by road. That Maun was far and away the busiest airport in Botswana, more so than even Gaborone's, testified to the immense impact of eco-tourism on the country. It also marked the turn-around point for Austin. Bidding Maun good-bye, he headed back to the capitol. He climbed high in order to glimpse the northern edge of the Delta. The maneuver returned its dividend as he was now able to see herds of zebra and water buffalo, a veritable smorgasbord of delights for the higher food chain. On final approach to Gaborone Airport, he saw the greatest of safari sights – the magnificent elephants whose girth and majesty never fail to captivate. The red fuel reserve light reminded Austin that the moment was drawing to a close. All things had their limit, especially in the African wilderness, and his limited supply of fuel seemed only fitting.

Africa is old in a way no other place is. Europe or China... they had epochs and *antiquity*, they measured time in *thousands* of years. But as soon as Austin stepped out of the plane he realized time was very different here. In Botswana, time is measured in *millennia*, in the ebbing and waning of *life itself.* Accordingly, Austin wondered if anything he or the doctors did really mattered when confronted with nature, a force which simply wipes the earth clean from time to time just like his cleaning lady dusting his house. Rather than gloating in his wheeling and dealing, Austin wondered how on earth to make sense of it all.

Just behind him was the belly of an epidemic, a beast that would consume whole populations, whole countries, whole villages. What the hell was that? But when you're in Africa, you realize that AIDS is much, much more than this or that political agenda. It is time doing some housecleaning and dusting us off precisely as it has done throughout the millennia. Was a two hour meeting going to change that? When Pickett first said this, Austin thought the musician was just ranting on. But now that he was standing boots on the ground, standing on *terra firma*, he knew exactly what Pickett was talking about. AIDS was *eschatological*. You might, might be able to control the disease, but you could never control time. The ultimate monolith, time will roll over every human pretense. Interestingly, this was how a lot of people approached classical music – as a glimpse into the infinite. For the first time in his life, Austin understood the real definition of "tragedy"- the inevitable failure of the human struggle against time. Medicine, science, and politics were just different forms of this struggle.

Austin blinked heavily and shook himself from his thoughts. After all, as much as death prowled the corridors of this hospital, so too did life. Great advances were being made in the treatment of AIDS and HIV in general. For example, doctors could now actually prevent transmission of the disease from mother to fetus with new drug cocktails. Was this really futile? Of course not! How could saving a completely innocent child be considered a failure of any sort? It was almost too much for Austin to sort out just then. One thing was clear. If we didn't have the daily pursuit of excellence and "progress" – no matter how illusory – what did we have? We had *nothing*, that's what. No matter what you thought of politics, of science, of progress in general, at least we were *trying*, and that made all the difference. As with music, the answer lay somewhere in the middle. In fact, the answer *was* the middle.

Austin shot out a baseball–style spit and stepped into a cab.

Chapter 22

The Mall was nothing like Austin expected. Everyone in Gaborone knows the Mall. It is one of the major retail hubs in the city. Located in the Dilalelo district between Independence Avenue and Kenneth Kaunda, the Mall was the center of urban retail commerce. If you asked someone where you could buy this or that, they would always mention the Mall as an option. Interestingly, though, the Mall was surrounded by numerous foreign consulates, countless other government buildings, the palatial Zales diamond building, and two Christian churches on Merafe Street. The Mall would hardly be reflective of life in Gabs without Christian missionaries somehow involved in the loop.

Because everyone mentioned the Mall in the same breath with shopping in Gaborone, Austin figured the Mall would be a newly constructed, Western style *homage* to conspicuous consumption. Indeed, the Mall was cited as the "modern one" as compared to lesser shopping alternatives. This was hardly the case, however. In fact, when the driver pulled over to let him out, Austin figured he had misunderstood him.

"No, I said the Mall, please."

The driver smiled at him. "The Mall, yes. This is the Mall."

"This is the Mall? Really?"

The driver smiled again and nodded. "Yes, this is the Mall." He handed Austin his card. "Call me when you are ready, and I will come to collect you."

"Thank you," said Austin. He took the card and slipped it into his wallet with about seven others. "OK, thanks." Austin stepped out onto the dirty sidewalk and couldn't believe his eyes. He was struck immediately by two thoughts. The first thing he thought was "are you kidding me?" followed immediately by "this reminds me of South Street in Philly." Perhaps it was the goats roaming around. Or it might have been the large number of men just sitting around in the middle of the day doing nothing in particular. Then again, it may have been the Evangelical puppet show using third-grade theology which literally *enthralled* fifty people. Whatever it was, Austin put all thoughts of doing some tourist shopping out of his mind.

The scene was almost carnivalesque, and the various sideshow attractions were set about performing their daily routines. No sooner did Austin dismiss the idea of picking up a new Armani suit than he spotted a young boy talking with some guy who made Bill Clinton look like a saint. The two couldn't have been more than twenty-five feet away right out in the open. There was really nothing distinctive about the kid. He was wearing shorts, sandals, and a plain red shirt. But the older guy... now there was a man who liked the center stage. He was very dark, bald, and clearly had been coming from the airport. About a dozen duty-free bags were piled by his feet. He wore a white shirt embroidered with a blue and red dragon that was right off the pages of *GQ*. His clean-shaven head was accented by large Dior sunglasses. The diamonds dotting the frames sparkled in the sun. So did the gold grill he was sporting. In other words, his gold teeth were even brighter than his frames and the rhinestones in his oversized belt buckle. His baggy, oversized jeans epitomized a trendy, hip-hop style. Austin found himself in the middle of Africa standing face-to-face with the King of Bling.

Austin looked on as the man pulled a knot of fifties from the pocket of his oversized jeans. He peeled one off and handed it to the kid, who squished the bill into a ball and stuffed it into his pocket without saying a word. That was quite a bit of money, and Austin assumed that drugs were involved. But he was wrong. For no sooner did the man put his wad back in his pocket than he started taking off his jeans right there in the middle of the Mall. Austin looked on in amazement as the man undid his huge belt buckle, unzipped himself, and dropped his Lucky 7 brand jeans around his ankles. What was even more interesting was that no one seemed to notice.

Ah, but then Austin realized the guy had *another* pair of jeans on underneath. That's right... under the first pair of Lucky 7's was a second pair, this time Diesel brand. The man lifted each foot and the boy took the first pair of jeans off, folded them neatly, and put them in an empty shopping bag he was carrying. The two repeated this process *five times*, and each time the jeans underneath were less and less baggy. It was amazing. The guy was shedding pairs of jeans he had apparently bought overseas and smuggled back on his person. So it wasn't drugs after all. The guy was into smuggling knock-offs. The quantities were small – only five pairs at a clip. But the street value must have been about $500 and that was cut rate. They would command more on E-Bay. Now multiply this by however many mules like this guy were out there running goods for the big boss.

It didn't take Austin long to figure out that counterfeit merchandise – flat-out stealing, really – was alive and well in Gaborone. Orchestrated by the Russian mafia (in other words, government officials), manufactured in China for cents on the retail dollar, and run through third-world channels no one could monitor, counterfeit goods were a visible part of the retail life here. If Austin had any doubts about the extent of the black market, all he had to do was take a look around. There were countless guys selling phone cards and cell phones right there amid numerous advertisements for Orange and Vodafone. How could this be? In Gaborone, you could buy any cell phone you liked on the street. All of them were authentic and all of them were mysteriously "rerouted" through Africa by the Russians. This was common knowledge. You could then find a mainstream service provider like Vodafone or Orange and set up your typical service.

Or you could just go around the entire corporate system of usage fees, service charges, taxes... the whole thing. You could just go to the Mall, buy a generic track phone with no corporate affiliation whatsoever, and buy a phone card which enabled you to use the cell phone independent of any provider. In effect, large service providers were efficiently replaced by $10 black-market phone cards from Eastern Europe. In Gabs, the Russian mafia was the new cell phone company of choice. Why subscribe to a service, why be taken advantage of by large multinational conglomerates when communication is your right? Instead, let the will of the people rule the day! In Botswana, the people just up and do things far more than they waste time worrying about doing things. Oh, and of course your phone wouldn't work without a "sim card" which allows you to tap into the worldwide wireless network, so to speak. Without a sim card, you couldn't use your phone because you couldn't "tap" into a service network. It's no different than "stealing" cable. What harm did it really do to Comcast? Not to worry though… you could buy a sim card anywhere on the street. You see, in Africa the "will of the people" amounted to taking what was needed to get by. Pay no attention to the wizard behind the curtain.

The more Austin shopped the Mall, the more he realized that the long arm of the wizard was everywhere. *Nike* flip-flops for five bucks… *Marlboro* Reds for two dollars a pack… *Lucky* 7 jeans for fifteen dollars. *Gucci* frames, *Louis Vuitton* backpacks, *Juicy Couture* sweat suits, *Adidas* sneakers, *Timberland* boots… whatever happened to be in that month's shipping container arriving via China. So if Austin was expecting a Western style mall, he at least got Western materialism. The only problem was that all of it was stripped of its glitz and panache. Large, upscale build-outs were replaced by faded, dirty window displays peppered with dead flies. It was like a dumpster diving in Beverly Hills – without its proper *haute couture* camouflage and inflated social positioning, everything was just crap. This was the truth behind the scenes.

Austin was less struck by the bargain-basement prices than he was by this realization. As he thumbed through a pile of Calvin Klein boxer briefs (a dollar a piece), he realized that one was just like another. The name brand – the marketing – made all the difference. But there was really no difference at all, at least not in the quality of the merchandise. Generally speaking of course, most people bought the packaging. Austin was startled by how… *naked* the merchandise was. Back in the States and at that very moment, millions and millions of dollars were being spent on marketing, on transforming ubiquitous "merchandise" into lifestyle vogue. From the customers' perspective, short-term happiness sealed the deal. But in the end, did any of it really matter? No worries… another short-term fix would appear on the horizon.

Now, all this might strike someone as a bit bizarre, a bit too close to the source so to speak. But Austin had hung around Philadelphia enough to know that all the African guys hawking "brand name" knock-offs on every corner didn't just fall out of the sky. They came from somewhere, they had a history, they had a family. Most importantly, they had "connections." The thousands and thousands of African men mysteriously found their way to America's cities as part of a huge worldwide sales and distribution network for black market, "redirected," and knock-off merchandise. Austin had long since stopped wondering why the cops or, more importantly, why the INS didn't crack down and put a stop to things, especially in a city like Philadelphia. After all, illegal immigration and laundered money played such an integral role in 9/11.

The parallel to the investment business was not lost on Austin. In fact, had Austin told the doctors what he *really* thought about their so-called investment advisor, it would have sounded like a critique of the sales racket per usual. The Princess Diana Hospital *needed* growth of income. Quite literally, there were lives depending on it.

As a matter of fact, most advisors at large firms are instructed time and time again to actually *avoid* making their own investment decisions. There's too much risk in it, especially now in this environment of litigation. Instead, brokers are encouraged to *gather assets* and pass them to the "professionals" to manage. In other words, leave the investing to professional money managers at the mutual funds. As Johnny taught Austin from the beginning, Johnny found immense success in matching a client to the most suitable investment strategy. How better to gather assets than by developing a unique and successful investment strategy? Moreover, Johnny *was* managing assets in ways not available in a mutual fund – in this case, for pure growth of income. Had Johnny been managing the hospital's money over the last decade, they would have made tens of millions of dollars more. Instead, one bond replaced another, and another, and so on. If their bonds were underperforming, they were simply swapped for different ones. It all looked very busy and very studious to Stone. What did he know? He was a *doctor,* not a money manager.

Johnny also learned early on that *not* providing unique insight and a clearly delineated investment strategy for his clients would create distrust. During his first few years working in the market,

226

Johnny placed most of his clients in mutual funds or managed-money portfolios. But he lost accounts almost as quickly as he won them. The simple fact was that his clients did not *need* Johnny if all he was going to do was put their money into vehicles they could get anywhere and for much cheaper. It was no different from buying a five dollar pair of Nike flip-flops instead of a $35 pair of Nike flip-flops if they were both the same thing. It was only the buyer's perception that varied, not the product itself. And that perception could sour very quickly, even toward someone as successful as Johnny Long.

Over time, however, Johnny's business grew and grew despite short-term market fluctuations. Why? Because the way Johnny Long managed money was successful. This in itself was critical. You have to deliver results, especially when managing people's money. Johnny taught Austin something he never would have imagined on his own. Most mutual-fund managers *do not* want to significantly outperform their competitors. They want to outperform their relative *indexes.* But they don't want to blow each other out. Instead, they prefer to stay huddled in a pack with everyone essentially buying and selling the same things. At first, Austin thought this was counter-intuitive. But the more Austin thought about it, the more he realized that no one wanted to run too far ahead of the pack where he would be vulnerable to criticism in the same way a gazelle who strays too far from the herd is vulnerable to preying lions. What people remember more than their profits are the flash-in-the-pan blow-ups. A trendy fashion – whether in clothes or mutual funds -- will not be in vogue for very long. And when it is forgotten, it is long forgotten.

Financial advisors were no different from fund managers in this regard. Financial advisors at large firms were trained to stay in the herd. It's much safer there. Why take risk picking stocks on your own – why stray out into the open – when you can stay back in the pack and put your client's assets in mutual funds or bonds. In this way, nothing could ever really be the broker's fault, right? There will always be a hot fund out there, but for the most part, one was like the next, just with a different name. It was no different than clothing -- different label, same crap. How could a client complain if the fund you picked for them was more or less the same as any other out there. When it came to the handful of hot funds that were scorching their way to the front page of *Barron's*, the broker's response was always the same – "It's too volatile for you." In many cases it was; in others, it wasn't. But when you're looking in the rear-view mirror, so to speak, it's always a matter of retrospect and remorse.

But there was more to Johnny Long's success than this. He did things just the opposite. It made sense to him this way. Like many of his clients, Johnny did not aspire to be mediocre. Sure, he could make a nice living for himself by huddling in the middle of the pack just like his clients could have made decent money in an unmanaged S&P 500 Index fund. This made no sense to Johnny, however. For Johnny, investing was a matter of risk to reward, and he sought to maximize his returns first and foremost. The perceived risk – often misconstrued with the Beta or volatility – was secondary to returns over a three-to-five year period. The *real* risk as Johnny Long saw it was in *not* meeting your clients' long-term objectives. Then you're really screwed because you can't go back in time.

Johnny's strategies never went out of fashion because, like a fine Brooks Brothers suit, they were rooted in classic beliefs that overarched short-term market fluctuations. Consecutive multiple earnings-estimate increases drove growth stocks up significantly over time. Similarly, repeated dividend increases drove utility stocks much higher over time. This was a fact proven again and again by anyone who did the research. And yet, in leveraging this vital information for his clients, Johnny stood alone among his peers. There is nothing so intuitive and logical as investing for growth, income or otherwise. And yet, there is perhaps no business as counter-intuitive and illogical as the brokerage business. In brokerage, fashion is everything; in investing, *profits* are what count.

The great difference between Johnny Long and countless other advisors was that Johnny had a *strategy* for approaching things. More than anything else, having a strategy meant *having discipline*. No matter what, you could always fall back on this. Johnny was disciplined in what he bought and when he sold, when he cut loose of a losing endeavor. Before he arrived in Africa, Austin never even thought about Johnny's wisdom outside of investing. But that was about to change. And the catalyst was quite unexpected – a business trip to Africa? Who would've thought. But personal growth usually happened for Austin this way. It had to sneak up on him and catch him off guard. Change can be painful, and Austin preferred pleasure to pain.

There was something about standing in the middle of the world that made this all crystallize right there for him. Changing your perspective will often do this. That's why he liked to travel. In fact, that's why Johnny sent him on the trip in the first place... to change Austin's perspective on things, on life, on himself. Tucked away in his mind Austin had a golden goose, one which had laid him a golden egg several years earlier. In a country where the world was afraid to look too closely, Austin regained his focus. In the epicenter of death and disease, Austin felt renewed. As he stood there watching the missionaries' childlike puppet show about Jesus multiplying fish and loaves, he felt a bit guilty for feeling this way. He felt way too privileged for receiving this wisdom... as if he bought his way to personal redemption.

In a moment of childlike innocence, a man standing next to him cried out in joy when the Jesus puppet began citing scripture. The man was neither embarrassed nor ashamed, neither guilt-ridden nor cynical. Instead the man was genuinely rejoicing in the power of the Lord. It had nothing to do with silly-looking hand puppets and everything to do with *faith*, belief in an order of things. If nothing else, the coming of Livingstone was the coming of *order*. Politics of imperialism aside, the cold hard fact is that people thrive, aspire, and succeed within a system, within an order. The history of human civilization is far more complex than the simple domination of one man over another. People will always resist power in their own little way. Look at the cell-phone black market running free in the Mall.

And so standing there next to this African man who was weeping over the meaning he discovered through hand puppets, Austin let his guilt go. He no longer worried about his presentation or letting Johnny down. He forgot all about his tumultuous breakup. For the first time since his mother died, he forgave himself for being off at a prestigious university when she passed away. The guilt in him that continually fretted about not practicing his music enough evaporated. He could actually feel the weight lift from his shoulders. *Literally...* he could feel his posture change. When he was in school, he worried about not having money. After his mother died, he worried about making money. When he made millions, he worried that much more about *not losing it*. It never ended, the worry.

The weeping man made it so obvious to Austin. That was why Johnny was always so happy and relaxed in his own skin. Both this man and Johnny saw something far greater than investment strategies and hand puppets. Austin finally got it. The strategy he had just presented to the board implied far more than how to buy stocks and bonds. One could actually extend the strategy to one's own life. Austin bit his lip and thought it over. There was a cacophony of voices in his head, as if new neural networks were forming by the second and conversing with one another. It was an Ah-ha moment, the second one Johnny had gifted him with over the years.

The weeping man picked up his torn and filthy plastic bag and started walking away singing. The puppet show wasn't quite over, but apparently he had gotten what he needed. Austin wondered where the man was headed. Did he have a family? Kids? Was he homeless or did he live in one of those shanties along the road? The man wore tattered sandals, but perhaps Austin was stereotyping him? At any rate, the fact was that this man was on his way to something. Moreover, there were only so many "somethings" he would get to over the course of his life. Yes, there are only so many things we get to do in the course of one lifetime. Thriving within a *fixed* amount of time… *that's* the trick to leading a happy life. There was no doubt in Austin's mind that Johnny Long lived his life the same way he managed money – according to a strategy.

Austin watched the weeping man disappear around a corner heading toward the sun. Austin wandered off into the crowd and grabbed a seat on a vacant bench under a shady tree. The sun was starting to beat down intensely, but Austin was undaunted. He wanted to think some more about Johnny Long. It had been a while since he evaluated the important people in his life, and he figured he might as well start with Johnny. After all, Johnny had done so damned much for him. Austin thought hard about the idea that Johnny lived his life according to a certain strategy. Austin wasn't sure. He had never thought to ask his mentor. The real question was whether or not Johnny's rules for investing – what to buy, when to sell, and what to do with the proceeds – could be applied to other decisions in a person's life. Austin bit his lip and shook his head. "I don't know," he said to himself. He couldn't see it, it wasn't there. Oh, he knew the answer was out there somewhere. He was even pretty sure the answer was "yes." But it wasn't clear for him. What *was* crystal clear was the *question itself.* Could Johnny's Three Questions be applied to the way a person lives his or her life? OK, so he had a big question to ponder on his return flight. But damned if the answer didn't elude him.

Austin's mind shifted to a favorite line of his. It was from the movie *The Bobby Fischer Story* starring Ben Kingsley and Lawrence Fishbourne as two master chess instructors vying for a young student's loyalty. What a wonderful trope for chess itself! Anyway, the young student is toiling away against Ben Kingsley and is stymied. He simply can't figure out his master's gambit and is growing increasingly impetuous. Sensing the frustration mounting in his young student, Kingsley says, "Wait until you see it. Don't move until you see it." Of course, the boy moves rashly and sets free his master's endgame. But that line stuck with Austin for years.

Austin had been through so much in his young life, but sometimes he felt like he saw so little whereas Johnny seemed to see everything, every angle, every opportunity, every possibility. It was easy for Austin to imagine himself seated across from Johnny playing white or black, it really didn't matter. How often Austin was tempted to move his money to someone else when the market went south for a while. But Johnny always talked him down. "Just wait," he would say. "Understand what's going on before you make a move." Stocks are like chess pieces. They move because people are doing certain things based on the information available. OK...

Wait until you see it. Don't move until you see it.

Chapter 23

Once back in the States, it took Austin a while to decompress. Visiting Africa is like deep-sea diving. Both excursions take you into a completely foreign element. You can't breathe underwater, you can't move the same, you can't see the same, the sea creatures have a completely different anatomy and chemistry... everything is alien, hostile and deadly. Putting a person underwater is no different than tossing a fish onto the deck of a boat. At the same time, though (and thanks to human ingenuity) scuba diving is also one of the most relaxing, soothing experiences. The rest of the world melts away. Scuba diving is somehow liberating, invigorating, rejuvenating. Such is the power of the sea.

Visiting Africa made a similar impact on Austin. Like the sea, Africa had an element of danger that you could not overlook. If you did, you could get very sick or even die. Death and disease were everywhere. Less obvious – but no less significant – was the constant danger of sleeping unprotected with the wrong person. One mistake made on one night after one too many drinks could alter the rest of your life. Still, there was something about being in Africa that put Austin at ease... more so than ever before. Even a city as "developed" as Gaborone had its dangers. Nevertheless, Austin soaked in a tremendous amount of simple good will. His priorities shifted. For the first time in a long time, he wasn't worried about his life, his money, or his future. Just like when you're scuba diving, the rest of the world melts away while you're in Africa.

When he stepped into a cab at the Philadelphia Airport, Austin felt a sense of longing. He actually missed Gaborone, not so much for the sights as for the freedom he felt while there. Ironically, everything went smoothly in Botswana, yet his bags were lost back here in the States. So typical. Not to mention how rude everyone was, especially the people working for the airline. Austin noticed this right away. Back in Botswana, everyone Austin met seemed just happy to be standing wherever they happened to be standing. In Philly, especially at the airport, everyone seemed disgruntled about something.

Since his luggage was lost, he decided to head straight to Johnny's office. As the cabby pulled away from the curb at breakneck speed and hurtled toward the city, Austin began to worry that he would lose the peace with himself he had discovered over the past few days. But he did have good news to report to Johnny. He would be pleased with Austin's performance. And Austin didn't even know if Stone had contacted Johnny or if they had decided to move their money. It was all very exciting, and Austin had to take care to transition from one culture back to the other. Too fast, and he might get the bends, so to speak.

Austin breezed into Johnny's office holding a cheesesteak in each hand… peppers, onions, mushrooms, cheese whiz, the works. Moira must have been out to lunch. She was not at her desk so Austin was spared the usual flirtatious interlude that could consume as much as 15 minutes of his appointment time with Johnny. Johnny looked up from his screen.

"What's up, Mandingo? The weary traveler is back from the dark continent."

Austin held up the cheesesteaks. "I shot and killed these for us, B'wana."

Johnny smiled and shook his head. "Scarfing down a cheesesteak is your idea of reassimilating, huh. Don't you just love this country? No one has indigestion like we do."

Austin sat down at the table in Johnny's office and feverishly unwrapped his cheese steak. Johnny grabbed a Diet Pepsi and an Amstel Light from the mini-fridge. He poured the beer into a travel mug and placed it down next to Austin's food. "Welcome home," he said. "I cannot wait to hear all the stories which I am *sure* you have. From the looks of it, you didn't eat much."

Austin laughed and swallowed his mouthful of sandwich. "Actually, the food was great. Pretty normal bar food." He took a swig of beer. "I think my tolerance has doubled though. They drink like fish. From the moment you get off the plane to the moment you leave the country. It's unbelievable. Look at me... I'm still drinking."

Johnny unwrapped his food and popped open his diet soda. "So you went to Western-style places?"

"It's all relative, believe me. The hotel had an upscale steak house... exactly what *kind* of steak was best left unexplored. It was good and tough. Mostly I hung out at local hang outs like this place called the Bull and Bush. That's where you meet people, you know?"

"So you met a lot of people in Botswana?"

"Batswana. That's what you call the people in the plural. They're great. Such a difference from Philadelphia it's unbelievable. Everyone here seems so grumpy, man."

"Well, that's because the women don't walk around half naked."

Austin almost choked on his food. He wasn't really expecting that sort of thing from Johnny Long. "Maybe in the annals of *National Geographic* or out in the countryside, but the city is remarkably... I don't know, normal for lack of a better word?"

"Really? I honestly had no idea what to expect. The doctors I speak to from the Penn program say there are some beautiful homes, but it's still primitive as a whole."

Austin thought it over while chewing. He took a long sip of beer to wash it down. "Well... I was thinking about how to best explain it to people. The downtown area where there are some new office buildings reminds me of one of those quasi-suburban cities that pop up outside Philly or New York. Like White Plains, New York, or something like Conshohocken around here. Here and there are some really regal government buildings, embassies... like that." Johnny was following right along while he ate his cheese steak. "There aren't many two-story houses. They're pretty much all ranchers. Some of them, like you said, are really nice. If you have a house proper, you live in a gated community. Black or white, it doesn't matter. Gated communities. What's really weird is that every, I mean *every,* house is walled in and topped with razor wire. It's a little creepy actually."

"Really? I was told that Botswana was the most peaceful and safest country in Africa. I would never have sent you there if I thought it was dangerous."

"No, no, no," said Austin. "It's really not like that at all. I was going to say that outside of the areas I just described, the rest of Gabs – Gaborone – looks pretty much like the suburbs of Philadelphia. That's exactly how I would describe it. You can get along pretty easily. It's not too, too alien from the appearance of things."

"Everyone speaks English, right?"

"That's the thing. It's like being in Philly. Actually, I think there are *fewer* people who speak English in Philly." They both got a good laugh out of that one.

"But seriously, it *is* a little strange to be out in the middle of nowhere with a bunch of Batswana who speak the Queen's English. Honestly, with no language barrier, I don't know why more people don't visit."

"So was it what you expected then?"

Austin shrugged. "How the hell did I know *what* to expect." He took another swig of his beer.

They spent about an hour discussing the social nuances of Gaborone as Austin interpreted them. Johnny sat mesmerized while Austin told him about the colorful people he met along the way. It all sounded right out of a Saturday afternoon movie... but it was all true. Of course, Austin embellished some of the finer details to drive home his points, but the facts were the facts. Sometimes a story is as real as it is... a story. No doubt some people would say that Austin's account was overblown and romanticized with all his talk of super-successful investment strategies, exotic African women, caricature South African war vets and the like... all very superficial on the outside. But that was just it, that was precisely what Austin found so amazing about his journey. It really *was* an adventure. In fact, he had been on one ever since he met Johnny. It never stopped. This trip to Botswana was just the most recent leg in a much bigger journey of discovery. It would be easy to dismiss Austin's story as some rich guy's aggrandizing self-promotion. But the facts spoke for themselves. There was a reason why Johnny's clients swore allegiance to him. There was a reason why Austin and Johnny stayed connected over the years. There was a reason why Austin could simply up and go to Africa without notice and seemingly fit right in. When a system works, it spreads like wildfire. People who care only to focus on the burned aftermath miss the point entirely.

And so Johnny sat transfixed as Austin spun out his world of hope and optimism juxtaposed against the backdrop of poverty, HIV, and mortality. In all honesty, Johnny lived vicariously through Austin. Sure Johnny was rich, richer than Austin by far. But he was still a family man, married for three decades, and stuck behind a desk servicing his clients more often than not. For Johnny, though, Austin represented change, new blood, excitement. Sending Austin to Africa was certainly not necessary; Johnny could have closed the deal by phone. But he *wanted* to send Austin as a sort of proxy for himself. He was a second pair of eyes through which Johnny could see the world anew, and it was not the world of luxury hotels, fine dining, and high-powered meetings so much as the grittier side of life that Johnny wanted to visit through Austin.

When Austin finished his story, Johnny stood up, went over to the mini-fridge, sat back down and poured Austin another beer. "So let me get this straight," he said. "Fifty percent of the population is HIV positive?"

Austin pursed his lips. "That's the whisper number, yeah."

"So it's like flipping a coin?"

"I guess you can look at it like that."

"And one of the first things you do is sleep with someone without protection."

Austin smirked. "Let's just say that I prefer to live... dangerously."

Johnny shook his head. "I don't know how you do it, Austin. I really don't. You have balls, I'll tell you that."

Austin laughed. "Well, at least until they shrivel up and fall off from whatever you think I caught out there."

"I suppose raisins have a certain appeal for some."

"Oh that's gross! And anyway, that's why you sent me out there... to poke my nose around where you haven't been. You know... get my hands a little dirty. See what I could bring back."

Johnny laughed. "Ha! Poke your *nose* perhaps. But not other things! And I certainly didn't want you to bring back a disease."

Austin held up his hand. "OK, OK... I'm trying to digest here. And you can relax... I also brought back a drinking habit. See what you've done to me. Hmph... some advisor you are."

Johnny snapped his fingers. "Ah! Speaking of which... don't you want to know what Dr. Stone said?"

Austin sat up straight. "You heard from him already?"

Johnny looked up over Austin's shoulder toward Moira's desk. "Moira? Can you bring me that e-mail from Dr. Stone in Botswana?"

Apparently back from lunch, Moira popped in the door as if she had been standing there listening the entire time. She handed Johnny the e-mail and started giving Austin a little neck rub. Johnny held up his hand in mock seriousness. "Moira, please. You need a body condom before you touch him."

Moira bent down and whispered in Austin's ear. "Yuck!" She chuckled a little and then walked out.

"Thank you *so* much Johnny. Really, if there's any other work I can do for you, please.... Don't ask."

"Well, Dr. Stone said your presentation went over really well."

"It was a little touch and go at times. This Dr. Silvia guy was a real ballbuster. I suppose in retrospect, though, it's perfectly understandable. He didn't know me from a hole in the wall."

Johnny opened up the hospital's file that was already sitting on the table. "Well whatever you did, Dr. Stone said you presented to the board a clear argument for making a change... although you were somewhat overdressed."

Austin laughed. "My God, I was sweating. I'm sure they had quite a laugh over that. I must have looked like I had Ebola or something."

Johnny laughed. "Don't joke. You may."

"So then you were trying to kill me off by sending me to Africa, huh? Was that the plan?"

"It's part of the game," said Johnny. "You get a free trip to Africa, I get a new account."

"I see," said Austin. "Well, whatever. As long as it worked out for you. I'm always glad to help, Johnny. You know that. And it's a good sized account."

"Yes it is. Fifty million."

"Wow, that's like a million in commissions a year."

"Yup! About four hundred grand a year in income."

"Christ, I'm in the wrong business."

"Oh yeah? What business is that? I thought you were an investment advisor?"

"Well, I mean... had I known that your Growth of Income Strategy would garner so many assets, I would have focused entirely on marketing that over the past few years."

"It's funny you say that," answered Johnny. "Thinking back, if I had it to do over again, I would do only the Growth of Income Strategy. There's just *so much* bond money out there that advisors ignore because they don't make any money selling it."

Austin was pensive for a moment. "Money, yes... speaking of which... an all-expenses paid trip to Botswana is nice and all, and don't get me wrong... the chance to contract a whole host of exotic diseases is a once in a lifetime opportunity – especially if you catch one - but I think I would prefer splitting the account, no?"

Johnny raised an eyebrow. "Wait a minute... so you're saying that you want to be compensated for winning the account? But I'm the one who had the contact, and I'm the one whose strategy they are using."

For a minute, Austin thought Johnny was being serious and his stomach knotted. Then he heard Moira snort in the background and realized Johnny was busting his chops. "Oh, kiss my ass old man! A million in commissions a year! That's like... 200 grand a year for each of us!"

"Just for doing the client a tremendous service," Johnny added.

"God I love this country!"

"When it works right, everyone makes a *lot* of money Austin. But remember... when you muck around with people's money like a lot of the schmucks out there, you can lose a lot too, and then it's no fun at all. Market corrections aside. The name of the game is to make money."

Austin's hairs were standing on end. "Just what I wanted to hear, Johnny. Like I was saying, let a little fall my way. You know, trickle down to the little folks."

Johnny tapped some keys on his keyboard and squinted at his screen. "'Little folks, huh. From what I see, this 200 thousand you're talking about brings you close to what... six, seven a year without stock bonus?"

"Geez... Mr. Cheapskate."

"Of course, we'll share the account, Austin. You did an amazing job. If it weren't for you, I would never have landed the account. You pretty much handed yourself $200,000 a year in extra income. Which means you can buy the new Diamondstar D-Jet." Johnny shook his head. "Only fly solo partner. Flying passengers is one risk you should *not be* willing to take."

Austin stood up and clapped his hands. "Damn I'm happy! Well, if you'll excuse me, sir, my liver is going through withdrawal and needs more alcohol immediately. If you need me, I'll be somewhere within arm's reach of a bottle of scotch. Cheers!" He winked and was out the door.

"Hey!" Johnny called after him. "I expect you back in the office first thing tomorrow morning, Austin! Austin... I know you heard me! I'm not handling your clients for another week without being paid!"

Austin turned over his shoulder. "Live and die by the sword, brother man!"

It was true, Johnny loved mentor-mentee repartee like this. One of his goals in sending Austin on this little mission was to refocus his young prodigy. Not to mention help him earn a nice chunk of yearly income to boot. Austin had no parents, and Johnny Long was more or less the only older, successful man who was close to Austin. Johnny was the closest thing to a father Austin had for many years. Johnny thought of the trip as a sort of business camp for Austin. It was the least he could do for the boy. It would have been easy for Johnny to have simply managed Austin's money like any other client's, made money for Austin, and sent him on his way. But Johnny was never like that, not even with his other clients. He believed his role as a trusted advisor included *educating* his clients. As much as anything else, Johnny saw himself as a teacher.

The dilemma out at the Princess Diana Hospital was exactly the sort of challenge Johnny sought. There was so much at stake. Sending Austin was part of his plan from the beginning. True, Johnny had been talking with Stone for several months prior to Austin's arrival. Johnny knew the hospital was in serious trouble without him. The sooner the account came over, the better. Of course, he never advocated market timing. Still, he would feel much better about the hospital's future once the money was under his management. The sense of security and self-confidence Johnny felt because of the success of his strategies made coming to work each day a joy. This new account was just the latest uptick in an otherwise steadily appreciating life. Johnny clicked over to his e-mail and started writing Stone. He informed the doctor that the assets were expected in house tomorrow and that they needed to discuss the changes as soon as possible.

The next morning when Stone read the e-mail, it was as if a tremendous boulder under which he had been pinned was suddenly lifted off him. He felt like he could breath again. It seemed to him an eternity since he could simply focus on patients and running the hospital more efficiently. With Johnny's help, Stone could be a doctor again. If you've ever been worried to death about money, you'll only begin to feel the stress, anxiety, and frustration Tony Stone felt. Imagine controlling something like $50 million. It would totally consume you morning, noon, and night. Would you sleep regularly?

Would your stomach begin to burn from the acid building up? Would Viagra even be enough to resuscitate your sense of manhood? Stone had suffered from a sick and twisted lie over the past few years, and now it was finally over. Have you ever felt so relieved that a few tears flowed? Stone cried just a little.

He knew full well, too, that his colleagues were feeling the same way. Silvia may have tried to keep up appearances in front of Stone, but Silvia discussed it with the chief often. Usually toward the end of the month, Sylvia would find a way into Stone's office with two cups of Earl Grey. He would make some small talk, but then inevitably turn toward his concern for the hospital's fiscal well-being. It was terribly distracting for Stone. He hated money problems (he had always had more money than he needed), and became a doctor to heal people, not to worry about money. He actually found himself thinking about the account while with patients. This realization absolutely horrified him. It violated everything he believed in politically. It had to stop. He was not only miserable, he was offensive to himself as well.

Accordingly, Pantelia was on board with any solution allowing her to be a doctor again. She knew full well that Silvia would be more of an impediment than anything else. Sure, Stone had the authority to transfer the assets to Johnny without Silvia's consent. But Silvia could still make things very difficult for Stone, and that certainly wouldn't move her closer to her goal of becoming strictly a doctor again. Stone, too, was concerned about Silvia's propensity to make trouble and start pissing matches. Silvia knew powerful people in the government and could ultimately pull the strings to have Stone sacked. There would be some resistance from Stone's supporters, but Silvia could overcome it with allegations of corruption and fiduciary incompetence.

Truth be known, however, Silvia sought nothing of the sort. He went into medicine because he loved research. His bedside manner was somewhat lacking, but he always kept patients prioritized. He came to the Princess Diana Hospital because he could conduct AIDS research more or less unfettered. He was attracted to the huge influx of grant money and became quite good at securing it, so much so in fact that he was tapped by local government officials to be the Director of Inpatient Operations. Part of his responsibilities included securing grant monies from the WHO, the UN, and other large multinational organizations. Without this money, the hospital would cease all operations.

As a result, Silvia found himself becoming more of a government employee than a scientist or doctor. His days consisted more of shuffling paperwork, scripting grant proposals, and kissing assorted asses than his ego could tolerate. True, he was quite good at navigating the politics. But he went into medicine for other reasons, and he quickly grew tired of living in the neighboring shadow of Harvard and Baylor right next door. Silvia knew that if Stone failed as chief, the government would tap him as successor. No way! So although Silvia made a public spectacle of his disappointment with the portfolio's performance, he secretly wished for a viable alternative that would free him from becoming even more of a government stooge. Johnny Long *had* to get the job done.

And so the news that the assets had more or less transferred to Johnny Long was welcomed by all three doctors, albeit for very different reasons. The one thing they did share, however, was a deep and painful desire to be doctors once again. It meant something different for each of them, but they shared a common yearning to practice medicine as they once envisioned it. Not to mention the fact that *none* of them came to Africa to be quagmired in bureaucracy. Just the opposite in fact. Oh, and worrying about *money* over medicine was not what they saw as adventure in Africa. Johnny Long and his young protégé represented a way out for each of them. Each secretly vowed to themselves not to let the opportunity slip away.

Johnny sensed this from the start. He was originally referred to Stone by a friend, Dr. Eric Abramson, who was very influential at UPenn. Abramson was the one board member who was not at the meeting. In fact, Austin didn't even know he existed. Nevertheless, Eric Abramson existed. He existed in a strange sort of orbit... six months in the States and six months in Botswana away from his family. When he was in the States, he was Dr. A. often seen whizzing around campus on his razor skateboard or drinking a seemingly bottomless latte while scurrying through the echoing hospital hallways.

Abramson played chess. When he was in Africa, he looked as if he walked straight out of the jungle with Livingstone. He was even known to wear a pith helmet, especially when watching cricket. More often than not, though, he was spewing ancient Latin invectives and pontificating about the need for operational metrics. The last time he played a "sport", he broke his pinky rebounding a basketball. His eyebrows – particularly his left one – seemed to be borrowed from a Scottish Terrier, his hair from Karl Marx. Yes, he wore Birkenstocks with black socks and khaki shorts when he was not working. But that was a rare occurrence indeed. He was *always* working, sliding out of one lab coat into another with the dexterity of Houdini escaping from a chained box.

In short, Abramson was one of the most renowned physicians on the East Coast. Not a week passed without a recruiting call from Boston or D.C. Interestingly, though, his sense of investing was as bad as his sense of fashion. Well, it might be better put another way. Abramson could not have cared less about money and fashion. It wasn't his thing... it bored him and sometimes even appalled him. You know the fact was that he really never had to worry about money - it followed him wherever he went. Men as brilliant as Abramson needn't worry about money very often. The son of a successful Park Avenue psychiatrist (who was himself the son of a successful Park Avenue psychiatrist), Abramson never had to question his wealth. When you grew up in Scarsdale, New York, acquiring wealth was never in question – it was assumed.

Abramson was always something of a free spirit, though. He could choose to be – he was by far one of the most brilliant teens to pass through the Scarsdale school system in quite some time. Harvard undergrad... Columbia Medical... this was not unusual for an ambitious kid from the Manhattan suburbs. What was unusual, though, was that Abramson graduated *number one* in his class at Columbia Med. *That* attracted attention, even in New York City. He was one of the top-ranked medical students in the country. The competition for top residents among well-placed hospitals is no different than the fight for the top graduating MBA's among Fortune 100 companies. While his friends and co-students (bright as they were) pined, ass kissed, and cashed in every one of their daddy's chips to get the internship they wanted (believing that it determined the rest of their lives), Abramson turned away some of the most attractive suitors.

It came as quite a surprise to his family and friends when he decided to specialize in internal medicine of all things! Freud must have turned over in his grave and assumed the fetal position! It was as if he was scoffing at the entire medical profession, not to mention his family's paternal lineage in psychiatry. What was next... would he vote Republican? But as usual, Eric knew best what Eric wanted. He went on to enjoy great renown at the University of Pennsylvania, where, among other things, he founded the hospital's program at the Princess Diana Hospital in Gaborone. He was doing what he wanted to do.

When Stone confided in him about the hospital's "financial dilemma" as Stone put it, Abramson was as worried as he could be. He was not angry about the hospital losing money (although that *did* wind him for a day or two). No, he was astonished by the thought that a ridiculous money shortfall – as insignificant as thirty or forty million – threatened not only to derail his life's work, but also to close an entire hospital at the very epicenter of a devastating worldwide epidemic. It was one of the few times that Eric Abramson was heard to utter profanity so vile, he would feel guilty kissing his mother with that mouth had she still been alive.

Of course, he called Johnny at home right away, rousing Johnny from a sound sleep in the process. From there, the rest was history. People like Abramson – people with money but no investment know-how – came to Johnny one after the other. The chain of referrals was long and prestigious, and led all the way up to the Saudi Crown Prince. Without exception, all of Johnny's clients were successful in what they did for a living. But when it came to managing the wealth they had accumulated, they might well have been playing pin the tail on the donkey.

Now, these folks could have chosen a number of very successful people to manage their money. But aside from Johnny's strategies and the great acclaim they heard from this or that friend or colleague already with Johnny, there was something he had that could never be learned, taught, acquired, or faked. Simply put, Johnny Long cared as much about his clients learning something as he did about gathering assets. As much as his strategies were his golden goose, his genuine concern for his clients' edification through wealth accumulation was the real secret behind his success. People just *trusted* Johnny Long to do the right thing. Sure he had a falling out with a client from time to time, especially when the client wanted to diverge from the strategy. That would not be in their best interests, and Johnny told them so. If they chose to invest according to a different style, they were free to do so… with someone else. Johnny would not knowingly invest a client's money in a way that was inferior to one of his methodologies. It was an ethical issue for Johnny.

Chapter 24

For the first couple of weeks after the account moved over, Austin kept in touch with Stone. Shortly thereafter, though, things settled down, and Johnny became the primary contact. As with all his clients in the Growth of Income Strategy, Johnny checked in with Stone when it was time to repopulate the portfolio with the new top-ten list. When the $50 million in cash came over, Johnny immediately purchased equal amounts of the top ten stocks on the list, including Pinnacle West, ConEdison, Nstar, Entergy, Nisource, and Exelon. Remember, Johnny did not market time. When the money came in, he invested it. Who's to say when it is the "right" time to buy? A stock's price is always priced on information already out. What happened next week – good or bad – would not happen until it happened. If the news was indifferent and the stock you were going to buy went down, you'd be pleased. But if the news was good and the stock went up without you owning it, you'd be furious. The strategy was the strategy. Dividend changes *in the future* would determine what Johnny did with the stock. Therefore the present was as good a time as any other, and there was no liability for being out of a stock that was climbing.

At first, the portfolio took a dip. No sooner had Johnny bought $5,000,000 worth of Exelon than the company cut its dividend. Out it went. Of course, the stock was down at the open about 11%, and the position lost about $500,000 just like that. Similarly, NiSource, the number ten stock on the list, was replaced by Questar. Out went NiSource at a 5% loss... that was $250,000. But those were more or less the only changes Johnny made for the first several quarters. In the mean time, First American Investors analysts raised dividend estimates on three stocks in the strategy – Pinnacle West, ConEd, and Entergy by about 8% each. That represented a 2% *increase* in overall yield for the portfolio net of the short-term trading losses. The hospital's income was beginning to *grow* already! At the same time the three stocks *appreciated* some 12% due to the dividend estimate increase or about $1,800,000. So after a couple of quarters – and an initial dip of $750,000 – the portfolio was up a little over $1,000,000 in principal. Just as important, though, the *yield* on the portfolio was up about 8%.

Think about that for a second. Whereas the hospital's money would have otherwise been stuck in a *fixed* rate of return, it was now getting *increasing* dividends *and* an increase in total portfolio value as an added benefit of the increasing dividends! Nothing could have made Stone and his colleagues happier. Robert Silvia was actually seen smiling in public on more than one occasion and was rumored to be dating a beautiful 23 year old Batswana nurse known for having the prettiest hands on the nursing staff. Even Eric Abramson sent Johnny a gift – it was a nice donation made in Johnny's name to the World Wildlife Fund. This was the thing about working with Johnny Long. At first, there was always volatility and, frankly, a little nausea. But as things settled down, his clients began *living* again. In this case, Stone, Silvia, Pantelia, and Abramson became *doctors again*.

About nine months later, Johnny e-mailed Austin a link to a London Times story. Dr. Tony Stone was dead. A chill ran down Austin's spine as he heard Stone's voice echo in his head. It was three days before Austin cried. This latest bit of news unleashed a flood of raw emotion Austin had kept pent-up. It wasn't just word of Stone's death; it was his *entire* African adventure. He kept it pent-up because he literally had no mechanism for interpreting the other-worldliness of it all. He decompressed all at once.

Apparently, Stone was visiting with a friend in Johannesburg. Authorities found Stone and another man, the owner of the home, bound to a chair and gagged. The other man, a black South African named

William Bender, was a big player in the construction business. They had both been tortured terribly and then executed. Oddly, there was a sizable amount of cash in Bender's bedroom that remained untouched. Nothing was overturned. There was no sign of forced entry, although a neighbor said she heard some loud voices, but nothing too unusual. British authorities stepped in to investigate Stone's murder, but the chief investigator on the case from the Johannesburg police department suddenly took a fortnight vacation, and the case went nowhere. It was assumed that poor Tony Stone chose the wrong time to visit his friend. It was one among three murders in Johannesburg that day. It became just another cold case file, just another death story.

Abramson was devastated. He was in Botswana at the time and was the last to see Stone before he was murdered. Stone's last words to him remained crystal clear – "I've got a great idea to present in the meeting Monday!" And off he went with a new spring in his step. That was the last anyone ever saw him alive. Going through Stone's notes in the days that followed, Abramson discovered Stone's "great idea." Now that the portfolio was appreciating and income increasing, Stone put together plans for setting up HIV treatment centers throughout the countryside. The costs were nominal, as all services would be provided on an outpatient basis. The plan was Stone at his very best. When Abramson told Silvia about Stone's last wishes as it were, Silvia turned beet red and stormed off throwing his clipboard down the hallway. How dare those damned savages lay a finger on Tony!

When Abramson returned to the States, he was inundated with questions from his colleagues. Unfortunately, he had no more information to offer than was available in the Johannesburg papers. But he had an idea of his own, a way of honoring Stone and his plan for bringing life to the Botswana countryside. As he had done once before when the Princess Diana Hospital was at issue, Abramson roused Johnny Long from his sleep. They worked out the details right there on the phone.

Abramson would see to it that several million was raised, with Silvia's help, and put aside specifically for the Tony Stone Wellness Endowment. Silvia used Stone's death as an occasion to ratchet up his expectation level for government giving. He never forgot Austin's words, "Most people just don't know that there is another way." Silvia took these words to heart and began almost demanding higher levels of giving from government agencies, including the IMF. He was like a man possessed, bringing in more money than ever before. More money for the hospital meant more money for Johnny to manage. More importantly, though, it also meant more income for the hospital.

Abramson also orchestrated a regular program of visitation to the Princess Diana Hospital for all interested students at Penn Med. At the same time, Johnny purchased a beautiful house close to the hospital. The visiting students from Penn would stay at this house while doing their rotation. Of course, the house was named the Stone House after the late doctor. There was never a shortage of students who wanted to visit the hospital, especially to work in the countryside. Indeed, it did not take long for Stone's outreach program to get into full swing. Silvia raised the money and Johnny put it right into the Growth of Income Strategy. The money it kicked off in dividends was enough to cover the outreach program and provide the Stone House and visiting students' financial support elsewhere. It was Stone's dream come true.

There was no way Austin could have known what lay in store for him that day when he boarded a flight to Botswana. All he knew at the time was that he was going to make a presentation pretty much like any other except he had to travel halfway around the world to do it this time. Boy, he couldn't have been more naïve. That was, after all, why Johnny Long sent his mentee in the first place. There was so much of the world that Austin hadn't seen and couldn't imagine without experiencing it for himself. This was really no different than Austin's showing Stone and his colleagues a totally different way of managing their money.

What Austin learned was something he never expected to learn, even working with Johnny. He was amazed at how Johnny's strategies affected people's *lives* for the better. When he started working at First American Investors, Austin had absolutely no idea money or investing could do so much good for people. Johnny was quick to point out time and time again that money could do as much bad as good. It's really about the people exchanging it. But this was twice now that Austin had witnessed amazing things from Johnny and his work – once with his Growth Stock Strategy and now with his Growth of Income Strategy.

Austin would never forget the death that imbued every person's life in Africa. And yet, he somehow had a *positive* feeling about his whole experience. Even Stone's death brought about goodness much larger than any one man's life. It was a sort of... *sacrifice.* Austin realized that he and Johnny Long could walk into anyone's life and make it better... much, much better. But only if that person was willing to walk with them. It was a matter of *faith* as well as sacrifice. And of course, everyone had to walk with the analysts.